CARTES de VISITE
IN NINTEENTH CENTURY PHOTOGRAPHY

WILLIAM C. DARRAH

D1709731

W. C. DARRAH, PUBLISHER   GETTYSBURG, PENNSYLVANIA

INTERNATIONAL STANDARD BOOK NUMBER   0-913116-05-X
LIBRARY OF CONGRESS CATALOGUE NUMBER   81-69489

TO REMEMBER THE MULTITUDE OF LITTLE-KNOWN AND FORGOTTEN PHOTOGRAPHERS WHO RECORDED THEIR NEIGHBORS AND COMMUNITIES, THEREBY ENRICHING OUR HERITAGE.

PREFACE

This book is a companion volume to *The World of Stereographs* published in 1977. Like its predecessor, its main objective is to advance our knowledge about a neglected type of photographic image, in this study the *carte de visite*—the most popular format from 1860 to 1885.

The narrative is organized in three sections: a description of cartes de visite and their history, a subject guide and survey of the diversity of cartes, and a summary of the methods used in the identification and interpretation of cartes.

Each section can be used independently as a unit, avoiding extensive cross-reference. This entails some repetition but always in either brief form or by amplification.

The information presented here is based upon personal examination of 40,000 images produced by nearly 14,500 photographers. The *documentation* of this book, therefore, is a combination of actual images, photographers' imprints, and notes in contemporary professional periodicals. References to published supporting evidence are given as footnotes.

Hopefully this book, the first serious attempt to survey cartes de visite, will be useful to collectors, archivists, librarians, historians and others interested in photographica or history of photography.

The images reproduced herein have been selected to illustrate the narrative, not for beauty or rarity. A few of the original images have faded or are in otherwise inferior condition. They have been used because they are the best available examples. I have made an effort to use images that have not been reproduced in other books on the history of photography and to introduce the work of many little-known able photographers.

Although the carte de visite has been considered in its proper world-wide context, the reader will recognize an American emphasis. The reason is a purely practical one—95% of the purchasers of this book will be Americans. I have tried to recapture the fullness of Victorian enthusiasm for cartes de visite. Some readers may question why so many of the illustrations have religious and sentimental connotations. That's the way it was. These are examples of what was typical or popular.

No work such as this could be accomplished without the help of many individuals, especially because there are no comprehensive institutional systematic reference collections of cartes. Collectors, dealers, archivists and librarians have provided me with cartes, shared their experience and knowledge, and assisted in other ways. It is impossible to thank each one individually. Acknowledgement of the generous help of these who made it possible to undertake the project was given in *The World of Stereographs* (page 237). To these many friends, I again express appreciation.

Five individuals have been especially helpful: George H. Moss, Seabright, N.J., who loaned me his entire collection of cartes; Henry Deeks, Cambridge, Mass., who shared his knowledge and found for me many images in the pursuit of information; Robert Cauthen, Leesburg, Florida, who also sent me many images, loaned two precious albums and many rare images; John Hess, North Andover, Mass.; and Russell Norton, New Haven, Conn.

Many other persons have given invaluable help. I am grateful to dealers in photographica who were patient to the point of indulgence, in finding material for my wants: Howard C. Daitz, Keith de Lellis, Marjorie Neikrug, all of New York; Ronald Lieberman, Glen Rock, Pa.; Robert G. Duncan, Holyoke, Mass.; Jack L. Nelson, Galesburg, Ill.; David C. Wheeler, New Milford, Conn.; Larry Rakow, University Heights, Ohio.

Among those friends and colleagues who shared information, family albums, and otherwise gave assistance, special thanks to Laurie Baty, Philip Chen, David Delling, Bonnie (Mrs. Warren) Douglas, Paul Galvani, Nicholas Graver, Stephen Guglielmi, Joe Henggeler, Larry Jones, Gordon Kibbee, Richard T. Rosenthal, Glenn Skillin, Mason P. Smith, Dr. Mary Margaret Stewart, Mrs. Carroll Voss, and Nigel Lendon of Balmain, Australia.

Images graciously loaned for illustration are credited in the legends accompanying them.

I owe a debt of gratitude to the staff of Gettysburg College Library, especially Anna Jane Moyer, Readers Services Librarian, for various services and courtesies extending over many years.

Ann Harnsberger has again assisted in working over the rough manuscript and Linda S. (Mrs. Harman) Spence has skillfully typed the manuscript, the fifth she has done for me.

Mahlon P. Hartzell, who has previously managed the printing and production of four of my books, has served as coordinator for this one.

To Helen Hilsman Darrah, I express love and appreciation for a lifetime of encouragement, sharing, and help.

All shortcomings and errors in this book are solely my responsibility.

William C. Darrah

Gettysburg, Pennsylvania
August, 1981

TABLE OF CONTENTS

PART ONE:

THE HISTORY AND DIVERSITY OF CARTES de VISITE

CHAPTER ONE
BACKGROUND

This book is about one kind or style of photograph known as the *carte de visite*. Cartes de visite flourished for almost a half century, 1857 to 1900, and survived into the 1920s. They quietly effected a revolution in photography and a greater intellectual revolution that placed the photographic image on par with the printed word in human communication.

Seeing a photograph is a form of literacy. To look at a photograph is to read it. One may glance at an image as a note or a headline, scan it as a poem, or ponder it as a profound essay. There are many points of view, from technical to esthetic. The greater one's experience, the more one is able to read in a photograph. The more too, one will question it.[1]

Photography was the first modern technologic invention to sweep the world. Daguerreotypy was developed in 1838–1839, but impetus for its rapid spread was the perfection of a method by which many copies could be produced from a negative image on glass.

Concommitant with this discovery, the practice of photography shifted from the pursuit of art to the promotion of commerce. The professional photographer became the proprietor of a business that increasingly demanded quantity. The beginnings of this commercialization are to be found in the early years of daguerreotypy, but by 1860 the movement had become irresistible.

Commercialization extended far beyond the photographer and his studio. Experimenters and inventors fought over patent rights in the grab for profits, while industrialists struggled to monopolize the manufacture of photographic supplies.

Uncountable millions of photographs were produced between 1854 and 1890. Man's vision of the world and its peoples was transformed by seeing— vicariously and imperfectly—images of the real world.

Thus, it was that the faces of the world's leaders in every field of endeavor became familiar. Thus too distant lands and majestic scenery, frontier settlements, and native peoples became known. How otherwise could Americans visualize Indians, cowboys, sod houses and wagon trains?

The photographic image conveyed the horrors of war far from the carnage on the battlefield. Emotions may be visible.

As spectacular as these information-laden images were—and still are—the impact upon society was cumulative, the subtle creeping invasion of printed images into every facet of our daily lives, displacing words by pictures in the dissemination of knowledge.

John R. Green, a British historian, wrote

> "The six penny photograph (the carte de visite) . . . is the greatest boon ever conferred on the poorer classes . . . Anyone who has seen the array of little portraits of the boy who has gone to Canada, the girl who is out at service, the little one with golden hair that sleeps under the daisies, or the old grandfather in the country, will feel with me that the six-penny photograph outrivals such philanthropic claims as schools, museums, and shoeblack brigades."[2]

History of photography has many aspects. It records discoveries and inventions—chemical, optical, and mechanical—that reduced ideas to practice. It records and interprets images of every description, their subjects, formats, and functions. It records and evaluates the men and women who made the discoveries, produced the images, and otherwise contributed to the evolution of photography. Lastly with hindsight, it assesses the relations of photography to the totality of human experience.

In the mid-1850s, five types of photographic images were being produced: daguerreotypes, calotypes, ambrotypes, tintypes, and albumen paper prints from glass negatives, named in order of importance.[3]

---

[1]For several points of view relating to communication, information, and the nature of photographs see:
Szarkowski, John, *The Photographer's Eye.*
Jussim, Estelle, 1974, *Visual Communication and the Visual Arts.*
Jay, Bill, 1980, *Negative/Positive: A Philosophy of Photography.*
Crawford, Wm., *Keepers of the Light*, pp. 1-16.

[2]Quoted by Oliver, John, 1956, *History of American Technology*, pp. 442-443.

[3]Detailed descriptions of these processes, including formulae and procedures, can be found in Towler, J., 1864, *The Silver Sunbeam.* A modern reprint edition (1969, Morgan & Morgan) is available. Crawford, William, 1979, *The Keepers of the Light: A History and Working Guide to Early Photographic Processes* is an excellent source.

The daguerreotype was an image produced on a silver plate or a silver covered copper plate. This was the most popular type of photograph from 1839 to 1856. It was seldom produced after 1862.

The calotype, also called the salt or salted print, was introduced in England by Fox Talbot in January, 1839. This was essentially a paper negative-paper positive method by which multiple prints could be produced. Ordinary writing paper was sensitized with salts of silver, iodine and bromine. The image was subsequently fixed with gallic acid or sodium hyposulfite. The negative could be waxed to improve translucency and thereby obtain a more contrasted print. Hippolyte Bayard, France, 1839–1840, independently devised a somewhat similar process to produce direct positive prints. The calotype was rarely made after 1860.

The glass collodion negative-albumenized paper print process was introduced by F. Scott Archer in England in 1851. A collodion mixture with reactive salts was coated on a glass plate and sensitized with silver nitrate. The plate was exposed immediately while still wet and the image fixed as in the calotype method. Multiple copies could be printed. This method, which was used almost universally for the carte de visite until 1895, will be described more fully later.

The collodion method was applied to other materials and processes, only two of which concern us here.

The ambrotype was a collodion glass negative image treated with mercuric chloride or nitric acid to convert the black silver iodide to metallic silver. When placed on a black background, the image appeared as a silvery white positive. The format, not the process, was patented by James Cutting of Boston in 1854. The viewing of a silver image against a black background was demonstrated by John Hershel in 1840. Ambrotypes were seldom produced after 1864.

The tintype, also known as the ferrotype or the melainotype, was an image on a collodion coated sheet of japanned iron. It was introduced in the United States in 1856, by Hamilton L. Smith. Although the tintype survived into the twentieth century, it remained a cheap process that never competed with the paper print.

The daguerreotype, ambrotype, and tintype were unique, one of a kind, images. Copies could, of course, be made but each copy had to be a new photograph.[4]

In contrast, the calotype and collodion-glass methods were intended for the production of multiple copies. The positive images were produced by contact printing.

Processing of the negative on glass was much less troublesome than working with images on paper. After the plate or paper was exposed and the image was fixed, all traces of residual chemicals had to be removed by washing. Although albumenized paper was very thin and dense, it was porous enough to tenaciously hold absorbed salts. The calotype was especially prone to fading because of incomplete removal of chemical residues. The glass negative plate being non-absorptive, could be washed easily.

By 1858 the materials and methods used in the collodion glass plate-albumen paper process had become sufficiently reliable to attract hundreds of able photographers. Easier to manipulate than the daguerreotype method, much less expensive, and multiple copies provided advantages for the master as well as the novice. By 1860 every kind of material and equipment required by a photographer was being manufactured on a large scale: photographic grade papers, purified chemical reagents, camera lenses, studio furniture, etc. These were marketed worldwide through an elaborate system of wholesalers and jobbers. Standardization as well as commercialization dominated professional photography.

The ascendancy of the collodion negative-albumen print method owed its enormous financial success to the exploitation of two styles of images, the stereograph (1851–1943) and the carte de visite (1854–1925). Both of these formats were card mounted photographs. The stereograph was a pair of images so made as to appear three-dimensional when viewed through a stereoscope. The carte de visite was a single image, approximately the same size as one member of a stereo pair. The stereograph was applied primarily to scenic views while the carte was essentially adapted to portraiture. However, every conceivable subject was photographed in both formats.

These two complementary yet competing types of image were sold in incredible quantities. Between 1857 and 1865 thousands of photographers established galleries throughout the world and produced millions of negatives from which multimillions of prints were published.

The functions of photography had changed; the revolution had begun.

Historians have neglected this social-intellectual revolution. Green, an advocate of educational reform, quoted above, was contemporary with the carte de visite. Even those few historians of photography who have considered it, have dealt with limited aspects. The real pioneer was Robert Taft,[5] a professor of chemistry, who called attention to the potential significance of the carte de visite. Michel Braive[6] recognized the far-reaching effects of the democratization of the portrait and the social uses of the photograph. Gisele Freund[7] took a broader view, particularly the uses of photographs in twentieth century. She lamented the destruction of the art of photography by commercialism.

As yet no one has explored the totality of the uses of carte de visite imagery as a reflection of the peoples and the periods in which they lived.

It is a remarkable story. The international trade in commercially published photographs rapidly familiarized the likenesses of celebrated persons, historical landmarks, native peoples of the world, and the great works of art—all *before* the book, newspaper, or

[4]The one of a kind image reappeared in the third quarter of the twentieth century with polaroid type cameras.

[5]Taft, Robert, 1938, *Photography and the American Scene, A Social History*, 1839–1889, p. 150.

[6]Braive, Michel, 1956, *The Social History of the Photograph*.

[7]Freund, Gisele, 1980, *Photographs and Society*, translated from the French edition of 1974.

magazine could be illustrated by printed photographic reproductions. Therein lie the appeal and the eager demand for these images. Little wonder, then, that inexpensive "six penny" photographs, mounted for convenient handling and viewing, were treasured as collectibles.

Cartes de visite have been ignored by many historians of photography, belittled by some and even despised by a few. Most of the prejudices have their sources in the bitter feuds between so-called artist-photographers and the commercial photographers that aroused so much controversy a century or more ago. Even Gernsheim and Newhall deprecated cartes de visite as crude, conventionalized, and unimaginative—criticisms that have been repeated again and again.

Despite the abundance of cartes de visite surviving today, they are little known outside of the circle of collectors and dealers of vintage photographic images. Even among these, the diversity of cartes is seldom recognized.

The state of affairs is slowly improving. Collector and scholarly interests in photographic images, especially as related to local and regional history, have directed attention to the importance of photographs in many kinds of iconographic documentation.

The serious study of photographs has, until recently, been done almost entirely by art historians who, by choice, avoided commercially produced images in the search for individualism and expression. There are two consequences of this esthetic approach: (1) the works of very few photographers have been critically investigated, the same names being cited again and again in every major publication; and (2) many influential and outstanding photographers remain forgotten.

The surviving cartes de visite are the relics of tens of thousands of photographers who captured on glass the portraits of their neighbors and the activities of the societies in which they lived. To be sure, few of them merit recognition as artists but even the plodding artisans have left a truthful, irreplaceable record, a fragile and perishable heritage that deserves both appreciation and preservation.

CHAPTER TWO
CARTES de VISITE:
A PHOTOGRAPHIC REVOLUTION

"The year 1861 is memorable for a revolution in pictures . . . the card photograph has swept everything before it, and is the style to endure." So wrote the editor of the *American Journal of Photography.*[1]

"Cartomania" or "photomania" it was called. In England alone 300 to 400 million cartes were sold every year from 1861 to 1867. What was this novelty that so captured popular fancy that it literally changed the nature of professional and commercial photography?

The carte de visite is a small photograph, most commonly a portrait, mounted on a card measuring approximately 2½ × 4 inches. The image size varies but usually is about 2⅛ × 3½ inches. The style is also known as the card or album photograph, for reasons that will become evident.

Its origin and introduction have long been disputed. There are conflicting claims and ambiguous evidence. Whatever their respective merits, there is little question that the Frenchman A. A. Disderi introduced the name, the format, and method for producing multiple images, as many as ten, on a single glass plate, in November 1854. Figures 1, 2.

Curiously, a month earlier, the editor of *La Lumiere* (Oct. 28) described a visiting card photograph prepared by E. Delessert and Count Aguado and suggested various poses that might be appropriate for different kinds of formal and informal visits.

Sir David Brewster attributed introduction of the carte de visite to the Duke of Parma in Nice in 1857. The photographer, according to Hayden,[2] was Ferrier of Nice. Taft accepted this version.[3] The Duke was said to have placed his portrait on engraved visiting cards.

The earliest claim, although not made until 1862, was that of Hugh W. Diamond who reported that he had produced such photographs in 1852. Very likely Diamond had simply mounted images on a convenient size card which happened to approximate the later carte.[4]

The standardized dimensions of the carte image, 2⅛ × 3½ inches, was determined by the manner in which the negative was taken. The 4/4 camera with a repeating back produced eight images on a whole plate measuring 6½ × 8½ inches. Thus each image was an eighth plate. As soon as precut mounts were sold by suppliers, no matter what type of camera was used the images had to be trimmed to the card size. The sixth

and eighth plate daguerreotypes had been popular for a decade.

Many photographers had been experimenting with glass negatives and paper prints in the early 1850s. John McClees of Philadelphia, for instance, produced small images in 1853, perhaps earlier. His photographs ranged from 2½ × 3 inches to whole plate.[5] McClees did not contribute to the origin of the carte de visite.

Many characteristics of the carte de visite combined to give it unprecedented success. The small size was convenient to handle and view without an optical instrument, an advantage over the stereograph. Inexpensive, sturdily mounted, novel and diverse, these cartes became collectibles and placed in albums designed to display them, hence the name "album photograph." But the most significant feature was their purpose or function, to provide visual information. Despite the name, they were seldom used as visiting cards. Charles Seely stated that they were made in New York since 1856, a claim that may have support in a comment published in England, "The Yankee man of fashion . . . hands out photographs of himself instead of cards bearing his engraved name."[6]

Another tantalizing circumstance is related by an unidentified correspondent from Atlanta, Georgia, to *Humphreys Journal* (Vol. II, Nov. 7, 1859) who reported that he had exhibited "a pack of photographic visiting cards." The sizes of these cards are unknown, hence their relation to the standardized carte de visite remains uncertain.

Just as there is no serious question about Disderi's patent application, there is no doubt about his role in popularizing the carte de visite. An unverified story—no doubt embellished by tradition—relates how Napoleon III in 1859 en route with his troops to Italy, stopped at Disderi's Paris studio to have his portrait taken. Seizing the opportunity to make a handsome profit, Disderi sold thousands of copies. Almost overnight a new fad was born. The studios of Paris, not only Disderi's, were besieged by patrons who wished to have their pictures taken in the new style. Figures 3, 4.

Gernsheim[7] believed that A. Marion & Co. of London and Paris introduced the carte de visite into England in 1857 but that it did not gain immediate favor.

[1]N.S. 4: 360, 1862.

[2]*Dictionary of Dates*, 1868.

[3]Taft, loc. cit., p. 139.

[4]*Photographic Journal*, April 15, 1862.

[5]McClees, John, 1855, *Elements of Photography*, pp. 20, 30.

[6]Both Taft, P. and Gernsheim, P. mention unconfirmed and questionable references to American photographic visiting cards in contemporary periodicals.

Seely, 1862, *American Journal of Photography*, n.s. 4: 456; also *Practical Mechanics Journal* (London), 1855, p. 76.

[7]*The History of Photography*, 1955, p. 226.

1. Disderi, A. A. Ch. d'Azzeglio. A typical standing pose. 1860

3. Mayer & Pierson. M. Lauwoestine, Paris, 1860.

2. Disderi, A. A. M. Billault. A typical seated pose. 1860

4. Petit & Trinquart. M. Magnus. Paris, 1860. Pierre Petit was Disderi's chief competitor in carte portraiture 1859-1861.

Its appearance in the United States, ignoring possible claims of earlier origin, dates from the late summer of 1859, when at least two photographers began producing carte de visite portraits. Here again, we are faced with conflicting claims. M. A. Root,[8] writing in 1863, credited C. D. Fredricks with the introduction.

John Werge,[9] writing in 1865, gave the credit to George C. Rockwood. Rockwood, in later years, claimed to have been first and named the prominent persons who sat for him.[10]

S. A. Holmes offered 25 copies of "your photograph

[8]Root, *The Camera and the Pencil*, p. 381.

[9]Werge, *Evolution of Photography*, p. 200.
[10]*Anthony's Bulletin* 12: 159, 1880.

on a visiting card the London style, for one dollar."[11] This bargain rate prevailed for only a few weeks at which time Holmes raised his prices to those of his competitors, 25 to 40 cents per carte.

Certainly by the Spring of 1860, dozens of photographers in New York, Boston and Philadelphia were making cartes de visite, with many others joining their ranks. By the end of 1860, the style had become the major fashion throughout the country. Figures 5, 6.

The immediate impetus for the rapid world-wide popularity of the carte de visite was a combination of two inter-related circumstances, Mayall's portraits of the British Royal Family and the democratization of the photographic portrait.

J. E. Mayall, an American daguerreotypist who settled in England, published in August 1860 his "Royal Album," a collection of carte de visite photographs of Queen Victoria, Prince Albert and their children, photographed on May 17 and July 1 of that year. Each negative bore an inscription with Mayall's name and the date. Sixty thousand sets of these photographs were sold in Great Britain, the Colonies and the United States. Root attributed much of the early promotion of the carte de visite in America to this series. Figures 7–9.

Mayall, who was appointed Court Photographer, issued a second series of Royal Family portraits in 1861 and additional titles in 1862. Great numbers of original prints and pirated copies (with Mayall's name removed) were sold in England and the United States.

Queen Victoria enthusiastically collected portraits of her friends and kept albums of them. One of the Queen's ladies in waiting, Eleanor Stanley, recorded on November 24, 1860, her part in acquiring portraits: "I have been writing to all the fine ladies in London, for their or their husband's photographs, for the Queen; . . . I believe Miss Skerrett is right when she says 'the Queen could be bought and sold for a Photograph'!"[12]

Throughout Europe royalty and nobility patronized the galleries of well-known photographers to have their portraits taken—Paris, Berlin, Vienna. St. Petersburg. Royal personages named court photographers who, in turn boastfully advertised their Royal patrons. Figures 10–13.

Within weeks, the well-to-do, merchants, clergymen, soldiers, writers, the great and the near-great joined the ranks of the photographed. Now for a few cents anyone could have his likeness taken and, what was more persuasive, could have a dozen or more copies that could be placed in envelopes and mailed to distant relatives and friends.

In May 1861, Mayall began the publication of portraits of celebrities, joining a trend already well established in Paris, London, and New York.[13] A tremendous world trade in the portraits of the notable developed rapidly and continued well into the 1880s.

The zest for collecting knew few bounds. Enterprising photographers published thousands of scenic views—cathedrals, castles, street scenes, harbors, historic sites and natural scenery. In addition, photographs of the world's great works of art, especially paintings and sculpture, were published in this format.

While the ever-increasing diversity of cartes de visite catered to expanding demand, two new circumstances

[11]*Leslie's Illustrated Weekly*, Jan. 7, 1860.

[12]Stanley, Hon. Eleanor (Long, Eleanor Stanley), ed. by Mrs. Stewart Erskine, 1916, *Twenty Years at Court*, 1842–1862, p. 377.

[13]*Photographic News* 5: 228, 1861.

5. Fredricks, Charles D. Portrait of a gentleman. New York, ca. 1860.

6. Rintoul & Rockwood. "Mrs. V. H." New York, ca. 1861.

7. Mayall, J. E. Her Majesty, Queen Victoria, July 1, 1860.

9. Mayall, J. E. Princess Beatrice, July 1860.

8. Mayall, J. E. Prince Albert, July 1, 1860.

10. Claudet, A. Dutchess of Kent, Mother of Queen Victoria, London, 1859–1860.

moved the center of photographic excitement to the United States.

The outbreak of the Civil War, with the calls for volunteers to serve in the military, separated hundreds of thousands of young men from their families. Every hometown photographer made portraits of its sons in uniform while they were on leave or upon mustering out. Camp-following operators did an enormous soldier business, as did those who owned studios near the theaters of war. Millions of these soldier portraits were produced. Hundreds of thousands of them still exist.

A second circumstance, peculiar to the United States, was the westward migration, the opening of new lands for settlement. This large-scale mobility of peoples was a continuous process since the founding of the colonies. During the Civil War it was interrupted, but immediately afterward the rate of settlement increased rapidly, in part by the immigration of large numbers of Europeans. This movement of settlers created a de-

11. Pierson, L. Queen Sophia of Holland, Paris, 1862.

13. Levitsky, S. L. Edward, Prince of Wales, Paris, ca. 1863. Carte issued by LeJeune, successor.

12. Angerer, L. Franz Joseph, Emperor of Austria, Vienna. Negative 1862, issue ca. 1865.

14. A scenic carte. Chappius, P.E. House of Parliament, from Lambeth, London. ca. 1861.

mand for ordinary portraits. The family album became a treasured possession linking scattered relatives and friends.

The movement of Europeans to the United States and to many colonies created comparable demands for family portraits.

Carte de visite albums.

Albums designed to hold and display cartes de visite were introduced in 1860, although albums with blank pages upon which photographs could be pasted preceded them. Several types of albums were imported in the United States in 1860.

The basic design consisted of a series of thick reinforced leaves, with open windows, bound in sturdy covers. A card was inserted through a slot so as to position the picture in the open window. Usually, two cards could be placed back-to-back.

It is a moot question whether the first American albums were copyrighted or patented. O. G. Mason in the spring of 1861 copyrighted an album having on each

15. A soldier portrait. "Charles H. Burleigh, 51st Mass. Vol. Inf., 1862" Worcester, Mass. C. R. B. Claflin.

16. A family portrait. Wright, D. H. Three generations. Terra Haute, Ind. 1864.

leaf, front to back, a window for a carte and a window for the autograph of the person portrayed.

U. S. Patent 32,287 (May 14, 1861) was granted to F. R. Grumel of Switzerland, the rights to which patent were acquired by C. D. Fredricks. Two weeks later, H. T. Anthony and Phoebus obtained a patent (32,304) for a very similar album. Seventeen patents for albums were granted between 1862 and 1872, all of them essentially similar. A score of manufacturers produced huge quantities of them.

The most common types of albums were octavo size with 25 to 50 leaves, that is, holding 50 to 100 cards. There were also quarto albums holding up to 400 cards, although most held 120 or 160. Small duodecimo pocket albums, mostly intended for the soldier who wished to have portraits of his loved ones with him in battle, held from six to twelve cards.

The bindings were of buckram, plush, calf, tooled morocco, and embossed, studded with mother of pearl, bone, ivory, even with gem stones. The clasps were usually made of brass, although gold was used on the finest albums.

There were four common types of album collections, many fine examples of each can still be found intact.

(1) family albums, with portraits of loved ones: parents, grandparents, brothers, sisters, spouse and children. Often such albums contain pictures of a residence or farm, a church, and a cemetery plot. Most of these albums span only a few years but even these may show infants, a child at different ages, and wedding portraits. Such albums were assembled from 1862 to about 1905.

(2) celebrity albums: collections of portraits of prom-inent persons—royalty, nobility, statesmen, military leaders, performers, literary figures, scientists, physi-cians, engineers, etc. Often the album concentrates on a limited subject, such as, the Govenor, Cabinet mem-bers and legislators of Massachusetts in 1872; the Lutheran clergymen in Illinois, 1871-1873; and circus performers 1868-1870. Typically these albums date from 1862 to 1880, occasionally later, especially the-atrical collections.

(3) travel (topographic) albums: scenic cartes de visite illustrating places visited on a tour. In many cases the cards were purchased in shops catering to tourists. The views could be purchased as a series or set of unmounted carte prints which could be pasted on blank page albums. Several French publishers offered huge selections of unmounted prints and invited mail orders for them. Among the more unusual travel collections are those assembled by sea captains on long voyages and by naval commanders of ships on duty in foreign waters. Travel albums were especially popular from 1862 to 1885.

(4) topical or subject albums: collections on a specific subject or of a limited type. Examples include Civil War, works of art, architecture, humorous, sentimental, a College class (usually with portraits of one or more faculty members and views of the College buildings).

An album should be examined carefully because it is much more than a collection or selection of photo-graphs. It is a document revealing related people and events related to people. Even the impersonal pur-chased set of travel views tells something about the collector.

Generally, in a family album the name of the owner

can be established. Marriages, children, anniversaries, and clues to the activities of the family can be recognized.

Sometimes the album reflects the prevailing attitudes of the period in it which it was assembled. My favorite example is a tooled red morocco quarto album assembled by the Baroness Meyer de Rothschild and presented by her to M. Auguste Micaise in October 1863. The portraits are arranged in peerage sequence, beginning with the Royal Family, Queen Victoria, Prince Albert and their children, followed by their cousins, the Lords of Parliament, the Archbishop of Canterbury, and then the prominent men in British politics both in and out of office. The album is only half-filled because the back windows of each leaf remain open so that the viewer can read the identifications (and we can read the photographer's imprints) carefully, written on the back in the Baroness' hand.[14]

Formats related to the carte de visite

The small image of the carte de visite imposed severe limitations upon the photographer. The head size, especially in most portraits produced before 1865, was so small that sculpturing of the face was difficult. Of course, this worked two ways; small blemishes, such as moles or warts, could not be detected. By 1870, improved lenses permitted a shorter working distance between camera and sitter, resulting in a much larger image that filled up to half or more of the carte area. By 1874, it was possible to produce heads filling nearly seven-eighths of the area, that is, from sixteen to twenty times larger than in a typical 1860–1863 portrait.

In 1866 the cabinet card was introduced in England and in the United States before the end of the year. In this format the card measures 4½ × 6½ inches and the image 4 × 5½ inches, approximately three times the area of the carte. The portrait was more attractive because of its greater facial detail.

Editors of American photographic journals applauded the new style as a boon to the photographic business, which had slumped badly immediately after the War. However, in the United States, the cabinet portrait gained popularity slowly. Pre-1873 cabinet cards are surprisingly scarce. By 1876 about a third of the studio portrait business in the United States was cabinet, two-thirds carte de visite. By 1880 it was roughly half and half, although in the large cities the cabinet portrait was more popular. By 1890 the carte de visite had declined drastically, amounting to less than a tenth of the portrait trade.

Albums designed to hold both cartes de visite and cabinet cards appeared in the United States in the early part of 1867 and remained popular until 1910.

Another style, the Victoria card, enjoyed a very short period of moderate success. In this format the card measures 3½ × 5 inches and the image 3 × 4½ inches. Its intermediate size offered little advantage over the carte and none over the cabinet card. All Victoria cards I have seen date from 1872 to 1876.

[14]See also, Maas, Ellen, 1977, *Die Goldenen Jahre der Photoalben*, 163 pp., Koln.

From time to time other styles of portrait card mounts were introduced, usually with fanciful names, such as "Trilby" (1 15/16 × 2 13/16 inches), "Promenade" (3¾ × 7 inches), "Boudoir" (5 × 8½ inches). About fifteen styles were available from 1878 to 1900, but only the carte de visite and cabinet formats were successful.

The carte de visite era

The history of the carte de visite falls into three stages:

(1) early development, 1857–1861, marked by the patronage of royalty and nobility and the well-to-do, which bestowed respectability upon the inexpensive, mass-produced photographic portrait.

(2) rapid diffusion, 1860–1870, throughout the world and application of the carte de visite format to a wide range of uses in addition to portraiture. This was the period of "cartomania" that revolutionized the profession and business of photography.

(3) routine studio portraiture, practiced from 1865 to about 1905, with steadily diminishing use of the carte de visite format after 1880 until 1905, thereafter rarely to 1915, very rarely to 1925.

Three factors contributed to the decline of the carte de visite. First and foremost, the illustration of newspapers, magazines and books by photographic reproduction (half tone photogravure processes) displaced the photograph as a source of information and amusement. Secondly, the invention of the box camera and roll film eliminated the services of the photographer for informal family pictures and snapshots. Thirdly, the picture postcard introduced in the 1880s captured the market for scenic views.

The role of the carte de visite in the history of photography remains virtually unexplored. Although many contemporary writers and a few historians recognized the impact of the carte de visite, no comprehensive study has ever been attempted.

A few of the far-reaching effects may be introduced here.

The most obvious result was the universality of the portrait. No longer the privilege or luxury of the well-to-do, it became common property. The low cost of the carte portrait was, however, still beyond the reach of many laborers, particularly in Continental Europe.

The application of visual images to documentation, propaganda, advertising, education and entertainment demonstrated the utility of photography in the daily lives of people.

The dissemination of images of the world's fine arts, architecture, paintings, sculpture, enlarged the cultural outlook of generations to come.

All of these images became so familiar that scarcely a child with a few years of schooling could not recognize the portraits of Washington, Franklin, John Adams, Jefferson or Lincoln, or the United States Capitol, Washington's Monument or Niagara Falls. The likenesses of Longfellow, Dickens, Tennyson and Emily Dickinson, and the forms of the Leaning Tower of Pisa, the Arc de Triomphe and the Houses of Parliament became familiar to millions.

Yet, in many respects, the revolution in the photographer's business was of equal importance. He became a merchant and publisher of multiple copies of prints. The carte de visite was the mainstay of his business for two decades, his "bread and butter." This shift from artist-photographer to businessman-photographer deeply divided practitioners. Some, like Gustave LeGray, abandoned photography rather than become a mercenary. Nadar wrote: "The appearance of Disderi and the carte de visite spelled disaster. Either you had to succumb—that is to say, follow the trend—or resign."[15] Nadar chose to follow.

This division should be considered in perspective because it was only one part of the nineteenth century dilemma over the progress of technology. The photographers, who, for a multiplicity of reasons joined the band wagon, were participating in the march of progress.

Photography-heliography, sun-drawing—involved a machine, the camera. The instrument and its products were suspect with paradoxes: artistic-mechanistic, romantic-materialistic, the real world-unnatural manipulation, and more. Although the camera could not be equated with the steam engine or the power loom, the artist felt no less threatened by it.

One of the most remarkable aspects of a technology, *any* technology, is proliferation, the tendency to diversify and combine with other technologies with ever-increasing complexity and ever-increasing applications. Claudet in 1860 called attention to the "impetus photography had given to various branches of trade and science—glass-making, chemistry, optical lenses, etc."[16]

The development of a technology is as much determined by social influences as by creative forces within technology. Ideas, research, and invention may offer a new device, process, product, or even a theory, but society alone determines if it will be accepted and developed commercially or adopted as a way of thinking. The withholding of a patented idea from the public is just as much a social pressure because an industrial company is itself a social organization.

Society enthusiastically accepted photography, used its services and products, and supported it. The carte de visite offered challenges and opportunities to tens of thousands of photographers, many of whom gave it their best efforts.

[15]Nadar, 1900, *Quand j'etais photographe*, pp.194-196.

[16]*Humphrey's Journal, 12*: 108-110, 1860.

CHAPTER THREE
THE PHOTOGRAPHER AND HIS BUSINESS

Professional photography in the nineteenth century demanded a combination of skills more complex than most occupations. Operation of a camera was but a small part. Until the 1880s, the photographer had to sensitize his own glass negatives and printing paper, develop the negative and positive images, tone the prints and, when properly fixed, mount them on card stock.

A familiarity with chemical reagents, processes and apparatus was essential, even though one might have little scientific understanding of the processes involved. Trimming and mounting could be done by unskilled assistants, but most photographers worked alone or with the help of the wife and older children.

These aspects represented only the technical side of photography. The photographer was a merchant selling a product. However much he considered himself an artist or his work a service, he sold photographs, which ultimately determined success or failure in earning a living. Oversimplifications and generalization are hazardous, although there are common characteristics that mark the carte de visite era.

The numbers of professional photographers operating in the United States are staggering.

According to the United States Decennial Census summary reports, there were in

> 1860, 3,154 photographers,
> 1870, 7,558 photographers,
> 1880, 9,990 photographers,
> 1890, 20,040 photographers.

The progressive increase is impressive, but the numbers cannot simply be totaled. Photographers who operated for only a year or two during intervening years were not counted. A significant number of photographers were missed or not properly classified in the census tabulations.[1]

There are substantial data to warrant a minimum number of 60,000 American photographers between 1860 and 1890, and 100,000 between 1850 and 1900.

Despite this great number it is possible to derive several simple general attributes. There are four common denominators in the practice of photography: (1) the studio or gallery, a place to work; (2) the techniques involved; (3) materials and properties; and (4) trade practices.

Few photographers could afford to specialize. The great majority earned a livelihood by offering a wide variety of commercial services such as portraiture, indoor and outdoor photography, copying and enlarging. Many sold images published by other photographers, albums and stereoscopes to augment their income. Portraiture was, however, the mainstay of business for nearly all of them.

[1]Darrah, W. C., 1977, p. 237.

The Studio or Gallery.

The technical processes of photography could be performed anywhere with minimal equipment, as indeed they were. Portable galleries of every description, from push carts and horsedrawn vans to flat boats and railroad cars were used by itinerant photographers who criss-crossed the hinterlands of North America. A vehicle and a dark tent were the only special mobile equipment required by the photographer.

Most photographers established a permanent studio. Here again, galleries were of every description, from the barest minimum to lavishly furnished suites of rooms. The basic requirements were: an area to pose the sitter, a darkroom to sensitize the plates and paper, and an area to prepare and mount finished prints. Some storage space was also necessary.

Small-scale photographers, especially in villages and boom-towns, managed to operate in a single room, using one corner for posing, a partitioned darkroom and a curtained-off work area. More commonly, the photographer had three or four rooms.

The elite photographers in large cities maintained commodious studios with elaborate posing rooms, dressing rooms, waiting rooms, offices and processing rooms.[2] Many of these had thirty to forty employees, including four to ten camera operators. Figure 17.

The most critical requirement of the studio was natural illumination provided by a skylight of ground plate glass. In buildings taller than one story, the gallery had to be on the top floor. To minimize the effects of changing light intensity and quality from morning to evening, north light was essential. Mirrors and reflectors were used to focus light upon the sitter. Artificial illumination was not really practical until electric lighting became economical (post 1885).

Cameras

Most photographers owned several camera boxes, that is without lenses, that could be fitted with several lens systems, called tubes. For cartes de visite the four-tube multilens camera was most widely used. A. S. Southworth, Boston, devised such a camera (U.S. Patent 12,700, April 10, 1855) provided with a sliding, called a repeating, back. The photographer could take four images simultaneously by one exposure and then move the plate and take four more. If the photographer desired, he could uncap the lenses one at a time, changing the pose, and take eight different images. The 4-4 camera could also be used to produce two stereo pairs.

[2]For descriptions of fine studios see: Pritchard, H. Baden, 1882, *The Photographic Studios of Europe.* There are also published sketches of several celebrated galleries, e.g.,: Anson, *New York Illustrated News,* Dec. 8, 1860, Meade Brothers, *ibid.,* Feb. 16, 1861, et. al.

17. Studio sales room of J. Wesley Rothwell, Washington, Pa., ca. 1867. Photographed by J. H. Rogers, Brownsville. Rogers and Rothwell became partners about 1870. Courtesy of Henry Deeks.

Simon Wing patented a multilens camera (U.S. Patent 30,850, Dec. 4, 1860) with subsequent modifications that was capable of making up to 616 images, each measuring one half inch square on a single plate measuring 12 x 15 inches. This size image, called "gem," was applied especially to tintypes, commonly mounted as cartes. Special card mounts with a small window, patented by Simon Wing, were introduced in 1862.

Marcus Ormsbee and Wing manufactured and distributed several sizes of these cameras.

Another American, August Semmendinger, patented a four lens camera with repeating back in July 1861. Apparently independently, Disderi developed a multi-lens camera, ca. 1854, while Lake Price produced a four lens stereo camera in 1858. C. Jabez Hughes adapted the Price design to carte de visite portraiture.

The ability to produce multiple images so inexpensively created tremendous competition for large volume business.[3]

Portrait lenses were manufactured by many lens-grinding establishments and optical instrument makers. The better quality precision grades were produced by Voightlander & Sons, Thomas Ross & Co., Dallmeyer, Darlot, and Steinheil.

The portrait lenses used between 1860–1872 for carte de visite images allowed a working distance between sitter and camera ranging from 13 to 17 feet. The photographer moved the camera to obtain sharp focus, with fine adjustment by thumb screw.

[3]*American Journal of Photography*, n.s. 4: 85, July, 1861. See also *Photographica* 13 (4): 9–10, 1981.

Photographic Processes

The following condensed description of the glass plate albumenized paper method will place the carte de visite in its historical context. Despite many minor variations, particularly in the chemical solutions used, this method remained essentially standardized for nearly forty years.

The glass used for negatives had to be flat, free from defects and have a hard surface. The chief physical defects to be avoided were "blisters" (small elongate gas bubbles), "stones" (which are small opaque masses of undissolved sand or other mineral components), and "cords" (thin lines of opaque materials). Generally these imperfections could be easily detected by careful examination. Occasionally prints reveal blemishes in the negative glass.

The sheets were cut from glass manufactured by the crown, cylinder or plate methods.[4] The best glass plates were imported from England and France, although excellent quality was also produced in the United States.

Photographic plates, free from defects, were available in many pre-cut sizes from 2½ × 2½ inches to 20 × 24 inches, with the most common 2½ × 4 inches (single carte de visite) and 6½ × 8½ inches (whole or 4/4 plate). In 1872, Wilson, Hood & Company sold the whole plate size at 55 cents a dozen, $6.50 per gross.[5] Although prices fluctuated, they were remarkably consistent from 1865 to 1880.

Preparing the Negative

The glass plate had to be coated with iodized collodion. Unless the glass had been polished, the two surfaces were not uniformly flat. The photographer raised the glass to eye level and rotated it in the light to determine which side should receive the collodion.

The collodion emulsion was prepared by dissolving nitrocellulose (pyroxylon) in a mixture of ether and absolute (100%) alcohol and dispersing salts of iodine and/or bromine in it. There were many formulae, most of which called for ammonium or sodium iodide and cadmium bromide dissolved in absolute alcohol.

The photographer held the plate in his hand and poured on the corner sufficient collodion mixture to cover the plate. He then inclined the plate so that the collodion flowed evenly over it. Any excess was caught in a small wide-mouth jar. Although these plates could be dried in a dust-free place and stored for later use, they were usually sensitized and while wet exposed immediately. Dry collodion methods were chiefly used for outdoor work, but the contrast in the images obtained was nearly always inferior. Many scenic photographers used only the wet plate method.

The coated plate was sensitized by immersing it for 40 to 60 seconds in a bath of silver nitrate with a trace of potassium iodide. The wet plate was now ready for use.

The sensitized plate had to be kept in darkness and carried to the camera in a holder or case called a shield.

[4]See Woodbury, W. E., 1898, *Encyclopedic Dictionary of Photography*, pp. 221–223.
[5]*Illustrated Catalogue*, Oct. 1872, pp. 69–70.

The back of the camera had a ground glass on which the image was focused. The ground glass was removed and the shield inserted in its place. A slide which covered the plate was now removed and the plate thus exposed. Exposure time varied with the intensity of illumination, ranging from a few to thirty seconds, or more.

The exposed negative was placed in a developing bath, most commonly containing an iron salt or pyrogallic acid. When the image appeared to be clear and sharp, the plate was quickly rinsed and immersed in a fixing bath of sodium hyposulfite. The negative was washed to remove all residual silver salt and other chemicals and then dried. Negatives from which large numbers of prints were to be made were coated with transparent varnish to prevent damage to the image.[6]

Albumenized Paper

Albumen paper was manufactured by many photographic suppliers. Anthony by 1860 had become the largest producer in the United States. As demand increased, scores of competitors entered the market. Many made an excellent product. (Gutekunst, J. Walzl)

The finest paper stock were imported from France (Rives) and Germany (Saxe-Malmedy, Belgium after 1919). These were the only localities known at the time to have essentially mineral-free water, which was necessary for the manufacture of photographic-grade papers. Several high-grade papers were manufactured in the United States after 1865.[7]

The paper was coated with common salt and egg albumen, giving it a pleasing glossy finish. It was dried carefully and sold by the ream in sheets of various sizes. The photographer had to sensitize the paper before using it. To do this a sheet was floated, albumen side downward, upon a solution of silver nitrate and hung bias by one corner to dry. Because sensitivity decreased rapidly, paper had to be prepared freshly every day.

Positive images were contact printed. The glass negative with collodion surface up and the paper with albumen side down were clamped in a frame with an opaque back. Printing-out was accomplished in sunlight, usually on the roof or in the back yard of the studio. The photographer or an assistant examined the prints from time to time, until the desired intensity and contrast were obtained, at which point the frame was simply turned face down. Large establishments had racks designed to hold up to a hundred frames at adjustable angles to the sun.

Exposure time for developing the image varied with time of day, degree of cloudiness and season of the year. In winter, when the temperature dropped below 40° F (5C), development was too slow to be practical. On overcast days printing-out was slow and difficult, sometimes impractical.

The exposed print was fixed by immersion in a solution of hyposulfite and then washed thoroughly. The wet print was placed in a toning bath, usually a solution of gold chloride which imparted a characteristic brown color to the image. Some photographers preferred black velvet-like tones achieved with a lime bath or warm tones with an acetic bath.

There were many experiments with other types of sensitizing and toning. One such variant, of special interest in the carte de visite field, was the "wothley-type" invented by J. Wothley, Germany, 1864, and used by Col. Stuart-Wortley (ca. 1865–1868, England). The paper was coated with collodion and sensitized with uranium and silver nitrates. The cartes bear the imprint of the United Association of Photography, Ltd.[8] Figure 440.

Several other steps and processes were in common use. For instance, the negative could be intensified by chemical manipulation if desired. The novice photographer soon learned, however, that no poor negative could be transformed into a good one.

The painstaking procedures from preparing the wet plate to the finished print should make us admire the marvelous prints that survive after more than a century, especially scenic images made in the wilderness under the most trying circumstances.

The Negative File

The customer usually ordered prints at the time of sitting or when proofs were examined. Because it was assumed that reorders for additional prints might be received, a filing system for negatives was a necessity. The photographer, even one who operated for only a few years, accumulated negatives at an astounding rate.

Numbering Negatives

The most common practice was to assign a serial number to a plate and record the names of sitter and customer. Commonly, but not universally, the number was written on the card mount to facilitate reorders. There are many eccentricities in numbering systems. Photographers who took several poses on the whole plate often identified them as 1225a, 1225b, 1225c and so on.

Most photographers in the early 1860s advertised that additional copies could be ordered at any time, but after 1866, a time limit of one to five years was often stated. Occasionally, the photographer noted that all negatives not purchased by the customer would be destroyed. The files of negatives became such a burden that many photographers periodically disposed of obsolete plates and abandoned numbering them. H. P. Kirk (Mason City, Iowa) boasted "a fire-proof vault for the safe-keeping of negatives." Figures 18, 19.

W. H. Tipton (Gettysburg) claimed to have made 100,000 negatives, about 4000 per year. Many city establishments made 10,000 per year. Cummings (Lancaster, Pa.) produced about 5000 per year.

Cleaning old plates after removing the images to recover the glass was a common practice. Such salvaged plates could be reused.

By the mid 1870s, a trade in scrap photographic glass had grown up in larger cities. Dealers in scrap glass

[6]Towler, John, 1864, *The Silver Sunbeam*, Chapters 22, 27, 30–32. Morgan & Morgan reprint edition, 1969 available. For a brief but vivid description see Holmes, O. W., *Atlantic Monthly 12*: 3–6, July 1863.

[7]Woodbury, loc. cit., pp. 334–335.

[8]See also Gernsheim, 1955, *History of Photography*, p. 282.

Geo. G. Rockwood,
PHOTOGRAPHER
839 Broadway
NEW YORK.

Additional copies from the plate from which
this picture is taken can be had, if desired

Nº 23495

N.B. *Negatives will not be preserved longer than One year,
from the date of sitting, unless they are purchased, in which case
a deduction will be made in the cost of pictures printed from them.
In ordering duplicates, please send the Nº as above, with name.*

18. Imprint of George C. Rockwood, New York, 1861, noting that additional copies could be purchased.

19. Imprint of A. M. Allen, Pottsville, Pa., 1871, with serial negative number and ordering instructions.

routinely toured neighboring towns to purchase obsolete plates. The larger pieces were cleaned and sold as window panes, especially for greenhouses, or resold to manufacturers of small novelties, toys, cheap hand mirrors, etc.

Thus great numbers of negatives were destroyed.

The Carte de Visite Mount

As noted earlier, the distinguishing feature of a carte de visite is its mounting on a standardized card. Its manufacture involved the following steps:

(1) Trim the paper print to the desired size and shape, which was accomplished by cutting dies or a template.

(2) Thinly spread dextrin or similar paste over the entire back.[9]

(3) Place the print, properly centered, on the card and carefully press on the print.

(4) Weight the card and print to avoid curling or wrinkling—commonly with plate glass or polished wood blocks.

(5) Dry completely, usually within 4–12 hours.

While most photographers produced their own cartes de visite, usually with semi-skilled assistance, in large cities much of the mounting work was performed by commercial photoprinting establishments. Such services appeared in New York, Boston and Philadelphia about 1860 and rapidly developed in every major city in the United States.[10]

[9]In 1866, cards with dextrinized surfaces to which a slightly wet print could be affixed became available.

[10]Darrah, loc. cit., p. 17.

The enormous trade in photographic supplies gave rise to a highly specialized and standardized manufacturing-jobbing-retailing system of every item needed by the studio, ranging from cameras and chemicals to card mounts and printing services. E. & H. T. Anthony remained the undisputed leader until 1890 with Wilson, Hood and Company its chief rival, but hundreds of companies entered the field between 1854 and 1885.

In no other aspect of the carte de visite was this industrial standardization more evident than in the card mount. At first, nearly all cartes de visite were mounted on plain white bristol board averaging .010″ to .014″ in thickness. In the later 1860s slightly heavier stock was used (.012″ to 0.16″). About 1861, the face of the card was bordered by gilt lines, single or double, occasionally with more ornate corners. This general style persisted until 1870. Figure 20.

Thicker, softer card was introduced in 1866 but did not become common until 1870. The stock, measuring .014″–.018″, is usually calendered on the upper surface. Throughout the 1870s, progressively heavier card stock is used, so that by 1880, the average thickness ranges from .024″ to .028″. Figure 21.

Almost every year the manufacturers of card stock modified the pre-cut and finished cards offered to the trade. The colors, finishes, beveled edges, gilding and so on set fads and fashions in mounts, so much so that dating a carte de visite by style of card alone is highly accurate, usually ± one year. It must be cautioned, however, that a few photographers refused to follow fads and used distinctive mounts of their own. Figure 22.

20. Card mount, early to mid 1860s. Thin white card with border of one or two lines, usually gilt, red or blue. L. S. Weller, Antwerp, N.Y., ca. 1863.

22. Card mount, latter 1870s. Thick card, beveled edges, gilded; card pink but any color from white to black. S. Piper, Manchester, N.H., 1878.

The Imprint or Logo

Everyone who has examined cartes de visite and cabinet photographs has been tantalized by the striking variety of imprints on the backs of the cards. Almost, without exception, every photographer used imprints to identify his work. The imprint or logo served two functions: it claimed authorship and it advertised.

Again, from simple beginnings it became a device for incredible showmanship and, as such, a remarkable source of historical information. In the early 1860s, the imprint is usually a name and town, often with a street address or a vignetted name.

A photographer-publisher imprint was not new. Publishers of stereographs from 1854–1860 usually identified their images. Often the imprint was on a pasted label. a device also used on many early cartes de visite (e.g., Rockwood, Anthony, Broadbent).

Already by 1864 some photographers had recognized that the card back was a means of giving instructions about appropriate dress for sittings, claims of merit and awards, types of photographic services offered, price lists and almost any other idea deemed to be advantageous to the business. Logos included Masonic emblems, cameras, patriotic symbols, sketches of the gallery building—the advertising artistry seemed unbound. Figures 23–27.

The Photographer as Publisher

One of the most significant developments in the commercialization of photography in the latter 1850s

21. Card mount, early 1870s. Card buff to yellow, rounded corners, commonly with border lines in red. A. Marshall, Boston, 1872.

WHIPPLE,
96 Washington Street
BOSTON.

PROF. S. A. KING'S
Photograph Rooms,
No. 50 SCHOOL STREET,
(Next to the Parker House, - - - BOSTON.)

The Aeronaut calls the attention of his friends to his
Rooms, where he is prepared to do every description
of Photographing in the highest style of the art.

23. Simple imprint, 1860-1862. J. A. Whipple, Boston, ca. 1861.

25. Individualistic imprint. Balloon logo of S. A. King, Boston, 1861-1865. King and Black made the first aerial photographs, October 13, 1860.

24. Imprint with patriotic vignette, 1862-1865. J. C. Spooner, Springfield, Mass., 1863.

26. Gallery logo, widely used 1861-1866. T. Lilienthal, New Orleans, ca. 1863.

27. Imprint with suggestions for sitters. Will Thomas,
Owatonna, Minn., ca. 1878.

was the manufacture of multiple prints from a negative for public sale. The picture was produced not for a specific customer but for the open market. Publishers of paper stereographs were active before 1854, but in that year the London Stereoscopic Company ushered in mass production of stereographs. Figure 28.

While the majority of photographers earned their livelihoods by custom work, thousands became publishers, producing only a few score titles. On the other hand, there were hundreds of publishers whose trade lists exceeded a thousand titles. We shall become acquainted with the work of most of the great carte de visite publishers.

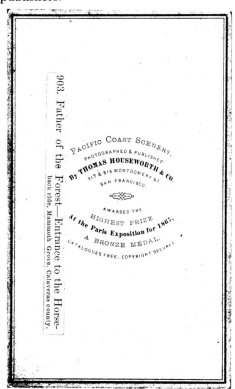

28. Imprint of a photographer-publisher. Thomas Houseworth & Co., San Francisco, 1868.

Publishing of cartes de visite, as of stereographs, required the use of copied negatives. In quantity production, simultaneous printing from ten or twenty negatives was common. Many publishers purchased negatives and produced copies without crediting the original photographer.

Copy negatives of high quality could be made easily. A glass positive was produced by contact printing and this positive used to print as many negative copies as desired. All quantity printing of stereographs and cartes de visite was done with multiple copy negatives.

Pirating

The ease with which copy negatives could be made, simply copying a good print—with some loss of detail—inevitably encouraged piracy of virtually every image having profit potential. Copyright (United States), registry (Great Britain) and depose (France) granted a claim or right to a photographic publisher, with recourse to legal action for violation, but there was very little actual protection.

This practice, rampant on both sides of the Atlantic Ocean, was but an extension of "the great age of piracy" that plagued book publishing from 1810 into the 1860s.[11]

The person responsible for the piracy was seldom known. The same image was often pirated by a dozen publishers. In most cases the cost of litigation would have exceeded the amount of damage or loss of income.

Some of the most respected photographers pirated images, to name only a few: Brady, Anthony, Gurney, Fredricks, Black and Carbutt. They did not hesitate to place their own imprints on them.

The great problem was the cheap copy issues turned out in huge quantities by unidentifiable publishers. These cards, which bear no identification, were sold for a few cents from 1863 to 1875. Any carte de visite of a well-known personality that has no imprint is a cheap copy. Every collector, archivist and dealer should recognize its true nature.

[11]Tebbel, John, 1972, *A History of Book Publishing in the United States*, v. 1, pp. 207–210.

Sometimes itinerant and small-town photographers mounted images on cards without an imprint. These were not produced from copy negatives nor were they pirated. Obviously, portraits of the members of a family had no sale value.[12]

Copy Services

The capability of the camera in copying became an important factor in studio work. From the very beginning of the carte de visite, photographers advertised that daguerreotype and ambrotype portraits could be copied and, if desired, enlarged. Thus everyone in the family could have a picture of a deceased loved one. Cartes de visite copied from old daguerreotypes are quite common. Of course, carte de visite portraits could also be copied. This became necessary when the negative was broken or damaged, or when the person wishing to have copies made, lived in a distant locality and was unable to obtain the original negative. Figure 29.

Many photographers advertised that they could copy drawings, plans and documents.

Montages or Combination Photographs

One of the curious productions of the early years of carte de visite photography was the montage, a photograph of several or many photographs, usually portraits (a college faculty, members of a state legislature, the British Royal Family). These were, of course, financial

[12]About 1% of the *original* cartes de visite I have examined have no imprint. Accumulations in flea markets and antique shops have many, because the cards bearing imprints have been removed or sold.

29. Copy services. Copy of a daguerreotype portrait. W. F. Allen, Winchendon, Mass. Carte 1863.

ventures. Some photographers experimented to see how many heads could be crowded into one image, and they achieved totals ranging from eighty to more than seventeen hundred, all recognizable with a magnifying glass. Many montages were made up of minute portraits taken with a Wing multilens camera. Figures 30, 31.

Prices for Cartes de Visite

Prices for cartes de visite in the United States remained nearly stable for twenty-five years, although there was a considerable range. The photographers' imprints on hundreds of card backs record these prices.

In the early 1860s, the price ranged from two to three dollars a dozen, although a few photographers charged as little as $1.50. The average price was less than twenty cents per carte. During the Civil War, 1864–1866, a federal tax was levied on each photograph sold in the trade. The two or three cent tax was almost always absorbed by the photographer. Figures 32, 33.

After the war, many small town photographers dropped prices to $1.50, or less, per dozen, but the costs of materials prohibited further price-cutting. Meanwhile, the fine studios in large cities raised their prices to $3 to $3.50 per dozen, deliberately appealing to a higher social clientele, a policy widely practiced in the 1870s.[13]

The same price range prevailed worldwide, probably because the cost of materials was internationally uniform. The equivalent average price, 12 to 15 cents in the United States, six pence in England, 50 centimes in France, contributed to the brisk world trade in cartes.

Other Aspects of the Photographic Business

Succesion

A well-located studio equipped with a skylight was usually rented or sold again and again to a succession of photographers, not only in large cites but also in small towns. Death, illness, change of occupation or removal to another location vacated the gallery, which quickly passed to a new proprietor. This was true in all countries. LeGray's elite studio on the Boulevard des Capucines in Paris passed to Bisson Brothers and then to Nadar.

To an incredible degree, the succession of ownerships is recorded by photographers' imprints. For example: C. T. Sylvester, successor to Ormsbee, Boston; I. H. Jordan, successor to J. H. Kent, Brockport, N. Y. (with the note, "Copies of Pictures from Kent's Negatives can be furnished on order."). Succession will be considered more fully in the Section on Documentation, page 180. Figures 34, 35

Generally, when a studio changed hands the negatives, being of value only in the home town trade, passed to the new owner.

Mobility

Consistent with the restlessness of young Americans generally, photographers moved from town to town,

[13]Price schedule printed on cartes by James W. Turner, Boston, 1876 and 1877.

DE UTGÅNGNE MISSIONERERNA.

E. G. Åkerlund.
Gravör & Fotograf från Stockholm

30. A pirated copy issue by John Carbutt, with his imprint on back, Chicago, 1870. Sold commercially to Swedish immigrants in Illinois and adjacent states.

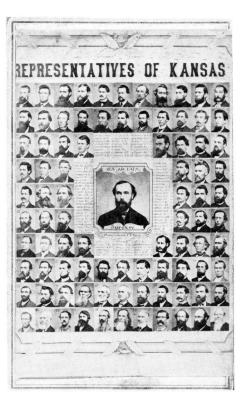

31. A montage. A composition of ninety portraits with a key to identities. Charles T. Smith, Topeka, Kans., 1869.

from state to state. Miltz & Swart began operating in Toledo, Ohio, about 1866, moved to Peoria, Illinois, in 1870 and thence to San Francisco, California, in 1872. Z. P. McMillan began photographing in Newark, Ohio, about 1862, moved to Galesburg, Illinois, in 1867, and finally to Red Oak, Iowa, in 1880.

Thousands of American photographers operated in two or more towns during their professional careers.

There are three striking patterns of this mobility: (1) movement from villages to larger communities to larger cities, each move resulting in a more successful business, as, for instance, J. H. Kent (Rochester, N. Y.); (2) movement from large city galleries to small communities, especially by young photographers who wished to become independent operators; and (3) the typical wanderer, "go west, young man." When lands were opened for settlement in Kansas in 1878, there was a veritable migration of Pennsylvania Dutch photographers, including M. A. Kleckner (Bethlehem) and S. G. Shaeffer (Hanover). California beckoned many

G. S. HOUGH,

PHOTOGRAPH ROOMS,

Corner 5th Avenue and Wood St.,

Pittsburg, Pa.

Card Photographs,   -   -   - $1,00 per doz.
4-4 or whole size in frame,   -   -   2,00 each.
4-4 or whole size Duplicate, without frame, 75 "

32. Imprint giving prices for cartes de visite. G. S. Hough, Pittsburgh, Pa., 1869.

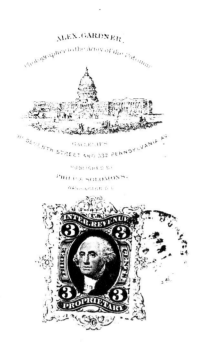

33. Civil War stamp tax. Alex Gardner, Washington, D.C., 1866. Note printed box for stamp.

35. Succession. Imprint of C. S. Roshon, Harrisburg, Pa., 1868. Note that the negatives of R. S. Henderson and of *his* predecessor, Burnite and Weldon, have passed to Roshon.

34. Succession. J. Q. A. Tresize imprint surrounding that of the previous gallery owner. Springfield, Ill., 1866.

photographers from New England (Taber, Spooner, Durgan) and from New York (Reilly, Howland).

Duration of a Typical Career

There is a widespread mistaken belief that the average photographer's career between 1860 and 1880 was only a year or two, a few at best.

Of approximately 11,400 American photographers known to me by examination of actual images, carte de visite, stereo and cabinet:

> 1,460 are represented by a single image, or by several similar card mounts and, therefore, can be placed only within a very limited time span;
> 4,475 are represented by card mounts spanning a minimum of five but not more than ten years;
> 3,820 are represented by cards spanning ten to fifteen years; and
> 1,700 are represented by cards spanning from fifteen to more than forty years.

These figures must be interpreted with great caution; they are only indicative. Many photographers who operated very briefly and thus produced few cartes, are unknown to me. These would lessen the average span. On the other hand, many daguerreotypists who began operating in the 1840s produced cartes de viste in the early 1860s. There are hundreds of these (including Ormsbee, Chute, Jordan, Southworth & Hawes) who, in my tabulations, produced cartes for only two or three

Mrs. J. F. BAUER,   BROOKLYN, L. I.

36. Imprint of Mrs. J. F. Bauer, Brooklyn, N.Y., ca. 1873. Mrs. Bauer was one of several hundred able women photographers operating in the United States between 1860 and 1890.

years. In these cases, their carte work represents only a brief phase in a longer career.

Part of the difficulty in deriving reliable chronologic data is the mobility mentioned above. Approximately forty percent of the photographers in the five-to-ten and the ten-to-fifteen year categories operated in two or more communities. Local business directories would therefore give only brief periods of activity.

Another factor which dare not be overlooked is mortality. In the period under consideration here, life expectancy for males over 21 years of age was less than 53 years. Many careers were cut short by chronic illness and early death.

In spite of these limitations, it would appear that a productive career of at least eight to ten years was typical.

Women Photographers

There is growing realization that in the nineteenth century photography offered many women a professional career. In the nineteenth century, several thousand women photographers practiced their skills in the United States. Every European country from England to Russia, from Norway to Italy, had successful women photographers. Denmark and Sweden in particular supported large numbers of them.

There are as yet only two checklists of women photographers but these preliminary lists suggest a

much more important role of women than has been previously considered.[14] Figure 36.

There are several patterns in these careers:

(1) widows who continued to operate the studio after the death of the husband, or established their own, sometimes for many years (Mrs. Charles Waldack, Cincinnati, Ohio).

(2) husband and wife teams, with the imprint indicating both were operators;

(3) sisters or daughters who learned photography in the family business and struck out on their own;

(4) assistants and colorists who acquired skills and found employment as camera operators, often in branch galleries; and

(5) women who paid for instruction in photography in order to find employment in the field or establish their own businesses.

Professionalism

The combination of technical, artistic and business skills involved in commercial photography made it imperative that the individual so engaged kept abreast of new ideas, improvements in techniques and changing fashions. This trend was in sharp contrast with the artistic tradition of individualism.

[14]Darrah, W. C., 1980, "Nineteenth Century Women Photographers," *The Photographic Collector 1*: (2): 6-10.
Palmquist, Peter E., "California Nineteenth Century Women Photographers," *The Photographic Collector 1* (3): 18-21.

37. A loaded imprint. National Photographic Association logo, succession, advertising, instructions for sitters, etc. J. G. Vail, Geneva, N.Y., 1872.

22

Technical manuals were essential tools of the trade, for in them one had formulae, instructions and warnings. Three of the best books were M. A. Root's *The Camera and the Pencil* (1864), with its emphasis on posing and images, and J. Towler's *Silver Sunbeam* (1864), with an emphasis on processes and methods. Earlier, Waldack published his *Treatise on Photography*, the third edition of which includes an appendix, *The Card Photograph* (1862). This thirty-two page sketch, also sold in pamphlet form, was the first full description of the carte de visite in an American handbook or periodical. Figure 37.

Professional journals provided news, suggestions and technical articles as well as forums for discussion and debate. During the earlier 1860s, *Humphrey's Journal of Photography* (1851–1870) was most useful and later, the *Philadelphia Photographer* (1864–1888) dominated the field. Somewhat less important was the *American Journal of Photography* (1858–1867), which merged with *Humphrey's Journal*.[15]

[15]A concise chronology of these journals and the various title changes can be found in Taft, 1938, p. 469.

Probably the most influential trend in professionalism was the organization of the *National Photographers Association* (1868), which held its first convention in Boston in 1869. Founded to improve the status of photographers, raise standards and fight unfair patent claims, it endeavored also to encourage friendly exchange of ideas and problems. By 1872 the Association's membership exceeded two thousand. The NPA logo was boldly printed on thousands of cartes de visite from 1871 to 1874, an expression of the enthusiasm of its members.

Many local and regional associations and societies were organized between 1863 and 1875, all of which contributed to the advancement of photographers. Local county fairs no less than International Exhibitions held competitions for photographs of every type.

With this view of the nature of the photographic business and how the photographer worked, we can turn to the incredible world of carte de visite images.

CHAPTER FOUR
PORTRAITURE

"Card portraits, as everybody knows, have become the social currency, the 'green-backs' of civilization."

Writing in 1862, Holmes observed:

"The sitters who throng to the photographer's establishment are a curious study. They are of all ages, from the babe in arms to the cold wrinkled patriarchs and dames whose smiles have as many furrows as an ancient elm has rings that count it summers. . . .

"Attitudes, dresses, features, hands, feet betray the social grade of the candidates for portraiture. The picture tells us no lie about them. There is no use in their putting on airs; the make-believe gentleman and lady cannot look like the genuine article. Ill-temper cannot hide itself under the simper of assumed amiability."[1]

The portrait business was booming. A large studio on bright clear days frequently had sixty to a hundred sittings, with the usual order for a dozen copies of each.[2]

Something of tremendous social importance was taking place. No longer was the portrait the exclusive privilege of the well-to-do. The carte de visite portrait, by virtue of its low cost, became available to the vast majority. This trend, begun in the mid-1850s with the introduction of the ambrotype and tintype (melainotype), was now at full speed.

There was no question that the cheapness of the carte de visite and the sheer numbers of them had a detrimental effect upon the quality of portraiture. A photographer simply had to sell many images to earn a living. It was the industrialization of an art. To make matters worse, the illusion of quick profit enticed many persons of little skill or talent to take up photography as a career.

Even so, there has always been a distinction between the practitioner who was determined to produce fine images and the mercenary whose goal was profit. Many photographers managed to balance both, thereby weathering economic ups and downs and leaving for us a record of beautiful accomplishments.

Even respected historians of photography, Gernsheim, Newhall and Pollock, have somehow failed to recognize the wealth of innovative protraiture in this format.

The often-repeated criticisms complain that carte de visite portraits were conventionalized, imitative, uninspired and cheap in every sense of the word. H. P. Robinson put it this way: "99 out of every one hundred photographic portraits are the most abominable things ever produced by any art."[3] Yet he fully recognized the revolution in photography that had been wrought by the carte de visite.

Fads and fashions came and went. Imitation there was. Conventions and artificialities were all too obvious. The real limitation, so easily overlooked, was the immobility of the camera. The photographer was boxed in by his equipment.

To circumvent the bare wall or screen, the photographer devised painted screens, scenery, papier mache rocks, cardboard balustrades, and accessories in endless variety. Staging the subject was, for forty years, a standard practice. The quest for originality and novelty at times led to ludicrous effects, but always the intent was to produce a pleasing picture. It dare not be forgotten that two generations admired them.

By choice, the art historian views photography in terms of art. The social historian, on the other hand, draws no such limits. If we are to understand, for example, the mood of a period, say, 1860-1880, we cannot ignore newspaper editorials, sermons, political speeches, dime novels, jokes and doggerel poems. These are day-to-day revelations of the emotions of the people, more accurate in many ways than the great books and poems that marked the age. How often have the most popular books of a decade quickly slipped into oblivion?

For similar reasons, it is not possible to measure the impact of photography unless we accept the carte de visite for what it was—the most popular and diversified type of photography produced in the nineteenth century.

Photographic portraiture rests upon two bases: the theory or concept of the portrait and the techniques employed in producing it. These bases remain today just as in the 1860s.

Root wrote: "To constitute a good portrait and, at the same time a pleasing picture, the original should be represented under such circumstances of position, arrangement, light and shadow, and accessories as shall suggest character, while also conducing to pictorial effect."[4]

Herein lies the fundamental difference between painting and photography. The painted portrait is an idealization of a personality, the artist's conception committed to canvas. The painter acquires a conceptual ideal of his subject through leisurely sittings, extending over days, weeks or months. He observes mannerisms, moods and attitudes, all of which meld in his mind.

In stark contrast, the photograph is an image captured in an instant, a fraction of a minute or of a second by a machine which is mechanically accurate. The image records the sitter, posed in artificial and unfamiliar surroundings. In large communities, he is

[1]Holmes, O. W., 1863, *The Atlantic Monthly 12*: 9.

[2]Bogardus, A., 1904, *Century Magazine 68* (1): 89.

[3]Robinson, H. P., 1869, *Pictorial Effect in Photography*, p. 82.

[4]Root, 1864, loc. cit., p. 143.

probably a stranger to the photographer. Self-consciousness might have been lessened to some extent by light conversation during the few minutes he was being posed and the camera adjusted, but some tension usually remained.

Artists and photographers wrote heatedly about these differences. At the same time, there was a strong tendency, almost an obsession, for the photographer to imitate the painter and the painter to imitate the supposed realism of the photographer.

The prime objective of the portrait is to depict the individuality and personality of the subject. The prime problem is *how* to display this individuality.

The photographer usually suggested the pose and selected the background and properties. Once he had the approval of the sitter, he was in full command. He turned the subject's head, placed the hands, adjusted the lighting and at the instant he felt ready, removed the cap on the lens tube and exposed the negative.

Unfortunately, it is not possible to narrate or discuss this seemingly simple procedure as a unit or an entirety. Instead, we must separate its components and consider each independently, without losing sight of the unity.

Four photographers strongly influenced the early development of carte de visite portraiture, Mayall, Brady, Disderi and Silvy. Mayall and Brady had long experience in daguerreotypy. The art of portraiture had been well developed by daguerreotypists. Close-ups of the human face were often wonderfully soft-textured likenesses, probably unequaled by modern photography, yet the majority of daguerrotype portraits are cold and stiff, lacking a sense of personality. Figure 38.

Mathew Brady preferred simple backgrounds, plain for the head or bust. Full standing figures were usually posed with a drape to one side, often with a fluted column resting on a base, strictly conforming to

39. Brady, M. B. Miss Hinckley. Note Brady's name on pedestal of column. Published by E. Anthony, 1860.

painterly tradition as shown in Thomas Gainsborough's standing figure of "Mrs. Graham." Figure 39.

Mayall, in photographing the Royal Family, adopted properties much like those of Brady but added balustrades and other furniture. In contrast, however, he placed the camera at a greater distance. The figures, individually and in groups, show a charming naturalness, despite the evident stiff posing. Figure 40.

38. Disderi, A. A. Cardinal de Bonald, Archbishop of Lyon, ca. 1860.

40. Mayall, J. E. The Prince of Wales, 1860.

Silvy, by many considered to be the greatest carte de visite portraitist, posed his subjects in lavishly decorated rooms, with period furniture, tapestries and art objects, all genuine and selected with taste. It is said that Silvy reserved one room for the exclusive use of the royal family. Occasionally he used painted backgrounds to suggest cultured opulence. In many of his portraits the front of the face is reflected in a mirror. Figure 41.

Disderi, concerned with the "whole man," portrayed the full figure seated or standing against a simple background with a velvet drape to one side. Usually the seated figure is engaged in some activity, writing at a desk, reading a newspaper or simply holding an object. Like Mayall, Disderi placed the camera at a distance to enhance pictorial effect. His concept of the portrait will be considered later.

The plain background has been called the Brady or American style as opposed to the more ornate European, really British-French style, but the distinctions are much overdrawn. By 1860, enough French and English carte de visite portraits by scores of photographers had acquainted American photographers with many styles. We shall see how quickly American practice deviated from the European.

Even prior to the introduction of the carte de visite to the United States, letters to the editors of photographic journals commented on the monotonous uniformity of portraiture and urged innovation and more attention to principles of art. Some correspondents emphasized symmetry and lighting. One common concern is evident: how to portray the character and individuality of the subject.

Root (p. 300) cautions: "the carte de visite . . . makes larger requisitions on the operator's knowledge of art, with its principle in regard to composition and arrangement than any other phase of photography that hitherto has been done."

"Expression is essential to a portrait . . . It is worse than worthless if the pictured face does not show the *soul* of the original—that *individuality* or *selfhood*, which differences him from all other beings, past, present, or future . . . Therefore he must detect and 'fix' the expression marking the *personality* of his subject." (p.144)

Root, who claimed to have taken 70,000 portraits, firmly believed that "the entire field of photography is well-nigh literally new and untried."[5]

Not all instructions were in general terms; some were explicit. Root, for example, explained the proper use of lighting. "Place the model in a very easy and graceful manner . . . such that every part is nearly in focus . . . Avoid as much as possible that silly clinging to uniformity in the position of the sitter . . . as of laying the hands folded together in the lap, or of fixing the thumb in the vest. Above all things endeavor to produce a variety of positions and paraphernalia in the respective members of the same family.

"Let me finally impress upon every photographer the absolute necessity of learning to *manage the light* before he can ever hope to be successful in the subsequent operation with chemical materials."[6]

There are four basic descriptive aspects of a portrait: pose, background, lighting and characterization, the last named being in part a result of the first three.

The pose determined the distance between subject and camera. Since the finished portrait would be a contact print from the negative, this was critical. Figures 42, 43.

There are only three types of studio poses: head or bust, seated or standing, although there are many variations of each. The seated figure may be half length to full length. The standing figure is usually full length. From 1860 to 1890, portraits were roughly equally distributed among the three posing types, although heads were somewhat more popular in the early 1860's and again in the 1870's, when improved lenses enabled the photographer to make images with the head nearly filling the print area.

Heads

It is rather surprising that the head was so popular throughout the 1860s, when the head size in the image was very small, ranging between 12 and 24 mm. (½ to 1 inch) and averaging about 18 mm. Figures 44, 45.

A larger head was introduced about 1867, and for the next six or seven years the common size was about 36 mm. The area of the head image had doubled, and it more than doubled again between 1873 and 1876, i.e., eight times that of a typical 1860-1864 image.

The image size on the negative was the function of three factors: focal length of the camera lens, distance between camera lens and subject, and the size of the subject. This may be expressed as a simple formula:

41. Silvy, C. The Prince of Wales, ca. 1862.

[5]*Photographic and Fine Art Journal*, 1858, *11*: 155.
[6]Root, 1864, loc. cit., pp. 32–33.

42. Silvy, C. Lady Topham, ca. 1862.

44. Southworth & Hawes. Vignetted heat of a young
woman. Boston, ca. 1861.

43. Brady, M. B. Secretary of War J. B. Floyd, later
a Confederate general. Brady copy negative, original
ca. 1858, carte issued by E. Anthony 1860–1861.

45. Broadbent & Phillips. Vignetted head of a child;
hand tinted. Philadelphia, ca. 1864.

$$S' = \frac{F \times S}{D}$$

where S' is the image size
S = size of subject
F = focal length
D = distance from camera lens to subject

For example, the Ross "quick acting carte de visite lenses" (late 1860s and 1870s) had these specifications:[7]

1. 1¾ in. dia.	4½ in. focal length	13-14 ft. working distance
2. 2¹/₁₀ in. dia.	4¾ in. focal length	15-16 ft. working distance
3. 2½ in. dia.	6 in. focal length	19-20 ft. working distance

To achieve fine sculpturing of facial features, it became necessary to pay greater attention to lighting. Illumination of the studio by skylight presented few complications because the problem was usually insufficient light. The great portraitist devised means for concentrating and directing the light. Illumination of the face to achieve the desired light and shadow was more or less a preference of the photographer but a preference that entailed difficulties.

The larger head size presented the human face in unprecedented detail. Blemishes not evident in a small image became conspicuous. Moreover, the skin is semi-transparent, under normal conditions slightly oily. In strong light the skin becomes more luminous.

Painters had individual preferences for illuminating their subjects. Rembrandt concentrated light on one feature, thereby producing strong shadowing. Holbein posed his subjects in full light, with almost no shadows. Leonardo da Vinci lighted his subjects from above, thus accentuating the nose, eyes and mouth.

Knowledge of the techniques of the master painters was part of formal training in art. After 1860, however, few persons entering photography had such education or experience. William Kurtz (New York) became famous in the 1870s for his beautiful portraits with "Rembrandt effects" as he devised reflectors to concentrate the light he needed.[8] Many American photographers experimented with the so-called Rembrandt portraits (e.g., William Notman, E. L. Brand) and advertised their skill in producing them. A. Bassano (London), about 1880, advertised the "Holbein" portrait both in carte and larger mount sizes. Figures 46–49.

As noted above, stronger illumination and larger images accentuated moles, pock marks and other blemishes. Whereas the painter could ignore them, the photographer was obliged to remove them from the negative.

Retouching was practiced since the late 1850s but was applied to the positive print. Retouching the negative did not become a standard practice until 1870, although it was done earlier. Retouching was usually performed by an artist, but several devices were manufactured to perform the work mechanically. The

[7]Wilson, Hood & Co., 1873, *Illustrated Catalogue*, pp. 9–12.
[8]For a discussion of Kurtz's work see Taft, 1938, pp. 336–341.

46. Putnam, George T. "Rembrandt effect," side illumination to increase sculpturing of the face. Middleboro, Mass., 1874.

47. Pierce, Wm., Mezzotint effect, soft focus by the Meinerth patented process. Brunswick, Maine, 1868.

48. Brand, E. L. & Co. Soft focus, side-lighting and symmetry; typical characteristics of Brand's portraits. Chicago, ca. 1873.

49. Kimball, W. G. C. A fine portrait from a skillfully retouched negative. Concord, N. H., 1874.

Getchell & Hyatt machine was attached to a sewing machine treadle and was capable of "all usual manual work, doing fine stippling and hatching." The Pierce & Hitchcock device was similar, but it was operated by a hand turning wheel. Most studios relied on hand retouching.[9]

Other methods were used to correct or avoid the cruel honesty of the camera. A widely adopted practice was the so-called Mezzo-Tinto patented by Carl Meinerth (Newburyport, Mass., U. S. Pat. 66726, July 16, 1867) devised to produce a soft image. This was accomplished by placing a plate glass or thin sheet of mica between the printing paper and the negative. A diffused focus resulted in a softness that resembled the so-called porcelain finish.[10]

Meinerth offered exclusive town rights for twenty-five dollars, single gallery rights for ten dollars and negotiated terms with operators in large cities who wished exclusive rights. He was able to sell more than 425 licenses, with a requirement that each carte de visite so produced bear a statement crediting the Meinerth patent and license number.

Meinerth was unaware that Sir David Brewster, twenty years earlier had demonstrated the "production of very soft and agreeable positive pictures by inserting sheets of paper or a sheet of glass between negative and print."[11]

The vignetted head was enormously popular in the United States in the 1860s but seldom appeared in Europe until the early 1870s. It was a bust picture "produced by shading off, in printing, the background and the drapery, so as to show only the head and shoulders seemingly clouded off."[12] Note that the subject of a vignetted portrait had been photographed in a seated pose and the image was printed by masking most of the negative. Masks could be purchased or homemade.

Delicate tinting of these portraits was quite common in the early 1860s: skin, cheeks, eyes, lips and hair. In the late 1860s only the cheeks were tinted.

The vignetted head gradually disappeared from the trade as images with larger heads were produced.

The Seated Pose

The seated portrait was favored by many photographers because the subject was more relaxed and it was easier to imply activity. The vignetted bust required no background other than that necessary to photograph the figure. Figures 50–52.

In the seated pose, the subject is surrounded by studio space which must somehow be covered or decorated. Simple screens or painted walls might suffice, but fashion dictated embellishment to enhance pictorial effects.

Disderi was especially successful in portraying his subjects in seated poses. Many English photographers

[9]See *Philadelphia Photographer 16*: 221-222, 1879.

[10]Darrah, W. C., "Carl Meinerth, Photographer", *Photographic Collector 1* (4): 6-9, 1981.

[11]*British Association for the Advancement of Science, Proc.* 1845.

[12]Waldack, C., 1862, *The Card Photograph*, p. 5.

50. Bierstadt Brothers. The seated portrait, note simple studio properties. New Bedford, Mass., 1861.

52. Hardy, James William. Lady knitting. Aldeburgh, Suffolk, England, ca. 1863.

also produced portraits with implications of activity, such as a gentlemen writing a letter, a lady knitting or a child holding a toy.

The Standing Full Figure

This popular pose was fraught with difficulties. The subject was obliged to stand motionless for a minute or more while the final adjustments were made for exposure of the negative. An iron head clamp, adjustable for height and with a tripod base, firmly held the subject in position. The base is evident in many images. Figure 53.

As with the seated pose, only more so, the back-

51. Whipple, J. A. George A. Rand. Seated portrait, three-quarters length. Note simple "American Style" background. Boston, ca. 1860.

53. Dow, James M. Full length standing portrait. Note painted scenery and base of head-clamp behind feet; also drape, pedestal and column. Ogdensburg, N.Y., ca. 1864.

ground must be contrived. The camera is at greater distance from the subject to show the full figure, thereby increasing the expanse of wall and floor. The painted background, a varied selection of furniture, rugs and decorative accessories became essential properties of every studio.

By 1863, manufacturing companies specializing in photographic supplies offered painted screens and curtains, papier mache rocks, walls and urns; also, columns, balustrades and fences of thin wood or cardboard, with an almost endless variety of small objects. Ornate tables with each of the legs carved in a different style were found in many studios. Posing chairs, backgrounds and head-clamps were as much a part of the business as the chemicals used in producing plates and prints.

Painted Backgrounds

At the time when the carte de visite was introduced, it was the usual practice to paint studio walls, at least in the posing area, a dull blue, buff or light gray color or to cover them with plain colored paper or fabric. The subject was thus photographed against a plain background.

An ornate background provided more than decoration; it could imply wealth, position or culture.

Painted scenery was sold by the square foot, in panels on rolls. A twenty-four foot roll usually had six scenes, but as many as twenty scenes might be in a roll sixty feet in length. A roll might begin at one end with a wilderness scene blending gradually into a lake or rural country-side, moving into an estate or garden, onto the steps of a mansion, into the drawing room and ending in

the library walled with shelves of books. There were military camp scenes, seascapes, sunrises and much more. Figures 54–58.

T. & W. Cummings (Lancaster, Pa., ca. 1862-1864) in the rich farming country of southeastern Pennsylvania, had a roll of painted backgrounds which included a fine barn and the corner of a handsome manor home with which to photograph their farmer clients.

The introduction of painted backgrounds is generally credited to A. Claudet, 1851, but there appear to have been occasional earlier uses of them by daguerreotypists. Henry Ulke is believed to have introduced painted scenery to the United States.[13] In Europe, the principal manufacturer of painted backgrounds and other studio properties was A. Marion & Co. (London and Paris). In the United States there were many suppliers. In 1863, John H. Simmons offered "fine backgrounds in endless variety." L. W. Seavey (New York, established 1865) became the largest supplier of painted backgrounds and papier mache acessories. Among his customers were Brady, Fredricks, Kurtz, Gurney and Sarony. Parisian photographers purchased Seavy's scenery, an indication of its superiority. Wilson, Hood & Co. (Philadelphia) in 1873 advertised: "We can paint Fancy Backgrounds from any design furnished and of any desired size."[14]

Many photographers painted their own or engaged a local artist to make their backgrounds.

[13]Brown, Paul, *Philadelphia Photographer 16*: 219-221, 1879.
[14]1873, *Illustrated Catalogue*, p. 61. Every issue of a photographic periodical carried advertisements by Ashe, Dayton & Co., Seavey, and Simmons, with testimonials by their customers.

54. Kinnaman and Howell. Standing pose; painted background. Findlay, Ohio, ca. 1867.

55. Truesdell, S. W. Painted background; lady with arm on Phenix posing chair. Kenosha, Wisc., ca. 1878.

56. Weller, L. P. Painted background, "seascape and sunrise." Oconomowoc, Wisc., ca. 1878.

58. Littleton, M. K. Typical painted "interior" scene, midwest United States, 1880s. Dexter, Kansas, ca. 1884.

57. Cummings, T. & W. Painted background, barn at left. The colonnade at the right merges into a manor scene on the roll. Many poses show only the barn or more of the manor house. Lancaster, Pa., 1862–1865.

59. Hughes Brothers. Home-made rustic properties, rustic fence, straw on floor, popular 1878–1885. Blanchard, Iowa, ca. 1880.

60. Eppert, C. Studio properties: papier mache fence. Terra Haute, Inc., ca. 1882.

By the late 1870s, the painted background became garish, bizarre and incongruous. Yet, even these reflect faithfully the fashions of the day.

Studio Accessories

Artificial rustic fences, gates and doorways, usually made of papier mache or cardboard, became standard studio equipment in the 1870s.

Cautiously at first, photographers began staging the portrait rather than merely posing the subject. Gradually the contrived scene became bolder. The deceptions used to create illusions were ingenious: porches, windows, rowboats, covered wells with oaken buckets, "snow," to name only a few.

Not all properties were make-believe. Many photographers maintained a large selection of costume jewelry, necklaces, large Christian crosses, combs and half-crowns to adorn female subjects. Potted plants, vases, cut flowers, books on a table, straw or buffalo skins on the floor were used at the photographer's discretion.

Whether one reacts favorably or abhorrently, is amused or disturbed, the fact remains: portraits made with these accessories were admired by those who produced them and those who purchased them.

Characterization

Disderi is sometimes credited as the first to portray "social types," but this is not true. Stereographs of native peoples of many lands and of contrived groups illustrating many traditional occupations were well

61. Clark, L. W. Studio properties: papier mache fireplace, mantle and andirons. Note various framed photographs. The posing technique approaches staging the subject. Streator, Ill., ca. 1880.

62. Bogardus, A. Studio properties: open window and balcony. A great many variants of this design were used in the United States and Europe, 1864–1875. New York, 1864.

63. Richardson. Studio properties: "row boat." There were about a half dozen types constructed of cardboard or thin wood. The men are standing behind the prop. Boston, 1866.

known in Europe and America before 1858. Disderi's manual explaining his methods was published too late and was too little known to have directly influenced the course of carte de visite photography in the United States,[15] although Root makes several references to it.

What Disderi did was to call attention to poses that

[15]1862, *Essai surl'Art de la Photographie.*

64. Schillare, A. J. Staging the portrait. Young girl seated among artificial flowers. Northampton, Mass., ca. 1878.

65. Mooney, Arthur. Staging the portrait. Girl beside oaken bucket and well: a combination of genuine and artificial props. Charles City, Iowa, 1877.

would characterize a profession or the position of the subject, the clergyman (priest or cardinal), the soldier (corporal or general), the statesman, the merchant. Indeed, instead of individualizing the subject, he was categorizing him.

Social typing unconsciously by-passes the search for the individual. Carl Meinerth instructed those licensed to use his mezzotint process to engage the subject in light conversation while setting up the camera, "to bring out whatever was inside" the person. A few years later Julia Cameron expressed the same sentiment.

Root's warning (p.143) "The portrait is worse than worthless if the pictured face does not show the *soul* of the original—that *individuality* or *selfhood*" is a clear indication of the American faith in the uniqueness of the individual, his independence. I have not found a similar expression related to the portrait in any nineteenth century European publication. Figures 66–69.

Disderi has been both applauded and condemned for his inventions and influence, praised for the changes in the practice of photography and condemned for the same reason.

"Disderi . . . single handedly destroyed the art of photographic portrait."[16]

The crimes with which he was charged may be summarized as standardized poses, typing of subjects, mechanized production of prints, and commercialization. For a few years the richest and most successful of all photographers, Disderi was bound to be resented.

[16]"Primitive French Photography," *Aperture 15* (1): 8, 1969.

66. Rowell, C. C. Characterization. Newport, N. H., ca. 1863.

68. Beal. Characterization. Note large head size common after 1871. Minneapolis, Minn., 1872.

67. Wyman, Henry. Characterization. Boston, ca. 1862.

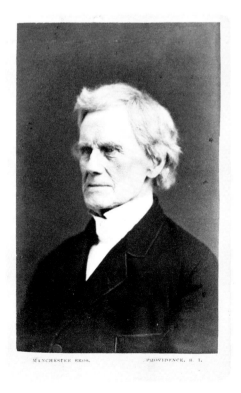

69. Manchester Brothers. Characterization, "Rev. Thomas Shepard, D.D." Providence, R.I., 1872.

It is very difficult to assess Disderi's influence on portraiture largely because he very cleverly promoted his own reputation and partly because many of his contemporaries viewed him bitterly.

Disderi's patent was "for improvements in photography." Multilens cameras and moving plate holders were independently developed by several photographers. Unquestionably from time to time Disderi tossed out suggestions and claims knowing that other photographers had already done them.

It is Disderi's approach to portraiture that concerns us here. Part III of his *Essai sur l'Art de la Photographie*, titled "Esthetic Photography" presents both a philosophical theory and a method.[17]

Although Disderi urged the photographer to "penetrate the true character" of the subject (p. 266), his criteria for a good portrait were almost completely lacking in references to individual characterization. He used the word personality but his own portraits seldom convey the emotional reaction characterization implies.

(1) a pleasing face
(2) appropriate presentation
(3) definition, light and shadow
(4) proportion
(5) detail of expression
(6) a beautiful resemblance (pp. 265–267)

The whole concept was technical, pictorial. Individuality, personality, and character were only implied.

There has long been a lively debate over personality in portraiture, by painters, photographers, psychologists and art historians.[18] American photographic journals from 1858 to 1864 carry many comments on this issue.

European photographers in the 1850s were fascinated by the large portrait, with its intimacy and charm. It was impossible to achieve such beauty in a small carte de visite image. That, however, hardly explains the stifling of imagination that marks the early phase of the carte de visite portraiture in Europe.

The character of the subject is shown primarily by the face, secondarily by the hands. Age, toil, health and the burdens of life are recorded in the eyes, the wrinkles and the mouth. Sadness, tenderness, pride, pain, all show through the physical features.

Julia Cameron, justly famous for the gentle characterization in her beautiful portraits, did not influence carte de visite portraiture in any way. She produced a few cartes and some of her large portraits were reduced to carte format for commercial distribution. As an amateur, rather deficient in technical skills, she was not appreciated by her professional contemporary peers. Nevertheless, Mrs. Cameron's portraits are among the most striking ever produced.

Considering, then, the instantaneous image caught by the camera, how can we reconcile the truth and untruth of the photographic portrait? It cannot record the whole person, nor can it reveal the real person.

There are great numbers of carte de visite portraits of men, women and children which show striking characters, beautiful in their individualities. Some were made by the masters like Gurney, Sarony, Mosher, Black, Kurtz, Nadar and Reutlinger, but greater numbers were produced by unsung small-town photographers scattered over two continents.

Some Portrait Conventions

Husband and Wife

Among the more abundant surviving carte de visite portraits are those of newly married couples and husband and wife at various ages. The most striking convention is the almost universally used pose of the husband seated and the wife standing, with one hand on her husband's shoulder. Mayall photographed Queen Victoria in this position, her hand on Prince Albert's right shoulder. There are fair numbers of portraits, especially newlyweds, with the partners standing, the husband usually to the right of his wife. Husband and wife, both seated, was a pose generally reserved for the elderly. Figures 70–72.

Brides in costume and bridal parties are occasionally seen. In the Protestant communities in the United States, weddings (and funeral services) were performed in the home. Traditional bridal gowns were usually worn at high church ceremonies.

70. Hollenbeck, O. A. Husband and wife. Note wife is standing with her hand on husband's shoulder. Oneida, N.Y., ca. 1864.

[17]1862, pp. 263–295.

[18]McCauley, Elizabeth A., 1980, *Likenesses: Portrait Photography in Europe, 1850-1870*, Albuquerque. See also McCauley, 1980, *A.A.E. Disderi and the Carte de Visite Portrait Photograph*, Ph.D. Dissertation, Yale University

71. Mora, J. M. Husband and wife. Image hand tinted. New York, ca. 1876.

Mother and Child

The madonna figure with all its charm has been the favorite pose for the babe in arms. Black, Fredricks, Whipple, Bogardus, and Gutekunst produced beautiful examples, capturing the affectionate beam of the mother. Figures 73, 74.

73. Sonrel, A. Mother and child, seated pose. Boston, ca. 1864.

72. Jones, T. M. Bridal couple, an unusual pose for this period. Moline, Ill., ca. 1878.

74. Whipple, J. A. Mother and child, standing pose. Boston, ca. 1868.

37

Children

Some of the most capable photographers flatly refused to take studio pictures of children. Many others advertised specialization in child portraits.

The chief difficulty was confining the child long enough to set up the camera and obtain a suitable pose. Usually the child was tied firmly to a posing chair by a broad sash. Because the same sash was used for many sitters, the design and color rarely matched the child's clothing. This incongruity marks the majority of these portraits.

A few photographers attempted to occupy the child's hands with a doll, toy or flower, but generally, they simply hoped for the best.[19] Figure 75–80.

By and large, although there are many lovely and "cute" portraits of children, most of them are at best mediocre.

Groups

A group, defined as more than two persons, ranged from a few to a great number. The most interesting are those relatively small groups which required the photographer to position the various individuals to obtain a suitable picture.

Occasionally the photographer strained for symmetrical balance, diagonal lines, or other geometric effects.

[19]See *Philadelphia Photographer* 3: 196, 1866; 4: 66, 1872.

STUART, PHOTO.   GLASGOW & HELENSBURGH

76. Stuart. "Thomas William Brown, age 8 months." Glasgow, Scotland, ca. 1872.

75. Smith, Miss C. We do not know if the photographer thought this was cute or gave up waiting for a more conventional pose. Note sash securing child to the chair. Lowell, Mass., ca. 1878.

77. Pach Brothers. Child portrait. New York, 1877.

C.D.MOSHER,   CHICAGO.

78. Mosher, G. D. Portrait of a young girl. Chicago, ca. 1876.

80. Wiklunds, A. "Sisters and brothers." Nassjo, Sweden, ca. 1895.

Family groups, parents and children, children alone, three or four generations, school friends, musical troupes, employers and their employees, a hunting party, a picnic of young friends, all are typical examples of this type of pose. Large groups include meetings, school children and clubs. Figures 81, 82.

Some Unusual Types of Portraiture

Mortuary

Portraits of dead persons, especially young children, were often the only pictures of the individual the family could possess. Child mortality until 1885 carried off one child out of five during the first year of life and two of five by the fifth year. Many cartes de visite show the portrait of a boy, age ten with a notation on the back "died 13 yrs 4 mos," or of a young woman of 18 or 20, "died age 23." Daguerreotypes of deceased persons had been common, cartes produced already in 1860,[20] simply continued the practice.

Death portraits of infants usually show the child as sleeping on a pillow or in a crib. Occasionally the body was held in the lap of a grieving parent, more often the father. Older persons were laid out as asleep on a bed or couch. Figure 83.

One photographer advertised, "We are prepared to take pictures of a deceased person on one hour's notice."

J.NOTMAN,   BOSTON.

79. Notman, J. Portrait of a boy. The Notman studios delighted in the use of artificial snow. Boston, ca., 1876.

[20]*Humphrey's Journal, 12*: 324, 1861.

81. Clark, J. A group of workmen. South Brisbane, Australia, ca. 1875.

83. Mortuary. Dead child. J. Hansen Jones, Hillsboro, Ill., 1872.

Self-Portraits

Many photographers, like painters, produced self-portraits, usually for family and friends. They are often autographed. Figures 84, 154.

Identification Cards or Passes

There is some uncertainty as to how early the card photograph was used as a means of personal identification. The most common examples were issued by the managers of exhibitions (1867–1885) to exhibitors and employees. The individual was permitted entrance by

displaying the card bearing his likeness and signature. Figure 85. See also page 137.

"Mug Shots"

The importance of identifying known criminals by means of portraits was recognized by some police departments in the early 1840s.[21] Daguerreotype files were maintained in France, Belgium and in the United States in the 1850s. The multiple prints from negatives greatly expanded the "mug file" system. Routinely, many police departments had the criminal photographed and the card annotated with his name, crime, date of conviction and punishment. Copies were sometimes sent to police departments in other cities. Figure 86.

Such annotated mug shots are quite rare, inasmuch as they were not intended for public distribution. Nevertheless, they do appear from time to time.

There are also portraits of well-known criminals that seem to have been commercially published. Notoriety of the subject apparently made the sale of the portrait profitable.

[21]Rudisill, Richard, 1971, *Mirror Image*, p. 112.

82. Downie, D. C. "The Ferguson Group—all Fergusons." Glasgow, Scotland, ca. 1875.

84. Rothwell, J. Wesley. Self portrait. Washington, Pa.,
ca. 1874. Courtesy of Henry Deeks.

86. Criminal "mugshot." "1025, John W. Gannon, convicted
of Robbery." From dispersed police file, Boston, Mass.,
1883.

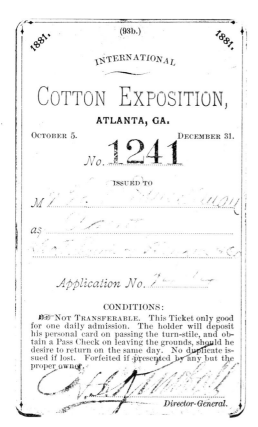

85. Identification Portrait. International Cotton
Exposition, Atlanta, Ga., 1881. Anonymous staff
photographer.

Spirit Photography

W. H. Mumler of Boston claimed that he was able to
photograph the spirits of deceased loved ones. He
convinced the gullible to the extent that for almost eight
years he produced them. Reputable photographers
branded him a charlatan and published descriptions of

87. Spirit photography. Ghost figures. Messrs. Lucas,
London, ca. 1865. Courtesy of Henry Deeks.

ten tricks that could be used to produce ghost pictures. A few of Mumler's images were quite convincing, but most were crude deceptions.[22]

Brewster had discovered that if a person stood in a position before the camera for a second or less while the exposure continued for a time thereafter, a "ghost" appeared on the negative. The person simply walked off the setting, resulting in under-exposure of his figure. Many humorous and sentimental stereographs utilizing this idea were produced between 1854 and 1858.[23]

Mumler, of course, had to use a copy negative of a portrait of the deceased in a new composed negative or print. His precise methods were never disclosed.

For quite different purposes, without deception, O. Erekson (Bridgeport, Connecticut) and G. L. Lape (New York) produced similar portraits, some serious sentimental mementos, not to deceive but to please the family, and some intended to be humorous, such as the ghost pointing an accusing finger at a person.

Spirit photography is mentioned here to suggest the ingenuity with which photographers explored the uses of carte de visite portraiture. Figure 87.

Other Uses of Portraiture

Routine portraiture, producing portraits pleasing to customers, was the basis and mainstay of a photographer's business. With rare exceptions, his livelihood depended upon it.

Carte de visite portraits of other kinds proved to be highly profitable ventures which benefitted the publisher, the retailer (often the independent photographer) and the subject. A tremendous world trade in the portraits of celebrities developed in the early 1860s, a business increased by the American Civil War. Portraits of the native peoples of the world were also sold in great numbers.

These types of portraits will be considered in the next three chapters.

[22]*New York Times*, April 13, 1869.
[23]*Photographic News 1*: 11, 1858. See also Darrah, *World of Stereographs*, p. 64.

CHAPTER FIVE
PORTRAITS OF CELEBRITIES

Disderi's portraits of Napoleon III earned him considerable reputation and handsome profit. Similarly, Mayall's portraits of the Royal Family enjoyed tremendous success, hundreds of thousands of copies being sold within a few years, earning him a royalty of 35,000 pounds from A. Marion, the publisher. The untimely death from typhoid fever of Prince Albert on December 14, 1861, at the age of 42, shocked the world. Seventy thousand carte de visite portraits by various photographers were sold in a week.[1] By the end of 1861, portraits of notable personalities were being commercially published by hundreds of photographers.

Certainly mere novelty and curiosity contributed much to this burgeoning world trade, but there were other reasons for this public enthusiasm. The world was rapidly becoming smaller. Commerce, colonization, migrations of people, the missionary movement and accelerated communication stimulated an awareness and interest in both nationalism and the world at large.

Several new practices were developing in photographic publishing, two of which were especially involved in the carte portrait business, the trade list and the fee and royalty agreement.

The publisher had to develop a trade list, a negative file from which a large variety of portraits and other subjects could be produced.

Larger publishers issued catalogues listing the titles and inviting mail orders from prospective customers. Assembling the negative file usually involved the employment of photographers to take pictures, the purchase of negatives—originals and copies by other photographers—and, commonly, pirating whatever seemed to be marketable.

Brady copied his collection of daguerreotype and other portraits on carte de visite negatives, from which he and E. Anthony published great numbers of prints, beginning in the winter of 1860–1861. Both Anthony and Brady purchased extensively and pirated often. For instance, "Brady's" portrait of Washington Irving was copied from a daguerreotype by John Plumbe (1847), and that of Edgar Allen Poe from a daguerreotype by an operator in the gallery of Masury & Hartshorn, and John Wilkes Booth from a carte by Silsbee, Case & Co., Boston, 1862.

The second publishing practice involved a financial agreement between the photographer and the subject. The person photographed was offered a flat fee ranging from 25 to 1000 dollars, depending upon notoriety, or a royalty based upon the number of copies sold. Gernsheim noted that A. Marion & Co. paid a royalty as high as 400 pounds ($2000) per 10,000 copies sold.[2] Sales of a single title often reached an enormous

volume. Probably the greatest recorded figure is W. & D. Downey's portrait of the Princess of Wales carrying on her back Princess Louise (ca. 1867).[3] Three hundred thousand copies, not counting pirated issues, were sold.

In March 1861, an English publisher advertised in *Humphrey's Journal* for negatives of Abraham Lincoln, James Buchanan and other American notables to add to his list. Current events often raised an individual to instant fame. The bombardment and surrender of Fort Sumter made Major Robert Anderson a national hero. For nearly two months, Anthony produced a thousand copies a day from negatives made by George S. Cook of Charleston.[4]

In November 1862, E. & H. T. Anthony issued a catalogue listing 2000 portraits plus 300 war scenes by Brady. The cartes de visite, printed from negatives of many sources, were grouped in eleven categories:

(1) Army and Navy
(2) Statesmen, lawyers, physicians and others
(3) Prominent foreign portraits
(4) The Clergy
(5) The Literary World
(6) The Stage
(7) Prominent women (only 37 listed)
(8) Copies of engravings and paintings
(9) Copies of statuary
(10) Miscellaneous
(11) Brady's Photographic Views of the War

Groups 8 to 11 were not photographic portraits, although many of the engravings and statues were of historical persons. This represented the most extensive coverage of American notables. Scientists and inventors were classed with statesmen and lawyers. Figure 88.

The Photographers of Celebrities

British photographers dominated the field, although many French and American publishers produced fine series. Nearly every country had at least a few photographers who issued portraits of persons of national importance.

The following British photographer-publishers produced fine series of portraits in the 1860s and early 1870s.

Bassano Alexander
Caldesi & Co. (Caldesi, Blanford & Co.)
Claudet, A.
Cundall & Co.
Debenham, W. E.
Downey, W. & D.

---

[1]See Gernsheim, H., 1955, *History of Photography*, p. 228.
[2]Gernsheim, 1955, loc cit., p. 227.
[3]*Photographic News*, 1885, p. 136.
[4]*Humphrey's Journal 12*: 9, March 1, 1861; *14*: 26, 1862.

88. E. Anthony imprint advertising Brady's Portrait Gallery. New York, 1861–1862.

89. Kilburn, Wm. F. Major H. Edwards, London, ca. 1861.

Duval, C. A.
Elliott & Fry
Fradelle & Marshall
Hills & Saunders
Hughes, Jabez (Hughes & Edmonds)
Kilburn, Wm. F.
Lock & Whitfield
London Stereoscopic (and Photograph) Co.
Mason & Co.
Maull & Polyblank (Maull & Co.)
Mayall, John J. E. (A. Marion & Co., publisher)
Melhuish, A. J.
Negretti & Zambra
Silvy, C.
Southwell (Thomas McLean & Co., publisher)
Watkins, John (John and Charles Watkins)

There were scores of others who published fine important photographs but whose trade lists were of smaller variety than by those listed above. Some were famous as portraitists of only a few celebrities. Charles Clifford, an Englishman residing in Madrid, was sent by the Queen of Spain to take a portrait of Queen Victoria. Clifford's "Regal portrait," said to be Victoria's favorite pose, was taken on November 14, 1861. This carte was published by Cundall, Downes & Co. Figure 93.

Thomas Annan produced a modest number of celebrity portraits. Among the better known is his seated David Livingston.

90. Mayall, J. E. Lord Canning, Govenor General of India. London, ca. 1861.

91. Elliott & Fry. Thomas Carlyle, London, ca. 1870.

93. Clifford, C. Queen Victoria, "The Regal Portrait of Her Majesty." November 14, 1861. Published by A. Marion & Co., London.

France

Many French photographers produced portraits of celebrities in the early 1860s. Disderi headed the profession but Mayer and Pierson enjoyed royal patronage. Mayer (successor to Mayer & Pierson), Pierre Petit—Disderi's closest rival for carte portraits—Levitsky, LeJeune, E. Desmarais, Etienne Carjat, Ernst Ladry, Maujean, Nadar (=Tournechon) and Reutlinger were the most important. From 1867 to 1875, Nadar and Reutlinger became not only the most prolific but also, because of huge sales, among the best known portraitists in the world. Frenchmen dominate their trade lists, but foreign leaders from all fields who visited Paris were invited to pose for their portraits. Both Nadar and Reutlinger preferred bust poses. Many of Reutlinger's portraits (1867–1875) are vignetted head and shoulders, reminiscent of the earlier American style. Figures 94–97.

Other European Countries

The most important German photographer of celebrities were L. Haase and Hanfstangl. Their cartes de visite of Emperor Wilhelm, Bismark, von Moltke and Franz Liszt, selected from many, indicate that they followed the publishing pattern established in England and France. Moser published portraits of artists, musicians and actors along with those of political personalities O. Brockmann (Dresden) also published an extensive series.

Gehmar Brothers (Brussels) became well known in England and America for their many portraits of the

92. Watkins, J. & C. Sir G. C. Lewis, statesman, versatile scholar, and man of letters. London, ca. 1862.

45

94. Reutlinger, Ch. Napoleon Joseph Charles Paul
Bonaparte. Paris, ca. 1868.

96. Levitsky, S. L. Empress Eugenie. Negative 1860,
carte issued by LeJeune, successor, Paris, ca. 1863.

95. Reutlinger, Ch. Mme. Adelaide Ristori, actress. Fine
portraits of Ristori were issued by American photographers during each of her four tours of the United
States. Paris, ca. 1868.

97. Petit, Pierre. Marshall M. E. MacMahon, president
of France. Carte issued by the Woodburytype Permanent Photograph Co., with credit to Petit, 1875.

98. Alessandri Brothers. Pope Pius IX, hand tinted portrait. Rome, ca. 1868.

children of Victoria and Albert, taken when on a visit to their great uncle King Leopold. Many foreign dignitaries posed for the Gehmars.

In Italy, no single portraitist of celebrities was outstanding and none issued a large list of titles. d'Alessandri, under special Papal patronage, produced many portraits of Pope Pius IX and of various church officials. These images, carefully hand-colored, were popular souvenirs for pilgrims in Rome. Schemboche (Rome and Turin), Alinari (Florence) and R. Rive (Naples) are noteworthy.

Victor and Ludwig Angerer and Emil Rabending (also as Rabending & Monckhoven) in Austria produced many portraits of Emperor Franz Josef and the Empress. Rosa Jenik photographed Archduke Franz Karl, father of the Emperor, and other nobility.

Most famous of the Austrian issues was a series of portraits of beautiful women, mostly actresses and singers, by Fritz Luckhardt (Vienna). In Russia, A. Denier (St. Petersburg) and S. L. Levitsky (St. Petersburg; Paris 1858–1866 q.v.), and M. Panov (Moscow) are best known.

Every capital city had its society and celebrity photographers who were ready to take portraits for the trade. To suggest the world-wide nature of this business, a few of the scattered photographers are listed below.

Malovich (Trieste)—portraits of Emperor Maximillian of Mexico and the Empress Charlotte
Abdullah Brothers (Constantinople)—systemati-

99. Mason & Co. Charles Dickens, London, ca. 1865.

100. Haase, L. Otto von Bismark, Chancellor of Germany. Berlin, ca. 1866.

101. Angerer, L. Ex-Empress Sophia, mother of Franz Joseph and Maximilian. Vienna. Carte issued ca. 1868.

102. Malovich, G. Maximilian, ill-fated emperor of Mexico, executed 1867. Negative ea. 1863, carte issued Trieste, 1872.

cally photographed political emissaries to the Sultanate and other prominent persons
Bourne & Shepherd (Bombay & Calcutta)
F. Chit (Bankok, Siam)—1870s
Yu Chong (Hanoi, IndoChina)—1870s into 1880s
Thomson (Singapore)
G. Leutzinger (Rio de Janeiro)
R. H. Klumb (Rio de Janeiro)
Cruces & Campa (Mexico City)
Fernandez (Mexico City)

Of particular interest to Americans are H. L. Chase and M. Dickson of Honolulu. Both published large numbers of portraits of native leaders, usually identifying them by native and Christian names; for example, two by Chase, ca. 1873: "H. R. H. Likelike, Mrs. Cleghorn, sister of the King," and "Pauahi, Mrs. C. R. Bishop, a Hawaiian Chiefess."

The United States
The popularity of celebrity portraits in the United States fluctuated, with two peak periods, 1860–1866 and 1875–1885. The earlier period conformed closely to the European fad, with statesmen, military, clerical, literary and theatrical figures. The second period was significantly different, being quite vulgar and leaning toward the queer and sensational.

To a surprising extent, the large-scale production of cartes de visite of celebrities was limited to barely a dozen publishers, although at least 600 American photographers are known to have issued such portraits.

103. Chit, F. "One of 75 children of the King of Siam by thirty-nine wives." Bangkok, ca. 1868.

104. Dickson, M. "Likelike, Mrs. Cleghorn, Sister of the King." Honolulu, Hawaii, ca. 1868.

105. Cruces & Campa. Marshall E. F. Forey, Commander of the French expeditionary army to Mexico. Mexico City, 1863. Courtesy of George H. Moss.

Simultaneously, in the summer of 1860, D. Appleton & Co. and E. Anthony commenced publishing pictures of notables. A. A. Turner Co. was photographer and printer of the Appleton issues. By early 1861 scores of photographers were producing them.

The outbreak of Civil War created a clamor of portraits of military leaders and statesmen involved in the war effort. The huge market for portraits of Major Anderson had already been mentioned. Preoccupation with the war delayed somewhat the broad coverage of contemporary American notables by the large publishers. Nevertheless, within three or four years, portraits of nearly all persons of prominence were available.

The following American publishers are known to have produced portraits of more than fifty celebrities during the 1860s.

Allen & Horton   Boston
Anthony, E.& H.T.   New York
D. Appleton & Co.   New York
Black (Black & Case)   Boston
Bogardus, A.   New York
Bradley & Rulofson   San Francisco
Brady, M.   New York, Washington
Carbutt, John   Chicago
Case & Getchell   Boston
Fredricks, C. D.   New York
Gardner, Alex   Washington
Gurney, J. & Son   New York
Gutekunst, F.   Philadelphia
Hallett & Bro.   New York
Hawes, J. J. (Southworth & Hawes)   Boston
Rockwood, G. C.   New York
Scholten, J. A.   St. Louis
Silsbee, Case & Co.   Boston
Soule, John   Boston
Whipple, J. A.   Boston

Gurney & Son and Fredricks, throughout the 1860s produced a continuing series of notables, from actors and singers in stage costumes to American and European authors. Fredrick's "Maggie Mitchell" and Gurney's "Rev. Dr. Flint" and "Charles Dickens" are typical.

In the 1870s and 1880s, Napoleon Sarony (New York) became the foremost American portraitist of celebrities. Although working chiefly with the larger cabinet card mount, he produced many portraits in carte de visite format. His favorite and best portraits were of theatrical performers, often posed in the costumes of a popular role. His staged poses possess a vitality rarely found in nineteenth century portraiture.

Mora, who began his career in the employ of Sarony, established his own studio about 1870. His excellent work is imitative of Sarony but is less imaginative, usually bust portraiture. Among his fine cartes de visite are several portraits of Dom Pedro, President of Brazil. Mora and Sarony tinted many custom and published portraits.

Some of these photographers produced unusual series, which are of only slight interest today, but

108. Appleton, D. & Co. George W. Curtis, editor of *Harper's Weekly*. A. A. Turner, photographer, 1862. Note dealer's blindstamp. Lawrence & Houseworth, San Francisco.

106. Silsbee, Case & Co. Edward Everett, clergyman, president of Harvard University, abolitionist, senator, Secretary of State. Boston, ca. 1860.

REV. PHILIPS BROOKS.

Entered according to Act of Congress, in the year 1861, in the Clerk's Office of the District Court of the United States for the Eastern District of Pennsylvania, by

McALLISTER & BROTHER, 728 Chestnut Street,

107. Gutekunst, F. Rev. Phillips Brooks, Episcopal clergyman. McAllister & Bros. publisher, Philadelphia, 1861.

109. Fredricks, C. D. Maggie Mitchell, actress. New York, ca. 1862.

110. Warren, W. Shaw. Charles Sumner, Senator and
abolitionist. S. B. Heald photo. Boston, 1872.

MLLE. ALBANI

680 BROADWAY, N. Y.

112. Sarony, Napoleon. Mlle. Emma Albani (Lajeunesse),
Canadian-born singer. New York, ca. 1874.

111. Warren, W. Shaw. Charlotte Cushman, actress.
S. B. Heald photo. Boston, 1873.

707 BROADWAY, N. Y.

113. Mora, J. M. Christine Nilssen, Swedish singer.
New York, carte ca. 1875.

important at the time they appeared. About 1862, Hallett & Bros. issued a series of the Methodist Bishops of the United States.[5] The portraits are photographically noteworthy for the fine delineation of the faces, bringing out striking differences in the individualities. Carbutt, just prior to giving up his studio in Chicago, ca. 1870, issued a series of Lutheran clergymen of Illinois. Gutekunst (Philadelphia) published portraits of many Lutheran clergymen of eastern Pennsylvania.

To be discussed in a later chapter, but deserving notice here, are the great portraitists of American Indian leaders, Whitney, Upton and Martin (St. Paul), Jackson Brothers (Omaha) and later in the 1870s, Zimmermann (St. Paul), Bennett (Kilbourne City, Wisc.), Morrow (Yankton, South Dakota), W. R. Cross (Niobrara, Nebr.) and F. J. Haynes (Fargo).

As noted earlier, about 1870 the demand for portraits in the United States shifted from persons who had achieved prominence by accomplishment, to those who gained notoriety or fame by exploit or oddity: the infamous, like Boss Tweed; the notorious, like Jim Fisk, and those born with severe physical defects or having extremes in weight, height or other anomaly. Such portraits were greedily photographed for profit. Figures 114–116.

When James Fisk, the speculator-financier, was murdered in 1872 by a business associate who was a rival for the amorous attentions of Josie Mitchell, a popular actress, thousands of carte de visite portraits of Jim and Josie were hastily printed from file negatives. In addition to legitimate reissues, thousands of pirated copies flooded the market.

[5]The most complete coverage of denominational clergy is F. E. Longley's series of 1100 Wesleyan ministers (1872-1874), England.

115. Eisenmann, Charles. I. W. Sprague, The Thin Man, with his family. Age 40, weight 46 pounds, height five feet five inches. New York, ca. 1877.

114. Hughes & Co. Millie and Christine, the Carolina Siamese twins. St. Louis, Mo., ca. 1863.

116. Baker, L. M. Ida Williams, age. 19, weight 515 pounds. Columbus, Ohio, ca. 1875.

The most remarkable publisher of this period, 1875–1885, was Charles Eisenmann (New York), who advertised with one of his imprints more than 2000 portraits. His trade list included fat ladies, bearded ladies, "human skeletons" (thin men), dwarfs, giants, three-legged, four-legged, armless and otherwise physically handicapped persons, many of whom were circus side show performers. Eisenmann also photographed acrobats, jugglers and clowns.

While most of the subjects who posed for those portraits were paid for the right to sell prints and probably benefitted to some extent from the publicity, these issues were always profit-ventures by the publisher. This practice was very different from the publicity portraits of screen stars that became a part of the cinema industry in the 20th century. By then, the tables were turned; the subject and his agent received the benefit while the photographer was paid only for his services.

The rush to photograph prominent persons begun about 1860, had, by 1863, covered the world. Few, if any, famous persons were overlooked. After 1863 men and women achieving promise were routinely photographed by enterprising publishers. A virtually complete portrait gallery of notables was available in carte de visite format.

The Celebrities

So far, this narrative has emphasized the photographers who produced the portraits of notable persons. Their combined work recorded the most influential and famous people of two decades.

To suggest the almost limitless span of this world wide portraiture, a dozen examples will be cited.

Claudet about 1859 photographed the Duchess of Kent, mother of Queen Victoria. Two poses in carte de visite format are known. Among other celebrities who died before the end of 1862 were Lord Canning, Governor General of India, who was photographed by Mayall. Maull & Polyblank published an excellent portrait of Lord Macaulay, who died December 28, 1859.

There are many portraits of Benjamin Disraeli. The earliest carte de visite known to me is that by Wm. Kilburn ca. 1862, but very likely there are earlier portraits. Hughes & Edmonds published group portraits of Gladstone and his cabinet, ca. 1869 and Disraeli and his cabinet ca. 1874. Figure 119.

The Earl of Derby, Chancellor of the University of Oxford and translator of Homer's *Iliad*, was photographed by C. A. Duval (Manchester).

Garibaldi, despite his avowed objections to portraits, posed for at least a half dozen photographers. A fine copyrighted example was published by Lacombe & LaCroix ca. 1865. Figure 120.

Louis Agassiz, the renowned Harvard naturalist, was photographed by Brady, Anthony, and Turner (for Appleton). Fine poses, seated and standing, were widely distributed.

Religious leaders were remarkably well represented. Cardinal Newman by J. H. Whitlock and several of Brigham Young by C. R. Savage and C. W. Carter.

117. Josty & Co. "Parkman, artist" Bristol, England, ca. 1875.

118. Elliott & Fry. Thomas Huxley, zoologist and evolutionist. London, ca. 1875.

119. Hughes & Edmonds. Rgt. Hon. W. E. Gladstone with his cabinet. London, ca. 1869.

121. London Stereoscopic Co. Adelina Patti, singer. London, ca. 1876.

120. Lacomb & Lacroix. Giuseppe Garibaldi. Geneva, Switzerland, ca. 1866.

122. London Stereoscopic Co. Miss Hargreaves, actress. Note Rembrandt lighting. London, ca. 1875.

The Patti sisters, Adelina (1843-1919) and Carlotta (1840-1899), famous operatic sopranos, born in Madrid but educated and trained in the United States, were photographed many times. The best portraits are by Fredricks (1860s) and Reutlinger (early 1870s).

Tom Thumb (Charles Stratton, 1837-1883), so named by P. T. Barnum after the dwarf in Arthurian legend, was one of the most popular celebrities. In 1863, his marriage to Lavinia Warren (born 1842) was heralded by Barnum as "The Wedding of the Century." Many cartes de visite of Tom, Lavinia and their attendants Commodore Nutt and Minnie Warren, photographed by Brady, were printed and sold by Anthony. Many pirated copies were distributed. Collectors should be warned that cards purported to have signatures of Tom Thumb and Lavinia Warren are not autographed, the names are printed facsimile.

Abraham Lincoln. Cartes de visite of Abraham Lincoln were issued by many photographers, most notably by Gardner and Brady. A tremendous number of carte portraits of Lincoln were sold in 1865 and 1866, mostly copy issues.

Lincoln scholars believe that they have been able to document nearly all of the known portraits and trace the original photographers. Critical research is sometimes necessary to verify a carte Lincoln portrait. The most familiar likeness of Lincoln is a portrait made by Gardner in November 1863, a few days before the famous Gettysburg Address.

Many photographers who obviously pirated an image did not hesitate to imprint it, thus implying authorship. For instance, Lincoln never visited Poughkeepsie, New York, but that did not deter Slee Brothers from publishing a Lincoln portrait under their own imprint (1865). Among the dozens of photographers who published pirated portraits and imprinted the cards were J. C. Spooner (Springfield, Mass.) and G. F. Bouve (Boston), who pirated a Gardner portrait (one of five taken in April 1865).

The problems of authenticating carte portraits will be understood by examining Gutman's exemplary study of known portraits of John Wilkes Booth.[6]

Minor Celebrities

Series of portraits of beautiful women were published by several photographers. Among the best known are the series by Loescher and Petsch, Berlin, and Fritz Luckhardt, Vienna. A large series was published by the London Stereoscopic Company in the mid 1870s. Rarer but especially noteworthy was Silvy's *The Beauties of England*, 1862-1863. The subjects were selected for their beauty, not their station. They range from acclaimed actresses to working girls, a point which distressed some high-born journalists who commented upon the portraits.

Portraits of the leading figures of the times are relatively easy to find. The collecting of album cards was widespread enough to preserve many copies of most portraits. Fine album collections frequently come to auction houses and dealers in photographica.

More important to scholars and historians are the great numbers of persons who locally or briefly enjoyed influence or were otherwise newsworthy, but of whom likenesses are rare or unknown.

When the work of small-town photographers is considered, the coverage becomes incredible. Artists, businessmen, local officials, lawyers, doctors, teachers, clergymen, inventors, heroes, even the victims of accidents are among the persons considered to be newsworthy.[7]

A biographer seeking a portrait of subject at a particular age should begin the search in the town of birth and the community in which he did most of his work.

Only five examples will be given:

Hiram Powers, American sculptor, settled in Florence, Italy. There are several portraits, the best by his son, L. Powers (Florence), ca. 1862. A fine portrait by Allen (Boston) may be a copy of an L. Powers print.

Bret Harte, American writer, spent much of his later life in England. A good portrait was issued by R. W. Thrupp (Birmingham), ca. 1880.

Othniel Marsh, Yale vertebrate paleontologist. A fine portrait was produced by Geo. C. Phelps (New Haven), ca. 1882. Figure 125.

Sir Morton Peto, English industrialist, described his tour in the United States, 1865, in *Resources and Prospects of America* (1866). A good portrait of him was produced by J. Beattie (London), ca. 1867. Figure 126.

Proceeding to lesser figures to show the range of possibilities:

O. L. Fairchild, editor of *Reese River Reville*, Austin, Nevada. An excellent portrait by H. C. Tandy (Austin), ca. 1868.

Another source for unusual portraits are the cartes de visite produced by photographers in the principal seaports of the world. Many American sea captains and United States Navy officers visiting foreign ports paused to have their portraits taken, sometimes as a memento to be mailed home, sometimes as a record of their arrival in the port.

Capt. Harris, S. S. *Marminster* wrote on the mount of his portrait, "Sailed from New York Saturday, June 15, 1867, reached Liverpool, June 27, 1867." This photograph was produced by Daniel Jones, Liverpool. (George H. Moss Coll., Harris Album)

Two London photographers, C. T. Newcombe and A. L. Henderson, were frequently patronized by American sea captains. Figure 127.

The officers and crew of U. S. Navy ships usually posed for portraits when anchored in distant ports. In 1867 the *U. S. S. Sacramento* visited Capetown.

---

[6]Gutman, R. J. S. & Gutman, K. O., 1979, *John Wilkes Booth Himself*.

[7]The title "professor" was used very loosely in America. Commonly it was applied to a high school as well as a college teacher. It was also given or taken by public lecturers, even traveling salesmen hawking patent medicines.

123. Downey, W. & D. C. P. Villiers. London, ca. 1862.

125. Phelps, George C. Othniel Marsh, paleontologist. New Haven, Conn., ca. 1880.

124. Appleton, D. & Co. Louis Agassiz, naturalist. A. A. Turner photo. New York, 1862.

126. Beattie, J. Sir Morton Peto. Clifton, England, ca. 1867.

127. Henderson, A. L. Charles Babson, captain of the *General Putnam*, Kennebunk, Maine. Photographed in London, February 11, 1863.

The same year, April 25, 1867, the *U. S. S. Aroostook* toured the Pacific. While the crew was in Takow (China, Formosa), S. S. Sidney photographed most of the officers individually in his studio and in groups on board ship. The *Aroostook* also stopped in Honolulu, where again the men had their portraits taken by Dickson.

There are portraits of American and German sea captains from the studio of Noble & Lopez (Callao, Peru).

Copy Issues

Pirating marketable portraits was so extensively practiced, even by reputable photographers, that scarcely a well-known image escaped plagiarism. Usually, all that was required was an image from which a copy negative could be produced. Mayall's popular portraits of the British Royal Family were sold widely in the United States, but as many, if not more, of the cartes had been pirated from copy negatives from which Mayall's name had been obliterated. Similarly, following Prince Albert's death, huge numbers of pirated images were sold in the United States, Anthony's issues among them.

As a general rule, the larger the publisher's trade list and volume of business, the greater the number of uncredited and pirated images. *Any* carte de visite of a prominent person that does not have a photographer's or publisher's imprint is a pirated copy. Even Silvy's superb portraits were occasionally pirated by London publishers of cheap cards.

The reverse is not necessarily true. Many portraits identified with an imprint are pirated copies. The so-called Brady portrait of John Wilkes Booth is an outright piracy of a portrait by Silsbee, Case & Co. Carbutt pirated portraits of the King and Queen of Sweden for sale to Swedish settlers in Illinois and Wisconsin, publishing them under his own imprint.

A high quality series of legitimately copied portraits was published in England in the mid-1870s by the Woodburytype Permanent Photograph Company. These magnificent mechanically produced prints include several hundred famous and lesser known personalities, mostly English but also continental European. Earlier issues of these woodburytypes bear a printed title and credit the original photographer. Later issues sometimes lack all identifications. These cards were sometimes offered as premiums by newspapers (e.g., *The Saturday Programme*, London, 1876.)

There are some unusual subjects in this series, for example, "Captain" Matthew Webb. Webb, famous for speed and distance swimming, including the English Channel, first to receive the Stanhope medal for heroism, was shown seated with his medals pinned to his sweatshirt. Webb drowned July 24, 1883, in an attempt to swim the Niagara Rapids. Figure 131.

Montages

Montages of celebrities in carte de visite format are quite common, appearing about 1860 and persisting to 1890. Disderi obtained a French patent for the carte montage in 1863 but he was in no way its inventor. The image is a copy of a composition made from two or more prints cut, trimmed and mounted in a design. Among the early montages are the British royal family, theatrical personalities by Disderi, Union generals, Confederate generals, college faculties, Lincoln and his cabinet and state legislatures.

There are some clever composites. About 1865, Anthony published a montage of the presidents of the United States, from Washington to Lincoln. Another montage was composed of the portraits of one hundred prominent women, with a key to their names on the reverse (ca. 1865, no publisher).

Historic Personalities: Reproductions of Paintings and Engravings

Photographers discovered almost as quickly as the carte de visite became popular that copies of works of art and portraits of historic personalities would be eagerly purchased by album enthusiasts. In short order, in Italy, France, Germany and England, engravings and paintings were copied extensively. Italian photographers were most active. The galleries of famous museums were systematically scoured for marketable subjects. The likenesses of Dante, Petrarch, Titian, Raphael, Machiavelli, of Popes, Borgias and Medicis became well known through cartes de visite.

In England, Queen Elizabeth, Henry VIII, Shakespeare, Mary Stuart, Cromwell, Newton, Robert Burns and Walter Scott were among the popular subjects. Ultimately, nearly every historic figure was available in

128. Dodson, C. L. (Lewis Carroll). Alfred Tennyson. Enlargement of the head from a print. Original negative 1857. Woodburytype Permanent Photograph Co. issue, 1875.

130. Elliott & Fry. Emily Fowler. Woodburytype Permanent Photograph Co. issue, 1875.

129. Melhuish, A. J. Princess Louise. Woodburytype Permanent Photograph Co. issue, 1875.

131. Woodburytype Permanent Photograph Co. Capt. Matthew Webb, celebrated swimmer, recipient of the first Stanhope medal for heroism. Photographer not credited. London, 1876.

carte format. Few of these English productions bear a publisher's imprint.

O. Brockmann, the Deutsche Photographische Gesellschaft, Moser and Sophus Williams were the most important publishers in Germany. In France, Neurdein and Desmaison were the best known. Several French series sold in the 1870s bear no imprints.

In the United States, there were a few publishers in this field, all active in the 1860s. McAllister & Bro. (Philadelphia), Charles Taber (New Bedford), J. H. Bufford (Boston), J. E. Tilton (Boston), Tomlinson (Boston), Stinson (Portland, Maine) and the Philadelphia Photograph Company were the most important. The subjects ranged from George and Martha Washington and other patriots to James Fennemore Cooper, Cotton Mather, and John J. Audubon.

The J. H. Bufford Company, print publishers, was one of the first American firms to produce copies of their large portraits of historic persons in carte format. The photographic copying was done by John Soule who was credited in the Bufford copyright notice, 1862, 1863. The series includes portraits of Washington, John Adams, Jefferson, Monroe, Jackson, etc., and their wives.

Appleton and Anthony imported huge quantities of the European issues and resold them, without imprints, throughout the United States. These cartes and similar ones, produced by unknown American publishers, are often found with printed or rubber-stamped dealer names (New York Photographic Company, Joseph A. Ward, Boston, etc.).

Present-day collectors have shown very little interest in these reproductions, chiefly because they are copies that contributed very little to photography *per se*.

In the history of education, however, these portraits represent pioneering in visual instruction and art appreciation, both of which profoundly influenced the course of public education in the United States beginning about 1865.

It is seldom recognized that virtually all encyclopedic books illustrated with portraits that were published between 1890 and 1915 relied heavily upon carte de visite portraits—originals and copies—for the pictures. For example, *The Dictionary of American Biography* and *Battles and Leaders of the Civil War*, 4 volumes (1885-1889) contain hundreds of reproductions of carte de visite portraits, scenes, and sketches.

CHAPTER SIX
NATIVE PEOPLES OF THE WORLD

Documentation of the native peoples of the world was one of the irreplaceable accomplishments of nineteenth century photography. The motivation for this activity came from several sources.

In 1839, the year Daguerre announced his discoveries, James Pritchard presented his famous paper, "The Extinction of Native Races," to the British Association for the Advancement of Science, meeting at Birmingham. In 1843, the Ethnological Society was organized to collect and systematize "all observations on the human race." Questionnaires were devised to assist military officers, colonial officials, missionaries and explorers in gathering useful data.

Still earlier, in 1837, the Aboriginal Protection Society, active in the movement to abolish slavery, had been founded in England.

The romantic nationalistic rediscovery of native dance, music, costume and folklore among the ethnic groups of Europe undoubtedly encouraged photographers to record some of these cultural traits.

Just how much these particulars directly influenced portraiture of native peoples is uncertain. Other factors also contributed to the trend.

The London International Exhibition of 1851, which did so much to promote photography, especially the stereograph, also opened the minds of visitors to the artistic and technological accomplishments of many nations and to the cultures of colonial native peoples.

During the 1850s and 1860s, European photographers scattered throughout the world, establishing studios in every commercial seaport. Within a few years, native photographers—as in India, Japan and China—joined the profession.

The westernization of areas under control of colonial administrators progressed rapidly. This was especially evident in many relatively thinly populated regions, such as the Hawaiian Islands.

In North America, the American Indians had been displaced from their traditional tribal lands by pressure from white settlements, a process that had begun before 1700. By 1860, the dislocation of Indian tribes involved nearly the entire continental United States. John Wesley Powell in 1873 warned politicians and scientists alike, that whenever the Indian came in contact with the white man, the Indian lost part of his cultural heritage and was spoiled thereby.[1] This consequence occurred wherever the European settled among peoples considered to be primitive.

Powell, determined to study the last unspoiled Indians in the United States, recorded their language and customs and photographed (Jack Hillers) these people in native dress and at their daily work and play, including the games of children.

In this light, we can begin to appreciate the amazing gallery of the native peoples of the world who were photographed in carte de visite format between 1860 and 1885. Ignored here are stereographs taken between 1856 and 1885, because most of them are scenic views showing native peoples, including many of American Indians, in groups engaged in some activity. Those stereo portraits photographed in studios after 1860 were nearly always available also in carte de visite format.[2]

Cartes de visite of native peoples fall into five categories:

(1) chiefs and leaders
(2) racial types
(3) native dress
(4) native occupations
(5) scenic, in which people are engaged in a characteristic activity such as marriage, religious gathering, etc.

These will be summarized by country rather than by type. In this way, the purpose for which they were produced and their importance today can be more readily recognized.

The family of man differs physically, racially, culturally and socially. Thus, the first impressions derived from these photographs are novelty and curiosity.

Races, in the scientific sense, are groups of people that share inheritable, measurable, physical characteristics. Such groups often have a cultural heritage (caste, class, dress, tools and customs) from which can be inferred relations to other groups. In the nineteenth century, the word race was used in a much broader sense than that defined above. Race included culture and language, whereas at present it is recognized that different genetic races can live together, sharing the same culture and language. The titles identifying nineteenth century images must always be interpreted in the sense that they were written.

The Natives of Western Europe

A steady stream of carte de visite portraits of colorful native types was issued by photographers in every country. The images follow a consistent pattern: men and women in native dress, usually in full-length standing pose. Often a young woman and young man, sometimes a bridal couple, are shown together. Typical occupations, such as spinning, haying and milking, are often suggested by a ball of yarn, a hay-rake or a milkpail in studio arrangements. Many photographers also used painted scenic backgrounds.

[1]Darrah, W. C., 1951, *Powell of the Colorado.*

[2]*World of Stereographs*, pp. 167–168.

Outstanding series in which the titles identify province and precise locality were published by A. Braun, Sophus Williams, P. Sinner and A. Jager.

Braun (Dornach, 1863–1875) published an extensive selection of studio portraits of peasant types from Switzerland, France, Germany, the Netherlands and Egypt. The images are usually found nicely tinted. Sophus Williams (Berlin) also published a large series covering most of the German states. P. Sinner (Tubingen 1860s and 1870s; Wilhelm Bonn, publisher) did a splendid series of southern German and Tirolean types.

A. Jager (Amsterdam) produced fine portraits of Dutch and Flemish types.

Many other photographers were active in this field. Also in Germany, O. Brockmann (Dresden) and E. Hattorff (Hamburg) issued striking portraits. Some of Hattorff's titles are outdoor scenes of people at work.

In Italy there were many publishers, but the numbers of titles by each are unknown. The most important were: Georgio Conrad (Naples), DeLuca Brothers (Naples and Sorentino), Roberto Rive (Naples), Sommer & Behles (Rome and Naples), Carlo Ponti (Venice) and C. Degoix (Genoa). There are many portraits of street vendors, urchins and workmen.

Malovich (Trieste) issued tinted portraits of northeast Italian, Albanian and Balkan types.

One of the most remarkable series was produced by William Carrick, an Englishman, who had a studio in St. Petersburg. Many of his subjects are staged at some activity such as drinking tea or gaming. The cartes which bear titles in Russian and English, or Russian only, are found tinted and untinted. A. Denier (St. Petersburg), A. Lorenz (Moscow), M. Panov (Moscow) and Posekin (Kharkov) also produced cartes de visite of Russian types.

Smaller but significant series were published in nearly every country.

K. Knudsen and W. Selmer, both of Bergen, produced tinted portraits of Norwegian types. Similarly in Sweden, J. F. Dahlgren (Stockholm), W. A. Eurenius & P. L. Quist (Stockholm) and Vogel & Dienstbach (Goteborg) issued fine series.

English native types were rarely published as such, instead, these must be recognized from photographs of people engaged in characteristic occupations. There are a few exceptions, such as Welsh women with traditional hats and men wearing Scottish kilts and hats, the latter being usually in ceremonial costume.

Throughout the world, local photographers used the opportunities to document the natives and commercialize their portraits. At least four photographers in Egypt did a brisk business: A Beato (Cairo, 1860s), W. Hammerschmidt (Cairo and Berlin), Schier & Schoeft (Alexandria) and Nicolas Koumianos (Port Said), all operating in the 1860s and early 1870s.

132. Braun, A. Swiss costume. Canton of Appenzell. Note painted kitchen panel and cardboard door. Dornach, France, ca. 1868.

133. Berillon, Ferdinand. Housewife. Bayonne, France, ca. 1874.

134. Rive, Roberto. Pigeon vendor. Note base of head clamp stand. Naples, Italy, 1865.

136. Hahn, Julius. "Young woman of the Vierland district." Hamburg, Germany, ca. 1870.

135. Ponti, Carlo. Oyster vendor. Venice, Italy, ca. 1865.

137. Sinner, P. Playing cards, Urach. Tubingen, Germany, ca. 1872.

138. Jager, A. Holland. Servant girl. Amsterdam, ca. 1865.

21. Koner fra Vos, Bergens Stift.

140. Selmer, M. Housewives from Vos. Bergen, Norway, ca. 1870.

139. Rogers, G. F. Fishwife. Broughty Ferry, Scotland, ca. 1874.

141. Knudsen, K. Bride from Vos. Bergen, Norway, ca. 1872.

63

142. Carrick, William. Russian types. Drinking tea.
St. Petersburg, ca. 1865.

143. Carrick, William. Russian types. Can vendor.
St. Petersburg, ca. 1865.

Two series of Algerian native types are known, one by J. Geiser, the other by C. Portier.

In Palestine, Syria and Lebanon, Bonfils was most active. His cartes were seldom tinted. Many European publishers offered portraits of peoples of the Holy Land without crediting the photographers.

Constantinople had several able photographers, but portraits of native types by Sebah, Abdullah Brothers, and Shishmanian are the only imprinted cards known to me.

Unmounted carte de visite prints for pasting in blank albums were sold in great quantity, mostly by French publishers. I have examined three fine folio albums (1860s) illustrating peoples of the Mediterranean region, Italy, Greece, Turkey, Palestine, Syria and Egypt, but without identifications of subjects or photographers.[3] It should not be difficult to identify the photographers.

There are extensive series of native peoples of the Far East, especially of Japan and China. Stereographs of native types were published between 1858 and 1862, cartes de visite beginning about 1862. Regrettably, most of the early series, i.e., until about 1868, do not bear a photographer's imprint. In the late 1860s and 1870s, some of the series have imprints. Pun-Lun (Shanghai and Hong Kong) produced beautiful portraits, found both tinted and untinted. In Japan, S. Suzuki (Tokyo and Yokohama, 1870s and 1880s) is noteworthy.

Several peculiarities among the Chinese and Japanese cartes deserve investigation. Most of the pre-1867 images seem to have been taken by European photographers. About 1880–1885, cheap copy issues of both Chinese and Japanese series appeared in the market. These often bear titles in characters only, suggesting that they were intended for local distribution and not for sale in Europe or America.

Bourne & Shepherd (Bombay & Calcutta) published the largest number of portraits of Indian types, including many scenic views in which people are at work. There are many similar cartes by other photographers, notably Sache & Westfield and Sache & Murray (Calcutta), Lindley & Warren (Bombay), Westfield & Co. (Calcutta), H. Chintaman (Bombay), Schwarzschild & Co. (Calcutta), etc.

There are many portraits of Hindus and Burmese who were photographed for American religious societies. The cartes were given away or sold to raise funds for missionary purposes. Occasionally these cards bear the imprint of an American photographer (Bogardus, Loomis, Gutekunst) who, most certainly, was not the original photographer but merely the one who produced prints from copy negatives.

Ceylon, through the work of two resident photographers, is exceptionally well illustrated. Slinn & Co. (Colombo) and A. W. Andree (Pointe de Galle) in the 1860s published large series of portraits of natives.

Australian aborigines have been documented by several photographers, but I have been able to examine few personally. G. Cherry (1860s) and S. Clifford

[3]G. H. Moss Collection, graciously loaned for study by Mr. Moss.

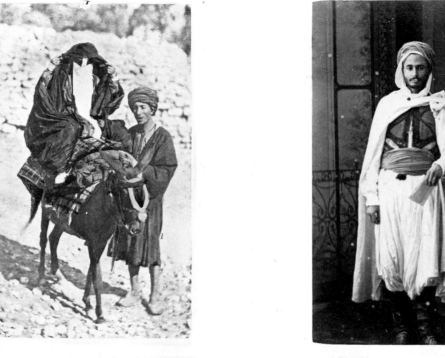

144. Hammerschmidt, W. Egypt. "Veiled woman riding a donkey" Cairo and Berlin, ca. 1870.

146. Portier, C. Algerian merchant, Algiers, ca. 1865.

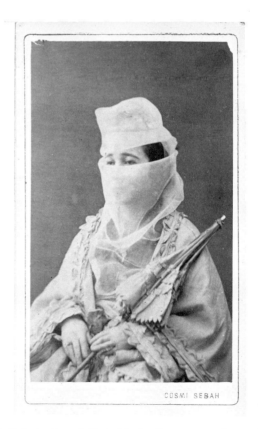

145. Schier & Schoeft. Untitled. Alexandria, Egypt, ca. 1867.

147. Sebah, Cosmi. Veiled lady. Constantinople, Turkey, ca. 1872.

148. Bonfils, Felix. Palestine. "Woman preparing and cooking food." Beyrouth,
ca. 1872.

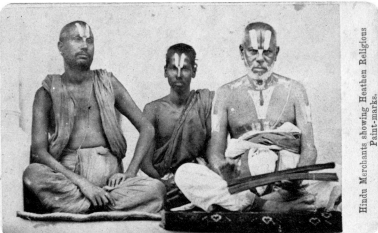

Hindu Merchants showing Heathen Religious Paint-marks.

150. Anonymous. India. "Hindu merchants showing heathen
religious paint marks." Note prejudiced caption.
Issued by the Children's Missionary Society of the
Lutheran Church. 1874.

149. Westfield & Co. India. Hindu lady, Bubee
Kesubchunder, Calcutta, ca. 1868.

151. Slinn & Co. Ceylon. Devil Dancer. Colombo,
ca. 1865.

152. Anonymous. Japan. "Doctor feeling pulse of a patient." Yokohama, ca. 1867.

154. Suzuki, S. Japan. Portrait of a young girl. Tokyo and Yokohama, ca. 1885.

(1870s), both operating in Hobart, produced fine portraits of Tasmanians.

New Zealand aborigines were photographed by Tait Brothers (Greymouth & Hokita), Thomas E. Price (Auckland) and J. Corbett (Auckland).

From South Africa, the most important portraits of natives known to me were produced by H. Kisch (succeeded by Kisch Brothers, Maritzburg, Natal 1870s and 1880s). Smaller series were published by J. Hesselson (Standerton, Transvaal) and W. B. Sherwood (Natal). All of the portraits are of negro types identified as to tribe and/or location.

153. Anonymous. Japan. "Fencers in ceremonial costume." Yokohama, ca. 1867.

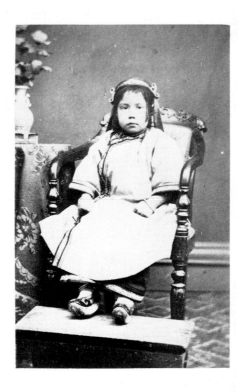

155. Pun-Lun. China. "Celestial child with bound feet." Hong Kong, ca. 1867.

156. Slinn & Co. Ceylon. Modliar and Lascoreens. Colombo, ca. 1865.

158. Farndell, E. Australia. Subai mother and child. Kenttown, Adelaide, ca. 1866.

157. Farndell, E. Australia. Subai tribesmen. Studio pose, note painted background. Kenttown, Adelaide, ca. 1866.

159. Rice, Thomas E. New Zealand. Maori Chief. Masterton, ca. 1872.

South America is generally poorly covered. A modest series of Peruvian Indians was distributed about 1870. A series of Bolivian and Ecuadoran Indians was published about the same time. There are two kinds of card mounts, but similarities of the images suggest that they may have been issued by the same unidentified photographer. I have seen two Indian portraits by Hermanos Courret (Lima, Peru, late 1860s) but do not know if these were titles in a series.

Pietsch & Dietze (Rio de Janeiro) published a small series of native types about 1870. They also sold in Brazil portraits of natives of Portuguese colonies in west Africa. A Pietsch & Dietze dealer's label or rubber stamp imprint is occasionally found on these superb portraits of Africans by an unknown photographer.

One of the most intriguing possibilities in recovering lost information is a large series of West Indian natives advertised by Felix Morin in two of his imprints used for nearly ten years (1870s). Some of Morin's logos give his location as Port of Spain, Trinidad, but others simply state "West Indies." I have seen only two poorly preserved images of laborers in Trinidad by Morin.

So far, this summary has been limited to portraits issued in series. Occasional images are to be found among the issues by hundreds of photographers in countries other than those mentioned above, such as Madeira, Mexico, Portugal, Rumania and Spain.

The American Indians

No one has yet attempted to record and index the known identified cartes de visite of American Indians and the photographers who produced them. The total certainly runs into the thousands, because at least three hundred photographers are known to have published them.

Merely to list the photographers' names and the tribes they documented would be a prodigious project. Among the most prolific were:

Bailey, Dix & Mead   Ft. Randall, South Dakota
Barker, A. W.   Ottawa, Kansas
Barker, G.   Niagara Falls
Bennett, H. H.   Kilbourn City, Wisconsin
Bennett & Brown   Santa Fe, New Mexico
Bonine, E. A.   Yuma, Arizona
Bratlee,   Devil's Lake, North Dakota
Britt, Peter   Jacksonville, Oregon
Carter, C. W.   Salt Lake City
Chamberlain, W. G.   Denver
Childs, B. F.   Marquette, Mich.
Collier, J.   Denver
Concannon, T. M.   Indian Territory (Oklahoma)
Cross, W. R.   Niobrara, Nebraska
Eaton   Omaha
Haynes, F. J.   Fargo, North Dakota
Hayward & Muzzall   Santa Barbara, California
Heller, L.   Fort Jones, California
Houseworth, Thomas   San Francisco
Huffman, L. A.   Miles, Montana
Illingworth, W. H.   St. Paul
Jackson Brothers   Omaha
Jackson, W. H.   Denver

Martin   St. Paul
McInnes, H.   Petosky, Michigan
Morrow, S. J.   Yankton, South Dakota
Muybridge, E. J.   San Francisco
Savage, C. R.   Salt Lake City
Upton, B. F.   St. Paul
Watkins, C. E.   San Francisco
Whitaker, G. C.   Leavenworth, Kansas
Whitney, J. E.   St. Paul
Winter, Frank A.   Ft. Shaw, Montana
Zimmermann, C. A.   St. Paul

Many of the photographers listed above produced portraits in both carte de visite and stereo formats. Heller issued stereo and carte series of the Modoc War (1873).[4] Some of the great western photographers of Indians, especially J. K. Hillers and Alex Gardner, renowned for stereograph and large plate images, are not known to have produced carte de visite Indian portraits.

J. N. Choate (1880s and early 1890s, Carlisle, Pa.), as semi-official photographer of the Carlisle Indian School (established 1874), produced many fine portraits. Probably these were made for the individuals themselves and for school records. Although these portraits were not available commercially, specimens occasionally appear in the photographica market.

Indian names

The titles usually written on the card mounts can be very confusing. The same subject may be identified as belonging to two or three different tribes. Among the plains Indians, a brave may be called a Dakota, Sioux or Crow. All are correct. The Sioux and Dakota refer to linguistic groups within which there are seven large tribes, within each of which there are smaller tribes. Usually, the name Shoshone is an inclusive name, while Ute or Bannock are restrictive names. Among eastern Indians, "Iroquois" bears a similar relation, there being many tribes within the group.

Anyone seeking to identify or document a carte de visite Indian portrait should become familiar with F. W. Hodges, *Handbook of American Indians* (2 vols. 1907-1910). Although now out of date, this massive work synthesizes the nineteenth century accumulated knowledge of the Indians.

Another problem confronting those researching Indian portraits is the spelling of names of personalities and tribes. Photographers had difficulty in translating names from phonetic sounds to the English alphabet and then dividing them into syllables.

In documenting a portrait with a restricted tribal name, it is relatively easy to establish relationships. The reverse, working from an inclusive name to determine a restrictive identity, may be very difficult.

The Indians have managed to preserve their tribal identities in spite of removal from their ancestral tribal lands and social pressures by white neighbors. Ab-

[4]Palmquist, P. E., "Photographing the Modoc Indian War: Louis Heller vs. Eadweard Muybridge," *History of Photography* 3 (2): 187-205.

160. Hull, A. C. Indian prisoners with shackled feet. Fremont, Nebr., ca. 1868.

162. Martin, O. "Old Betz." St. Paul, Minn., ca. 1868.

161. Cross, W. R. "Spotted Tail's Family." Niobrara, Nebr., ca. 1878.

163. Zimmermann, Charles. "Chief Hole-in-the-wall." St. Paul, Minn., ca. 1870.

originally, hundreds of small tribes were distributed over North America in small bands, numbering from a few hundred to a thousand members. These diverse tribes are classified by linguistic stock and by cultural traits. Sometimes, for convenience, they are grouped as woodland, plains, pueblo, etc. to indicate environmental-cultural relationships.

The most thorough photographic documentation of Indians in the carte de visite format includes tribes of the western Great Lakes region, especially the Chippewas and Winnebagos. The majority are studio portraits, but there are many fine outdoor views as well. Next in coverage are Indians of the Colorado-Utah-Dakota Territory region, followed by those of California.

Many photographers seem to have had a genuine sympathy and admiration for their Indian subjects. The studio portraits of proud chiefs and graceful expressions in the faces of some of the women could not have been produced otherwise. Whitney, Martin, Savage and Morrow are noted for their superb portraits.

Indian portraits commonly show hats or items of clothing, medallions, or weapons obtained from the white man. Sometimes a trifling object passes unnoticed. Such examples of cultural borrowing may be historically significant.

The ethnologist can also recognize cultural borrowing and discarding among neighboring tribes. For instance, in the Great Lakes region the Winnebagos occupied lands on the west side of Lake Michigan. Although ethnicly related to Siouxan tribes, such as the Iowa and Oto, they show cultural ties with their Algonkian neighbors, the Fox, Sauk and Menomonee. Figures 160–163.

164. Anonymous. Peru. Indian woman. Carte purchased in Lima, 1868.

The American Negro

Excepting such famous individuals as Frederick Douglass (Appleton, Anthony) and Edward Bannister (Manchester Bros., Providence, R. I.), portraits of few blacks were published commercially. There are, however, a fair number of portraits of well-dressed men and women by photographers in the larger northern cities and in southern cities like Richmond and New Orleans. Very few of the persons are identified, but some of them certainly achieved economic and social success.

During the Civil War, many blacks served as soldiers and civilian employees. Scenic views of southern states often include blacks working in the cotton, sugar and tobacco industries, as wharf laborers, etc. Black performers and side show actors were usually photographed. Figures 114, 166–168.

There are rare group portraits, among them the Fisk University Singers (J. W. Black, Boston, ca. 1872) and a one-room school, with fourteen children and a young woman teacher, probably in Georgia or northern Florida, ca. 1875, unidentified by title, photographer unknown. Undoubtedly there are many unrecorded cartes of black families and groups which are of considerable historical significance.

165. Pietsch & Dietze. Brazil. "Negro in her Sunday dress." Rio de Janeiro, ca. 1870.

166. Richmond Photograph Co. American Negro. Black gentleman. Richmond, Va., ca. 1876.

FANNIE VIRGINIA CASSEOPIA LAWRENCE.
A Redeemed SLAVE CHILD, 5 years of age. Redeemed in Virginia, by Catharine S. Lawrence; Baptized in Brooklyn, at Plymouth Church, by Henry Ward Beecher, May, 1863
Entered according to Act of Congress, in the year 1863, by C. S. Lawrence, in the Clerk's Office of the District Court of the United States for the Southern District of New York.

168. Kellogg Brothers. Fannie Virginia Casseopia Lawrence, a slave child, redeemed in Virginia and adopted by Catherine Lawrence, baptized by Henry Ward Beecher, 1863. There are many issues of this portrait. Hartford, Conn., ca. 1864.

167. Cosand & Musser. American Negro. Portrait of a black lady. Caldwell, Kans., ca. 1878.

Indigenous American White Groups

Many areas of the United States were and still are populated by the descendants of early settlers. Through intermarriage within the group, i.e., by inbreeding in the community, especially among religious communities, characteristic physical features, especially facial, have persisted generation after generation. The portraits of Civil War soldiers from parts of Maine, Massachusetts, Kentucky, Tennessee and Texas show remarkable regional types.

Quite similarly in some respects, the racial purity of recent immigrants and the first American-born generation produced by them is manifest by their portraits. Non-English speaking immigrants tended to settle by nationality groups, Scandinavians in Illinois, Wisconsin and Minnesota, Swedes and Norwegians usually separating. German groups often concentrated in industrial cities, forming large communities in New York, Brooklyn, Philadelphia, Pittsburgh, Cleveland, Cincinnati and St. Louis. Photographers, many who learned their skills in Europe, settled among their former countrymen. These photographers sometimes imprinted their cards in German and offered to mail, free of charge, portraits to relatives in Europe.

The influx of French-Canadians in Maine and New Hampshire, especially in the vicinity of Manchester and Nashua, was recorded by many local photographers, some of whom were French Canadians (G. Desmarais, H. Laroque).

As a final example, attention is called to portraits and group pictures of Chinese who settled in California and those who worked as cooks and laborers on the construction of the Central Pacific and Union Pacific railroads.

o o o

The carte de visite documentation of native peoples represents but a small part of the photographic anthropological record produced in the nineteenth century. Not only stereographs and large plate images, but great numbers of intermediate sizes were produced for mounting in albums and for official records. Some insight into the scope of this activity can be gained by considering the efforts to illustrate the peoples in specific countries, notably Russia, 1855–1885,[5] India,[6] and many others.

Collectors of cartes de visite at present are primarily interested in the portraits of aboriginal and non-European types. There is also a demand for images showing people at work, especially in primitive trades. Scholarly research in aspects of social change illustrated by photographic images is still very limited. The carte de visite as a historical or a scientific resource remains almost untouched.

[5]Morosov, S. A. "Early Photography in Eastern Europe—Russia," *Hist. Phot. 1* (4): 327–347, 1977.

[6]*Report of a Mission to Yorkund*, 1873 (photos by Bourne & Shepherd). See, Krauss, Rolf H., *Hist. Phot. 3* (1): 15–21, 1979.

CHAPTER SEVEN
THE CIVIL WAR

Photography was more intricately involved in the American Civil War than in any other historical event in the nineteenth century. The Federal government and, to a lesser extent, the Confederate government utilized photography for military intelligence, documentation, map copying, medical recording and other purposes. "Official" and semi-official photographers accompanying armies and troop units produced a great variety of scenic images. Further, independent photographers, many of them camp followers, took uncountable numbers of pictures.

Instead of a brief insurrection lasting a few months, the conflict settled down to a long drawn out war fought over an area nearly as large as Western Europe.

At the outbreak of hostilities, the regular army consisted of only 17,000 men. President Lincoln issued a call for 75,000 state militia for three months service on April 14, 1861. On April 17, he called for 42,000 volunteers for three years and 40,000 for the regular army. Following the Union disaster at Manassas (Bull Run) on July 21, Congress authorized a call for 500,000 men. Before it was over, nearly four million men had been engaged. The casualties were enormous, 500,000 killed or died of wounds and diseases.

This large-scale separation of men from their wives and families contributed greatly to the popularity of the carte de visite and the tintype, which was commonly mounted as a carte de visite. The card could be kept in a pocket, inside a Bible or placed in an envelope and mailed home.

Virtually every Union soldier had his portrait taken, most of them several times. Photographers with studios in towns through which soldiers passed or near which they were concentrated did thriving business, as did the camp followers. There are great numbers of soldier portraits by home town photographers. Millions of soldier portraits were produced, hundreds of thousands still exist.

There are five major types of Civil War cartes de visite:

1. Portraits of soldiers, officers and others directly concerned with the war effort

2. Scenic views: battlefields, camps, troops, prisons, naval vessels, materiel, and landmarks

3. Contemporary war-related: Sanitary Commission and its Fairs, mascots, medical cases, etc.

4. War propaganda: cartoons, patriotic, sentimental, etc.

5. Post-war related: military cemeteries and their monuments, battlefields, reunions and encampments, Grand Army of the Republic, etc.

Soldier Portraits

The most highly prized portraits, understandably, are fine daguerreotypes, ambrotypes and tintypes, which, being one-of-a-kind, are rare. Especially valued are the daguerreotypes and ambrotypes, because these were seldom made after 1861. Tintypes were produced in great numbers until 1880, thereafter, less frequently. Images showing weapons and other details are especially sought for.

The abundant carte de visite images show varying degrees of information. Full standing figures with epaulettes, stripes and insignia, especially when the subjects have a ceremonial sword, rifle or pistol or other equipment, may be particularly informative. Buttons on the uniform can often be examined in detail. Each state had its own design, thus permitting identification. On the other extreme, vignetted heads often show nothing more military than the kepi hat and the coat collar.

Some photographers posed their subjects standing against painted camp or battle scenes, replete with American flags and other patriotic symbols.

Autographed portraits are important, the more famous the person, the greater the demand for the signed image.

169. Marmu, C. Portrait of a Union officer. New Orleans, La., 1865.

170. Adams, C. P. "Charles Gilbert Ware." Pittsfield, Mass., February, 1862.

172. Kertson, M. "Sgt. Philip R. Floyd, Co. F., 35th Mass. Vol. Inf." Newark, N.J., 1863.

Military Leaders

The surrender of Fort Sumter, the attendant fame of Major Anderson and the huge sale of his portrait has been previously mentioned. He was only the first of many officers whose portraits were in great demand. Col. Ephriam E. Ellsworth, who was killed on May 24, 1861, by a civilian in Alexandria, Virginia, after taking down a secession flag, was similarly memorialized.

Anthony's catalogue listed as its largest group of portraits, military leaders and statesmen. Brady, Gardner, Gutekunst, Carbutt, Fredricks and Gurney are but a few of the photographers who produced many fine such portraits. Studios in Washington, in addition to Gardner's, also notable for portraits of officers and statesmen, were operated by Henry Ulke, John Goldin, R. W. Addis, G. F. Child, John Holyland, et al. Many were issued by Scholten (St. Louis), Black (Boston), Warren (Boston) and Bogardus (New York) but there were hundreds of other photographers whose soldier portraits are still common.

The great publishers produced portraits of Union and Confederate generals impartially. The more famous generals and statesmen were photographed many times, often by the same photographer. Studio portraits are quite common, portraits at field headquarters or in the field are rare. There are some well-known portraits taken by military photographers such as the bust of U. S. Grant by Brigham Bishop, Army of the Cumberland.

There are many unusual series of portraits. A. E. Alden (Providence) issued a considerable series of

171. Holyland, John. "Lt. H. H. Wood, Utica, N.Y., Co. C., 146 N.Y. Zouaves." Washington, D.C., 1863.

173. Anonymous. Confederate volunteer, "Lt. E. R. Ward, Co. A, 4th Reg. Tenn. Vols. Photographed in Atlanta, Ga., November, 1862." Courtesy of Henry Deeks.

175. Schaeffer, R. "Capt. R. Phillips, Co. B. 8th Reg. Mass. Vol. Militia." Baltimore, 1861 A very early war portrait; uniform pre-war. Phillips enlisted April April 20, 1861. Courtesy of Henry Deeks.

174. Brady, M. B. "Capt. E. H. Chapin, Black Horse, Cavalry." Washington, D.C., 1862.

176. Scholten, John A. Confederate Gen. Sterling Price. A reworked image by Scholten. St. Louis, 1862.

small portraits mounted singly or paired—as of Lincoln and Grant—on cards with an ornate embossed patriotic frame, ca. 1864.

So far as I am aware, no Southern publisher issued a large series of portraits of military men, although Anderson (Richmond) sold a series of copied portraits of Confederate leaders in the late 1860s, after the war.

The demand for the portraits of generals and admirals, Northern and Southern, led to the publication of a great variety of carte issues. By late 1862, lithographic reproductions of engravings, mostly copied from photographs by camera lucida drawing, were sold widely. Within another year at least seven companies were publishing these reproductions, the most important:

Elias Decker, New York; bust portraits nearly filling the card; good impressions.

J. H. Bufford, Boston; a large series; busts in a gilt oval frame, frame uniform for all titles; impressions fair to good.

Charles Magnus, New York; a similar series, busts in ornate red oval frame.

Wm. S. & A. Martien, Philadelphia; portraits in oval frame, mounts with olive-gray front.

L. Prang & Co., Boston; portraits printed in white oval; cards with pinkish gray front.

C. Bohn, Washington; fair to good impressions nearly filling the card.

Monument Photograph Company, Baltimore.

178. Williamson, C. H. U.S. Navy Commander J. Blakely Creighton. New York, 1864.

177. Anonymous. Capt. A. W. Greely, autographed. Greely later became an arctic explorer and achieved the rank of major general. New Orleans. August 16, 1866.

179. Williams, J. A. U.S. Navy Landsman, Lewis R. Price. Note painted gunbreech and recoil rope. Newport, R.I., ca. 1863. Courtesy of Henry Deeks.

Each of these series includes the well-known Union and Confederate ranking officers and each contains less familiar persons whose likenesses are seldom seen, e.g., Col. Crossman, Quartermaster Corps, Philadelphia (Bufford series).

These two major types of portraits, personal made for sentiment and military leaders produced commercially, represent only one phase of the war, really a tangent to the conflict, remote from its hardships and horrors.

The photographers who recorded the war—the camps, troops, marches, battlefields, the weapons, the wounded and the dead—are legion. Josephine Cobb[1] listed more than three hundred names, but this is very incomplete. Being compiled from official records in the National Archives, it excludes all photographers who did not have some official connection with the War Department.

There are five distinct degrees of relationship between the armies and photographers.

1. Army photographers specifically assigned to record military information, e.g., Capt. A. J. Russell.

2. Photographers who enlisted with local units and accompanied them in the war. There are several variations. Occasionally a local photographer, not an enlistee, went with the men without pay or for subsistence to take photographs as mementos and to send home to the families—presumably with some profit to the photographer, e.g., Wm. Kunstman.

3. Photographers, like Brady, who obtained official permission to engage in private business taking photographs of men and scenes, for profit.

4. Contract photographers who were employed briefly or part time to do documentary work for military hospitals, prison camps or as post photographers.

The best known contract photographers were those hired by the many army hospitals. Political pressures forced the Army to establish convalescent hospitals in nearly every state, chiefly to place the suffering veterans closer to their families (although there was considerable disagreement within the Medical Service as to the desirability of sending home men who would fully recover). In some general hospitals the services of a local photographer were secured (e.g., Klauber, Louisville; Wood Brothers, Albany), but in others the contracting party was from a distant location (as at Hospital No. 1, Nashville, where Manchester Brothers & Angell of Providence, Rhode Island, provided the photographic service).

J. C. Spaulding, "Army Photographer," Point Lookout, Md., who is not listed by Cobb, contracted to work at the Hammond General Hospital in the great hospital complex in and around Washington.

Medical documentation of injuries and healing by cartes de visite was a major project under the direction of the Surgeon General. More than a thousand such photographs were secured, from which hundreds were selected to illustrate *The Medical and Surgical History of the Civil War* (4 vols. 1870–1888).[2]

5. Camp followers, by far the most numerous. These itinerants set up a tent or parked a van as close to a camp as commanding officers would permit. During the long dull periods between battles, the photographer might remain in one location for weeks or months, taking many portraits in carte de visite or tintype format. With few exceptions, these strictly unofficial photographers made scenic pictures of troops and various war activities. Although a fair proportion of the cards produced bear an imprint, sometimes with a misleading statement, such as, "Photographer with the Second Army" or "Camp Douglas," many of these cards have no photographer imprint.

The official and semi-official photographers were keenly aware of the importance of their work. Certainly Brady had conceived a masterplan to preserve for posterity a vivid record of the war.

A. J. Russell, one of the first official Army photographers, was selected by General Herman Haupt to document the construction and operation of military railroads. He recorded his reminiscences as a war photographer in *Anthony's Photographic Bulletin*.[3] His comments have been quoted in whole or in part many times[4] but are especially pertinent here.

"The public does not and cannot realize the part that the camera served in bringing down the facts of the late war for future history; one cannot look back but with wonder and admiration on those few industrious painstaking men . . . who played their part well . . .

"The memories of our great war come down to us and will pass on to future generations with more accuracy and more truth-telling illustration than that of any other previous struggle of ancient or modern times . . ." Russell's appraisal remained true until World War I.[5]

Historians have probably recovered nearly all of the large-plate Civil War images, although every year "new" photographs are rediscovered. In 1978 a remarkable find of more than fifty stereograph negatives and a quantity of prints in various formats by William H. Kunstman was reported. Kunstman (misspelled Hunstman in Cobb, *loc. cit.* p. 133), a photographer operating in Nazareth, Pennsylvania, used the imprint "General Photographer, the First Division, Eleventh Army Corps, Army of the Potomac."[6]

[1]"Photographs of the Civil War," *Military Affairs 26*: 127–135, 1962.

[2]See also: Gladstone, William 1979, "Medical Photography in the Civil War," *Photographica 11* (2): 8–10.

[3]*13*: 212–213, 1882.

[4]Miller, F. T., 1910–1912, *Photographic History of the Civil War*, 10 vols, Vol. 1, pp. 30–54.

[5]See Haupt, Herman, 1901, *Reminiscences of General Herman Haupt*, p. 256; also, Gladstone, Wm., "Captain Andrew J. Russell: First Army Photographer, *Photographica 10* (2): 7–9, 1978, who points out that many of Russell's photographers have been erroneously credited to Brady.

[6]Roberts, Tom, *Bethlehem (Pa.) Globe Times*, Oct. 17, 1978, pp. 1, 7. Through Mr. Roberts, I was able to examine this remarkable collection.

180. Anonymous. "Part of Gen. Geary's Staff" . . . Lookout Mountain Summit on Christmas Day, 1863. Courtesy of Henry Deeks.

red according to Act of Congress, in the year 1862. by Barnard & Gibson, in the Clerk's Office of the District Court of the District of Columbia.

181. Brady, M. B. Gen. McClellan's Tent, Camp Winfield Scott, near Yorktown. May 1, 1862. Brady's Album Gallery no. 350. Negative probably by Barnard & Gibson.

tered according to Act of Congress, in the year 1862, by Barnard & Gibson, in the Clerk's Office of the District Court of the District of Columbia.

182. Barnard & Gibson. Servants of officers of staff. Camp Winfield Scott, May 1, 1862. Brady's Album Gallery no. 359.

183. Barnard & Gibson. Fortifications on the Heights of Centreville. Brady's Album Gallery no. 300.

184. Ennis, Geo. O. Construction of the Dutch Gap Canal, James River, Virginia. 1864. W. D. Selden & Co., publisher, Richmond. Courtesy of Robert Cauthen.

185. Ennis, Geo. O. View of the Burnt District of Richmond, 1865. W. D. Selden & Co., publisher. Courtesy of Robert Cauthen.

War Scenes

The largest and best known series of scenic cartes de visite was produced by Brady beginning in 1862, with additional titles until 1865. The exact number of titles in Brady's series is not known but probably exceeds 400. As noted above, the series was first offered for public sale by Anthony in the fall of 1862. The images copyrighted in 1862 were by Brady or, more usually, by Barnard and Gibson, then in his employ.

Brady's ambitious private venture to photograph the war with a large corps of cameramen in his employ are well known.[7]

The cards in "Brady's Album Gallery" were sold continuously for more than three years. There are at least eight variants in the typesetting of the printed labels, indicating a long period of manufacturing.

There were relatively few scenic series issued in carte de visite format. The best known are by:

> Selden & Ennis (Richmond), including fine views of Richmond, Petersburg and the construction of the Dutch Gap Canal. (Cauthen Collection)
> Barnard (Charleston), a considerable series including the vicinity of Charleston, Hilton Head, etc.
> John Soule (Boston), a series photographed in 1865 of the vicinity of Fort Sumter, Charleston and Richmond; identical to Soule's stereographic series and bearing the same title numbers.
> S. A. Cooley, Beaufort, North Carolina, many camp scenes, landmarks and groups of soldiers.

Very likely there are other series that, because only a few titles are known, remain unrecognized as such.

Late in 1861 Anthony issued a small series of scenes of Harper's Ferry, without acknowledgment of the photographer.

[7]Frassanito, William A., 1875, *Gettysburg: A Journey in Time.* Frassanito, William A., 1978, *Antietam: The Photographic Legacy of America's Bloodiest Day.* Cobb, Josephine, "Mathew B. Brady's Photographic Gallery in Washington," *Columbia Historical Society Records* 29: 33–36.

In 1863 Peter S. Weaver published a small series of views of the battlefield at Gettysburg. These were sold for some years as both cartes de visite and stereographs. The mounts most commonly found were produced between 1867 and 1872, without the photographer's name. Pirated issues were sold by Mumper and Tipton with their imprints in the mid 1870s.

George S. Cook's series of the ruins of Fort Sumter were produced in both carte de visite and stereograph formats.

The most important scenic cartes de visite, however, were not produced by these well-known publishers, nearly all of which have been reproduced in the host of books and articles on the Civil War. The rarest and historically most significant are the occasional and fortuitous images produced by camp followers and local photographers. Three examples will be cited.

Illustrated here is "A group of Cherokee Indians entering our lines at Nashville," T. M. Schlier photographer. The Indians are probably from the Tennessee-Georgia area. Figure 186.

D. P. Barr (Vicksburg), ca. 1863, published a fine view of the *U. S. Ram Vindicator* on the Mississippi River.

Union prison camp, Elmira, N. Y., a remarkable panoramic view by Moulton & Larkin. Figure 189.

Most frustrating are the hundreds of unusual, perhaps unique images that bear no photographer's imprint, in many cases not even a penciled title. Very probably these were produced by camp followers, many of whom did not bother with imprinting their card mounts.

The Moss Collection contains a fine image of a supply or sutler's wagon in camp. The two sides of the wagon are raised and propped open to display the contents. The only identification is a title "Quartermaster's Wagon."

Another tantalizing scene, showing a group of six soldiers is titled "telegraph detail," but nothing in the named picture suggests this assignment, dated 1862.

186. Schlier, T. M. "Cherokee Indians entering our lines at Nashville, Tenn." Nashville, 1864.

187. Bishop & Zimmerman. Ruins of Chambersburg, burned by the Confederates July 24, 1864. Chambersburg, Pa., 1864.

The photographer's imprint may be extremely important, often revealing elusive information. Furthermore, the information relating to the war may be found on a portrait of a woman or child, totally unrelated to the war. For example, in 1865–1867, A. J. Riddle (Macon, Georgia) advertised in his imprint:

"The same RIDDLE who photographed the maps for the Army of Tennessee, under 'Old Joe.'"

A card photograph of an earlier Confederate soldier portrait bears a pasted label:

"A. J. Riddle, Chief Photographer, Division of the West, Macon, Georgia." (Larry Jones Coll.)

So far as I am aware, this is the only confirmed "official" Confederate Army photographer. Most of the Confederate photographers seem to have done contract work.

Portraits of soldiers often bear imprints giving the Camp, Army or unit with which the photographer was associated (e.g., Camp Douglass, Camp Chase, Tenth Army Corps, Hunt's Brigade, etc.) A number of photographers had imprints of more than one camp address because they moved with the armies.

Despite the tremendous collector interest in Civil War images, at present it is almost impossible to estimate, or even predict, the extent of this carte de visite documentation of the war. To gain some crude idea as to what was available, I tabulated the scenic Civil War cartes offered for sale at the Civil War Collectors Show held in Gettysburg in 1978 and in 1980. The combined totals, tabulated shortly after the shows opened, reveal that approximately 175 different images were offered by 17 dealers in 1978 and 115 by 12 dealers in 1980. Approximately half of the cards bore no photographers' imprints. The only conclusion warranted by this meager sampling is that very many little-known scenic war views in carte de visite format exist, many of them not as yet reproduced in any printed publication.

The high proportion of cards without imprints is probably greatly exaggerated because cards identified by an imprint were withheld for the dealer's private collection, had been sold previously, or were reserved for sale to preferred customers or for auction.

War-Related Cartes de Visite

There are many other types of cartes that are directly or indirectly related to the war. Those most directly concerned include pictures of drummer boys and mascots, both often involved in combat situations. Drummer boys sounded commands, much like buglers. Collectors should be cautioned that there are portraits of boys with drums, patriotic poses but not military.

Famous mascots were photographed for carte issues, most notable "Old Abe," an American eagle, mascot of the Eighth Wisconsin Infantry and "Old Joe," the dog of the 102nd Pennsylvania Volunteers. Several photographs of these are known.

Tattered battle flags, proudly held by veterans were photographed for cartes to be distributed among members of the regiments. Figure 188.

National Military Cemeteries

Eleven cemeteries were established during the war or immediately after: Antietam, 1862, Gettysburg, 1863, Vicksburg, 1865, Shiloh, 1866, et al. Arlington National Cemetery (1864) provided for burial of military officers, government officials and their families. Cartes de visite of all of these are known.

National Military Parks

The designation of battlefields as national parks did not begin until the 1890s (Chicamauga-Chattanooga, Vicksburg, Shiloh, Gettysburg), although the sites of most of the great battles had been preserved and, to some extent, developed by local groups to attract tourists. The Gettysburg Battlefield Association, as early as 1868, sought to preserve and maintain this historic site. Markers and monuments placed by the

189. Moulton & Larkin. Union Prison Camp, Elmira, New York, 1864.

188. Purviance, W. Battle Flags of the 111th Penna. Vol. Inf. Pittsburgh, Pa., 1864. Courtesy of Nicholas Graver.

COL. CROSSMAN.
U.S.Q.M. Phila
J.H.Bufford Pub Boston Mass.

191. Notman, W. The confederate ship *Alabama* lost in battle with the *U.S.S. Kearsarge* off Brest, France. From a sketch owned by Capt. Semmes. Several issues of this image are known. Montreal, ca. 1865. Courtesy of Robert Cauthen.

190. Example of lithographed portraits of military leaders. J. H. Bufford, publisher. Boston, ca. 1863.

States and military units engaged in the battles studded the fields and lined the driveways long before they were declared national parks. Post-war cartes de visite and stereographs record the development of these battlefields in the 1870s.

The United States Sanitary Commission

This influential civilian organization was established by Congress in June 1861 as a result of public pressure. Prominent citizens, many of them medical doctors, were determined that the dreadful mortality due to filth and disease that occurred in the Crimean War, would not be repeated. They demanded the right to examine camps, hospitals and army medical services but asked for no financial support. Their outstanding accomplishments in improving camp sanitation, transporting sick and wounded, supplementing food supply and training nurses were achieved slowly in the face of great difficulties, especially by obstruction by military officials. Among their best known activities were "Sanitary Fairs" held in many cities to raise money for the work of the Commission. Cartes de visite of exhibits in their fairs are fairly common. Images of the Commission's boats for moving troops on the Mississippi and Tennessee Rivers and groups of workers in military hospitals and camps are also known.

Many local relief committees and societies were organized by women's and church groups. Most of these today are remembered only as names mentioned in contemporary newspapers or reports. At least one was recorded by a local photographer, D. C. Pratt, Aurora, Illinois, ca. 1863. The image shows an outdoor fair with a banner "Christian Relief Society," some twenty tables of foods and articles apparently for sale and about two dozen people gathered at opposite ends to give the photographer a clear view. Two men in uniform, much bunting and two American flags complete the picture.

Fund Raising

There are several instances of the sale of cartes de visite for the specific purpose of raising money to support war related charitable projects.

Bishop and Zimmerman published a small series of scenes of the destruction of Chambersburg (Pa.) on July 30, 1864, by the Confederates. The money derived from the sale was contributed to the relief of the sufferers.

Perhaps the story of the "Children of the Battlefield" is the most remarkable. An ambrotype of three young children was found clutched in the hand of an unknown Union soldier killed in the town of Gettysburg. Publicity about the incident aroused the interest of Doctor John C. Bournes (=Burns) of Philadelphia, who had several thousand copies printed in carte de visite format to be distributed throughout the Middle Atlantic and New England states in an attempt to identify and locate the soldier's family. Simultaneously, the carte photograph was redrawn for publication in religious magazines and described in newspapers. By mid November the soldier had been identified as Sergeant Amos Humiston of Portville, New York, 157th New York

192. Imprint of Butler, Bonsall & Company, General Rousseau's Division, 1863–1865.

193. Hollenbeck, O. A. Drummer Boy. Oneida, N.Y., 1863.

84

194. Warner, P. H. Dedication of the War Memorial,
Hopkinton, Iowa, 1866. Courtesy of Henry Deeks.

Volunteers. The first issue, photographed by H. C. Phillips & Brother, of course, had no identification of the children or their father.

Immediately upon location of the family, a wave of public sympathy led Doctor Bournes to publish thousands of portraits to raise money for the care and education of the children. At least five Philadelphia photographers printed cartes for the project Wenderoth & Taylor; Wenderoth, Taylor & Brown; J. E. McClees, F. Gutekunst, and Phillips). All of these 1864 to 1867 issues identify the children and indicate the

VIEW OF THE
RUINS OF CHAMBERSBURG,
Sold for the Benefit of
THE SUFFERERS.
....
PHOTOGRAPHED & SOLD BY
BISHOP & ZIMMERMAN,
Chambersburg, Pa.

195. Bishop & Zimmerman. Carte issued to raise money for victims of the burning of Chambersburg. See Figure 187, 1864.

purpose for which the picture was reproduced. The proceeds from the sale of cartes de visite and from membership in the "National War Orphan's Homestead" led to the establishment of the Homestead in Gettysburg (1866–1877), a few yards away from the grave of Sergeant Humiston. Mrs. Humiston served on the staff for several years while her children resided there. Figure 196.

A group portrait of three black children, "Rebecca, Charley, and Rosa, Slave Children from New Orleans," was sold in the North to raise funds for the education of black children in areas under control of the Union Army in Louisiana.

The Assassination of Lincoln

The assassination of the President by John Wilkes Booth occurred five days after General Lee surrendered at Appomattox. Within a week there appeared a crude montage, known as the "apotheosis of Lincoln," possibly first produced by Tomlinson. It was immediately pirated by a dozen photographers. The picture is composed of a bust of Lincoln in the embrace of a bust of Washington, the two enveloped in a field of clouds.

National mourning created a tremendous demand for portraits of Lincoln and of John Wilkes Booth and his co-conspirators. There was a rash of reprints, copy issues and drawings expressing the public sympathy. Booth, the actor, had his portrait taken many times by a dozen photographers. All of these earlier images were extensively pirated. Portraits of Boston Corbett, who shot Booth, also sold in considerable quantities.

Propaganda

Many political and patriotic cartoons and drawings were published as cartes de visite during the war years. Some of these are scornful depictions of Jefferson Davis, of members of Lincoln's cabinet and of "copperheads" (northern sympathizers of the Confederacy).

Patriotic paintings, such as G. D. Crewerton's "On to Richmond" and "All Quiet on the Potomac" were sold widely (1864).

196. Phillips, H. C. & Bro. "Orphans of the Battlefield," The Humiston children. This is a copy of
the first carte issue published before the identity
of the children was known. Philadelphia, 1863.

During the period 1862–1864, many photographers'
imprints reflected the patriotic mood of the country.
Vignettes of flags, eagles, shields of stars and stripes,
"Liberty" and other symbols embellished the card
backs.

Occasionally, photographers advertised their ability
to "copy portraits of loved ones lost in the war" (e.g., F.
B. Gage). Figure 197.

Post-War Related

Cartes de visite of the national cemeteries and
battlefield parks produced in the 1870s have already
been mentioned. Many local photographers published
views of landmarks, such as Appomatox Court House,
Lee's headquarters at Gettysburg and the like for the
growing numbers of visitors to old battle sites, especially children and grandchildren of veterans.

197. Imprint of F. B. Gage advertising his ability to copy
pictures of persons lost in the war. Note revenue
stamp. St. Johnsbury, Vt., 1864.

198. Bogardus, A. Sentimental, allegorical. Guardian angels
and cavalryman. New York, ca. 1863.

The veterans themselves maintained close ties. The Grand Army of the Republic, organized in 1866, held national and state encampments. For twenty years, annual encampments, veritable tent cities, were held in Gettysburg. Cartes de visite of these were published in the mid 1870s. In 1890 membership in the GAR reached 900,000. Great numbers of portraits of middle aged men show insignia of the society.

There are many portraits of the "old soldiers" in uniform with the GAR medal pinned on their breast pockets.

Many states, and communities including tiny villages, erected monuments in honor of the soldiers and sailors who served in the war. A surprising number of these memorials were photographed. There are cartes de visite of the monuments, their dedication ceremonies and the annual Fourth of July and Memorial Day gatherings around them. Figure 194.

These soldier monuments present remarkable examples of American enterprise. While many of the memorials were designed by the leading architects and sculptors, by far the greater number were quantity-produced by several manufacturers, beginning about 1867, continuing until the time of World War I. The "soldier boy" or "Citizen Soldier" was generally a modified copy of a bronze statue by Michael Millmore, Boston, 1867. A bronze cast could be purchased for less than 200 dollars, an iron one for only 50 dollars. The Grand Army of the Republic posts and other patriotic organizations raised the funds necessary to erect a statue on a suitable granite or marble base.

The Federal Tax on Photographs 1864–1866

Congress levied a stamp tax on many items of commerce to raise money for prosecution of the war. From August 1, 1864, to August 1, 1866, photographs were included under taxable products. A two-cent tax was levied on photographs selling for less than twenty-five cents, a three-cent tax on those selling for twenty-six cents to fifty cents, and a five-cent tax on those selling from fifty cents to one dollar. I know of no carte de visite that sold for more than seventy-five cents. In March 1865 the act was amended, including a reduction of the tax on cards selling for less than ten cents to one cent.

A few photographers charged a dollar per dozen, thus the cards were taxed one cent each. The great majority of cards bore two- or three-cent revenue stamps.

The law required that the stamp be cancelled with the initials of the photographer and the date of sale. This specific regulation was generally ignored. For convenience, many large studios used a rubber stamp, often without a date. Many photographers simply cancelled with an X or a few strokes by pen or pencil, a practice that was immediately accepted without complaint by the Treasury Department.

The presence of a revenue stamp places the card within the period of the tax. The cancellation often provides the precise date of sale.[8]

* * *

The documentation of the Civil War by photographs in carte de visite formats represents one of the few remaining untapped sources of contemporary Civil War information.

The many applications of photography to the war effort, military and civilian, show convincingly the extent to which the image became a part of the daily lives of people and the operations of society—all this in the short span of five years.

[8] See also, Fuller, Kathleen, "Civil War Stamp Duty, Photography as a Source of Revenue." *Hist. Phot.* 4: 263–282, 1980. There are several errors in this paper which, however, do not diminish its usefulness.

CHAPTER EIGHT
SCENIC CARTES de VISITE

The carte de visite format was primarily used for portraiture but photographs of every conceivable subject were published in this style. Scenic views were among the first cartes offered for sale in France and Italy and made their appearance in England and the United States in 1860.

There are five main types: landscape, topographic, architectural, reportorial, and sentimental. Because the functions of these are so different, each will be described briefly.

The pictorial landscape stereographs that make up a large part of early stereo history, owe much to the grand period of English and French landscape painting of the period 1800-1850. William Grundy, Gustave LeGray, and A. Braun followed the painterly tradition. The great American scenic photographers developed a distinct style. Carleton Watkins, John Moran, Charles Bierstadt, Thomas Houseworth, John Soule, and Eadweard Muybridge have left a rich legacy of stereographs.

Popularity of scenic cartes de visite in the United States was confined almost entirely to the 1860s and early 1870s. Not surprisingly most of the cartes were published by the well-known stereographers, some of whom were using the 4/4 camera and mounting the prints as two stereos or four cartes. There were many expert stereographers who used only stereo cameras. The novelty and appeal of the three-dimensional illusion is lost in the scenic carte de visite. Furthermore the image is too small to convey the grandure of an expansive vista.

The most beautiful carte de visite landscapes were published by English and French photographers: G. W. Wilson, F. Frith, V. Blanchard, F. Bedford, F. York, Bisson Brothers, and A. Braun, but there were many, many others in Europe and America who did superb work.

Topographic Scenes, i.e., descriptive or documentary views of the countryside, city, village, harbor, or ancient ruins. This type represents the largest proportion of commercially published scenic cartes. The publication of them in series was a remarkable extension of the concept of the "guide book" that had become popular with well-to-do tourists before 1850. John Murray in 1834 had begun publishing his famous guide books to the British Isles. Karl Baedecker developed the idea further, issuing tourist guides for nearly the entire world. In America, D. Appleton & Co. began to publish guides to the United States about 1850.

Photographic publishers were quick to produce stereographs and cartes de visite to illustrate the historical sites and landmarks cited in the guidebooks. In fact, the sequence of scenes in a series commonly coincides with the route in a guidebook. In the 1880s the guidebooks were often illustrated with reproductions of carte de visite photographs.

Architectural scenes, photographs of single buildings, of groups of related buildings, or details of construction. This is a varied category which includes many subjects that were photographed for a variety of reasons.

(1) Famous Buildings: Notre Dame Cathedral, United States Capitol, San Sophia Basilica, The Taj Mahal, Leaning Tower of Pisa.
(2) Famous Structures: Rialto Bridge, Venice; Arc de Triomphe, Paris; Washington Monument, Albert Memorial.
(3) New buildings, especially upon completion of construction. These were often produced as advertisements for the architect or builder, or for community promotion.
(4) Churches, schools, colleges—produced usually as souvenirs for members, advertising and fund-raising.
(5) Business establishments—banks, retail stores, mills, factories, etc. These were often produced for "grand openings," anniversaries, or advertising. Many of these images show the proprietors and employees lined up in front of the building.

Sentimental. Most commonly this type includes homes, farm buildings, often with surrounding grounds. Most of these "outdoor" views were made at the request of the family to have a keepsake of the old homestead to preserve cherished memories. There are also scenes of barns and stables, interiors as well as exteriors.

Reportorial are scenic cartes that record an event. These range from disasters such as fires, floods or tornados to celebrations and gatherings of people, including parades, public meetings, country fairs, beach scenes, etc.

It should be apparent that only one of these categories requires the photographer to follow the "rules" of art—the pictorial landscape. In the other types he has little choice over composition or arrangment. His greatest problem is to frame the picture within the size permitted by the carte format. At best, he could only consider light, shadow and total pictorial effect.

Actually, all of these purposes represent a single function, to provide information. While attractiveness and appeal might have added to the effectiveness of the image, they were incidental to the *purpose* of the image.

If we rate the purposes for which the scenic cartes de visite were produced, the following order of importance indicates the relative abundance of each type.

(1) Souvenirs for tourists and visitors, also sold in sets as "travelogues." Every city and town had one or more photographers who published series of local points of interest.

(2) Sentimental, family mementos of homes, the parish church, etc.

(3) Documentation, including "reportorial." Generally these issues were small and distributed more or less locally. The variety is great but most individual titles are scarce.

(4) Advertising, chiefly by manufacturers, hotel and resort owners, merchants and architects. The abundance of such cards is impressive.

(5) Fund-raising. These are relatively rare but frequent enough to deserve attention.

The sale of cartes de visite to raise money for a specific project seems to have originated soon after the introduction of the format into the United States and continued until the mid-1870s. Many missionary and Sunday School societies published scenes of their foreign missions and schools, less frequently of other subjects. Usually these were sold above cost to raise money to further a project. Sometimes the cartes were distributed freely to propagandize. The Methodists, Baptists and Lutherans were especially active in this manner.

Many churches financed in part a new building by selling cartes of the architect's rendering of the edifice and/or the finished structure. Some churches sold the carte for one or two dollars denoting "one share" in the building.

The carte de visite iconography of cities, towns and villages.

There is a consistent pattern of the scenic coverage of American cities and towns which is quite different from European communities. The official buildings (post office, city hall, court house, custom house) were invariably photographed as were churches and monuments. Every community with an educational or charitable institution—school, college, orphanage, hospital or prison, or an arsenal, religious colony, etc., would also have these photographed. Even small villages with a single church and a modest factory would have these illustrated.

In America there was great pride in mills and factories, bridges, and businesses. These were symbols of industry, enterprise, progress. Also typical of the American small town was the center square, village green, and "business" or "commercial" block.

There are spectacular panoramic views of small towns throughout the United States. Large cities generally did not have cartes of residential areas.

So far as I have been able to learn, no such complete coverage of small communities of Europe exists in either cartes de visite or stereographs. The scenes are more historical, more traditional. One is more likely to find views of the churches, birthplace of a notable, castles, sixteenth century buildings, and monuments. Commercial and industrial features, excepting busy harbors, are ignored.

The thriving tourist business in the United States expanded enormously after the Civil War. The White Mountains, Catskills, Adirondacks, Poconos, Nigara Falls, the Glens of New York, the seashore, Florida, Colorado, and California all figured prominently in the trend. Many photographers published commercial issues of scenic cartes for the tourists. The proprietors of inns and hotels distributed many of the cartes with their business imprint on the back.

The sum-total of these diversified types of scenic views is a vast number of different images. How many? Nobody knows.

In spite of this diversity, scenic cartes are relatively scarce, representing less than one-half of one percent of the cards reaching market today. They appear to be much rarer than the stereographs with which they competed.

It has been estimated that the number of different scenic stereographs exceeds five million (1851-1940) produced by some 20,000 photographers.[1] I have been able to document more than 800 stereographers who issued identical cartes de visite, but only 72 who produced fine scenic cartes but not known to have published stereos. However, undoubtedly there were many who published scenic views only in carte format.

It is difficult to explain why scenic cartes are scarce. Some plausible factors are: in Europe, the stereograph had become popular between 1854 and 1857, in the United States between 1859 and 1862. The publishing and marketing of stereographs were highly sophisticated before 1860. Many collectors may have preferred to enlarge their collections rather than to purchase views in a new format when they were available also in stereo.

Even though slightly more expensive, the stereo card offered more for the price. In 1865 in the United States, fine scenic stereographs sold from 25 cents (2.50 per dozen) to 50 cents for the best European issues. Good scenic cartes, American and foreign, sold for 15 to 25 cents. In 1873, the average price was 10 to 25 cents for a stereo, 10 to 25 for a carte.

The carte de visite was originally an *album* card, intended to be kept as such. The album had declined sharply after 1866 even though many designs of albums were manufactured (for both carte and cabinet views) into the twentieth century. The Wilson, Hood & Co. catalogue for 1873 offered wholesale, a large selection of American and European series of stereographs, but did not list cartes de visite of any kind.

Still another probable reason was the limited number of copies of the views taken by small town photographers. Even views of disasters and celebrations had only local interest. Every photographer was capable of taking outdoor views—and probably did. Most of these were rarely sold beyond the neighborhood.

Thus there are two major types of scenic views, the commercial issues produced in varying quantities, and the views taken for customers which were not for general distribution. Generally, the commercially

[1]Darrah, W. C., *The World of Stereographs*, 1977, p. 6.

89

199. Seeley, A. & E. England. Palm House, Kew Gardens. Richmond, ca. 1862.

200. Wilson, G. W. Scotland. Edinburgh from Colton Hill. no. 107. Aberdeen, carte ca. 1870.

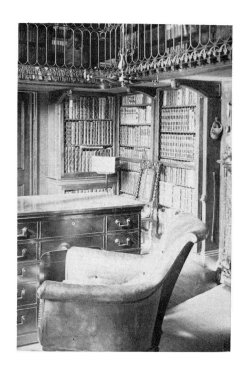

201. Wilson, G. W. Scotland. Abbotsford, The Study. Aberdeen, ca. 1865.

produced images are superior to the custom-made.

Pirating of scenic cartes de visite, excepting those related to the Civil War (e.g., Libby Prison, Castle Thunder, Fort Sumter) was seldom a problem. Apparently there was too little profit in making copies.

Geographic Synopsis

The following summary attempts to indicate the degree of coverage of various parts of the world. The principal countries of Europe and most of the United States had such large numbers of photographers issuing scenic cartes that only the most important can be cited. For many parts of the world, however, only two or three photographers are known to me. In terms of output these were minor, but in terms of regional history they may have considerable significance.

Great Britain

The renowned photographic publishers such as The London Stereoscopic Company, Negretti & Zambra, G. W. Wilson, Wm. Sedgfield, William England, Francis Bedford, F. York, Valentine Blanchard, H. Petschler,

and F. Frith produced varied series of scenic cartes, usually identical to their stereos. Bedford, for example, issued more than 3000 titles. Virtually every known stereographer also offered scenic cartes, among them: Thomas Annan, Archibald Burns, A. & E. Seeley, Hills & Saunders, Inskip, etc.

As with stereo, cathedrals, castles, great bridges, and historical sites predominate.

There are many superb scenic cartes by photographers not known to me as having produced stereographs:

C. Vos Bark	Bristol
P. E. Chappius	London
Charles Deana	Chatham
John Hawke	Plymouth

202. York, F. England. Windsor Castle. no. 62. London, ca. 1865.

Daniel Jones	Liverpool
Robinson & Cherrill	Tunbridge Wells
James Russell	Chichester

There is a mistaken belief that the sale of scenic cartes—indeed all cartes—was confined to the 1860s and early 1870s. Although there was a noticeable shift from commercial to custom work in the 1870s, this only slightly affected the great publishers. A steady demand for fine scenic cartes continued until the mid-1880s when the picture post card gradually displaced them.

H. Baden Pritchard (1882)[2] describes how Francis Bedford, Valentine Blanchard, and William England were still publishing huge quantities of their famous scenic cartes de visite and stereographs. Blanchard was selling his finest cartes at one pound and one shilling (= $5.25) per dozen.

France

Paris was probably the world center for photographic publishing in the 1860s, not only because of the large number of photographers issuing prints but also because of the many manufacturers of cheap original and cheaper copy issues. A fair share of this trade was in stereo and carte scenic views. The subjects covered France, all of Europe, the Near East and Japan, China and some India. Few of the copy issues bear a publisher's imprint, but many are marked with a dealer's stamp—including many American.

[2]*The Photographic Studios of Europe.* Available in a reprint edition, Arno Press, 1973.

204. Braun, A. Holland. Amsterdam, canal scene, no. 3908. Dornach, France, ca. 1864.

203. Bedford, F. North Wales. Bangor, Britannia Bridge in the distance. London, ca. 1862.

205. Braun, A. France. Mont Blanc, Chamonix Glacier no. 778, Dornach, ca. 1862.

208. Garcin, A. Switzerland. Church of Notre Dame, Geneva, ca. 1868.

206. Deplanque, Jules. France. Versailles Gardens. Paris, ca. 1863.

One of the most important publishers, A. Braun, was located not in Paris but in Dornach. Famous for scenic photography and still life arrangements, he later specialized in photographic reproductions of works of art. In the 1870s Braun opened a branch in Paris.

Braun's extensive list of scenic titles was published in both stereo and carte de visite formats. The titles and numbers are identical. A few examples are:

778	Valee de Chamonix, Mont Blanc
3873	Haarlem

207. Andrieu, J. France. Chateau de Chillon, no. 2286. Paris, ca. 1872.

3908	Amsterdam
4783	Erfurt.

Note that there was a run of more than thirty Dutch scenes. Braun's list exceeds 7000 titles. Numbering carte titles was not a standard practice, especially among the smaller publishers. Figure 209.

The principal photographers-publishers of scenic cartes were E. Lamy, J. Andrieu, E. Ladrey, Neurdein, A. Liebert, Collin, and Jules Deplanque.

As in England, many small-town photographers not known to have published stereographs, produced cartes of their localities. A few examples include:

E. M. DuFour, Dijon
L. Konarzewski, St. Jean de Luz
M. Paucault, Pau

Italy

Scenic views of Italy are among the most common foreign scenic cartes found in the United States. Probably curiosity about ancient Rome, Renaissance Italy, and Christian traditions, account for this preponderance.

The publishers of scenic views are, with few exceptions, the well known stereographers: D'Alessandri Brothers, Michel Mang, Spithover, and Oswald Ufer, in Rome; C. Ponti and Naya in Venice; Giacomo Brogi and L. Powers in Florence; Georgio Sommer in Naples; Degoix and Hodcend in Genoa; Emilia in Bologna; Giulio Rossi in Milan; Van Lint in Pisa; and Nessi in Como.

Many of the early superb scenes of Rome, especially ancient landmarks, published by Spithover were from negatives taken by James Anderson.

In the early 1870s a large series of scenes of Rome and its treasures in statuary was issued by an unidentified publisher. The card mounts bear a sketch of St. Peter's square on the back.

211. Ponti, Carlo. Italy. Venice, Panorama, ca. 1865.

As in other European countries, there were many small-town photographers who issued fine local views:

Hopfner, Halle
W. Kurtz, Wiesbaden
Hermann Priester, Hamburg
F. Rose, Wernigerode
Th. Schumann & Son, Karlsruhe
Steuer & Hautzendorf, Baden
A. Wille, Harzburg

Austria

Oscar Kramer, Franz Unterberger, Miethke & Wawra, C. J. Rospini, and Chizak issued extensive series of scenic cartes, for the most part identical to their stereographic images.

F. Fridrich (Prague), also well known for superb stereos, published many cartes of this city.

Switzerland

There is a wealth of scenic views of the Swiss Alps and of Geneva and Zurich, generally published for the tourist trade. The largest publishers were F. Charnaux (and Charnaux & Sons) and Garcin of Geneva; A. Gabler, Interlaken; and M. Vollenweider of Berne. Sometimes tiny villages boasted an able photographer. J. J. Rauch, Schuls, near Engadin, issued beautiful views of the vicinity.

209. Bisson Brothers. Imprint of the series. "Expedition to Photograph Mont Blanc and its Glaciers." Paris, 1861.

Germany

E. Linde, S. P. Christmann, Moser, and Sophus Williams, in Berlin were among the important publishers of scenic cartes. The Deutsche Photographische Gesellschaft, Berlin, produced scenic views but is better known for reproductions of art works in carte de visite format.

Nearly all of the great stereographers issued comparable scenic cartes: H. Krone, Dresden; O. Lindner, Frankfurt; G. M. Eckert, Heidelberg; F. S. Hanfstangl, Munich; Brandseph, Stuttgart; and C. Holzamer, Worms.

210. Ponti, Carlo. Italy. Venice, Rialto Bridge, ca. 1865.

212. Sommer, Giorgio. Italy. Naples, The Quay, ca. 1866.

213. Joulia, E. Spain. Bull Ring, Valencia. Note Joulia's
photographic van at right. Valencia, ca. 1866.

214. Jager, A. Holland. Scheveningen, sea resort.
Amsterdam, ca. 1866.

215. Schoenscheidt, J. H. Germany. Koln, panorama,
ca. 1872.

Erinnerung an Kiel: Der Schlossgarten.

216. Hinrichsen, Chr. Denmark, Kiel, Castle Garden, with
parked gun caissons. Kiel, 1862.

Attention is called to the availability of scenic views of Switzerland, Holland, Belgium and many other countries by the publishers of "world wide" lists, especially Lamy, Braun and Andrieu, of France, and Linde, Christmann and Sophus Williams of Germany.

Other European Countries and the Near East.
Only a few of many noteworthy photographers and publishers can be cited to suggest the degree of coverage.

Spain: J. Laurent, Madrid; L. Masson, Seville; E. Joulia, Valencia; F. Rojo, Malaga.
Portugal: Photographia Nacional, Lisbon.
Norway: W. Selmer, Bergen; Chr. Olsen, Christiana; Madsen, Frederickstad.
Sweden: Vogel & Dienstbach, Goteborg; Otto Petterson, Lund; J. F. Dahlgren, Mathias Hansen, A. Roesler, Stockholm.
Denmark: Chr. Hinrichs, Kiel (early 1860s).
Netherland: A. Jager, The Hague.

217. Kramer, Oscar. Austria. Vienna, St. Charles
Church, ca. 1868.

218. Hammerschmidt, W. Egypt. Mosque Mohamud Aly,
Cairo, ca. 1867.

219. Beato, Antoine. Egypt. Pyramids at Memphis. Note
the small oasis. Cairo, ca. 1865.

Belgium: DeChamps & Co., Ghemar Brothers,
Brussels; F. Tessaro, Antwerp.
Russia: N. Lorenz, St. Petersburg.
Greece: D. Constantine, P. Moraites.
Palestine & Syria: Bonfils, Beyrouth & Jerusalem;
Bergheim, Jerusalem.
Turkey: P. Sebah, Abdullah Brothers.

North Africa

Egypt. The cartes de visite of Egypt are exceptionally diverse, in large part due to the completion of the
Suez Canal. W. Hammerschmidt, Cairo, issued more
than 200 titles; A. Beato, Cairo; N. Koumianos, Port
Said; Schier & Schoefft, Alexandria. Koumianos
published unusual views of the dredging of the canal by
machinery.

Tunisia. J. Garrigues, Tunis.
Algeria. C. Portier, J. Geiser, Alary & Geiser,
Algiers; Trappe, Staoueli.
Madeira (Atlantic Islands). G. Silva, Funchal,
1860s.

Asia

In the mid 1860s hundreds of European photographers scattered over Asian seaports and established
studios. Many of the negatives (or copy negatives) were
obtained by European publishers who issued them
without identifying the sources. To complicate matters,
considerable numbers of stereographs and cartes de
visite without photographers' imprints, were sold in
Chinese and Japanese cities.

221. Bogardus, A. India. Scottish Orphanage in Calcutta.
Bogardus did not credit the source of his negative.
New York, 1864.

220. Portier, C. Algeria. Scene in Algiers, ca. 1866.

96

Japan

There are many unidentified scenic cartes of Yokohama and Nagasaki, ca. 1865–1870. H. Uyeno, Nagasaki and Nakasima, published a fine series in the mid 1870s and 1880s. K. Tamamura, Yokhama, published cartes of the city in the 1880s.

China

Pun Lun, Hong Kong, was active in latter 1860s and 1870s. S. Sidney, Takow, and F. Schoenke, Foochow are also noteworthy.

India

Bourne & Shepherd, Bombay and Calcutta, were the largest publishers of scenic views in all formats. Sache & Murray, Calcutta, issued fine scenic cartes in the 1860s. Chintamon Hurrychund, Bombay, published an unknown number of views of the area. See also, Encyclopedic Section, Religions page—157.

Straits Settlements. Lambert & Co., Singapore.

Ceylon

The remarkable coverage of the native peoples of Ceylon by Slinn & Co., Colombo, and A. W. Andree, Point de Calle, is matched by the scenic cartes of these excellent photographers. The plantations and country-side are beautifully recorded.

Australia

I have been able to examine very few scenic cartes of Australia, but there must have been many. The imprinted cards known to me are by William Bradley and Albert Lomer, Sydney, and E. C. Bell of Melbourne. There are also local scenes by G. Cherry, Hobart (Tasmania).

New Zealand

Tait Brothers, Hokita; W. H. Clark, Wellington.

Hawaii

M. Dickson, H. L. Chase, and A. A. Montano issued large fine series.

Latin America

Very few cartes de visite of South America are to be found in the United States, in spite of the fact that at least a score of American photographers opened galleries in several countries between 1855 and 1870 and extensive trade between the United States and Brazil and Chile. Portraits are much more abundant than scenic views, but this is typical.

Brazil, the best represented, had several excellent photographers. The most picturesque scenes were published in the 1860s by Photographia Brasiliera, Rio de Janeiro. C. Leutzinger and Henschel & Benque are better known.

Peru is fairly well covered. H. Courret, who operated a studio associated with Nadar, and V. Richardson of Lima issued nice series. Noble & Lopez, Callao, and Villaalba, Callao also published scenic cartes.

Chile. Bischoff & Spencer, Valparaiso.

Mexico. Fine scenic views were issued by Cruces & Campa, Mexico City; L. Zuber, Mazatlan; Carlos Clausnitzer, San Luis Potosi; A. Fahrenberg, Monterey. During the American civil war several Confederate sympathizers, Moses and Company, Constant and Stephen, established galleries in Matamoras and published scenic cartes during their stay.[3]

Guatemala. W. C. Buchanan, Guatemala City.

Panama. E. Herbruger, Panama, two fine series, 1860s.

Costa Rica. L. B. Fortino, San Jose.

[3]Collection of Lawrence T. Jones III.

223. Maunoury, E. Peru. Theater in Lima. Maunoury was a correspondent of Nadar whose initial logo is imprinted, ca. 1867. Courtesy of Henry Deeks.

222. Photographia Brasiliera. Brazil. Botanical Gardens, Rio de Janeiro, ca. 1864.

224. Herbruger, E. Panama. Grand Hotel, Panama City,
one of the "Isthmus Views" series, ca. 1865.

Cuba. J. B. Fernandez, Havana.
St. Thomas. Benjamin Wellcome.

The United States

Scenic cartes of the United States supplement to a remarkable degree stereographs which are much better known. There are striking differences in the coverage in the two formats. Except for John Soule and C. R. Savage, no publishers of an extensive list of stereographs produced comparable numbers of scenic cartes. There are no long runs of western cartes such as the stereos of the government surveying expeditions in the 1870s, nor the many series of disasters or the Centennial Exhibition at Philadelphia.

The great early stereo publishers, Anthony, Bierstadt Brothers, Stacy, Appleton, Beers, and New York Photograph Company, produced scenic cartes but discontinued them before 1865. Langenheim did not issue cartes. Soule published his extensive scenic series in both stereo and carte formats, with identical titles and numbers. His White Mountains and Boston scenes

are quite common but those of Niagara Falls and Yosemite are scarce.

The great wealth of unusual scenic cartes is to be found in the occasional issues by small-town photographers. Almost from the beginning, the scenic carte de visite in America was essentially a local product. Apparently they were not financially profitable, at least not nearly as successful as stereographs.

New York State and City have the best coverage. The early issues by Anthony, Stacy, Beers and Rockwood are heavily weighted on scenes of buildings, street scenes and Central Park.

The tourist resorts were frequently photographed, the following being typical:

Lake George—S. Beers.
Havana Glen—G. H. Marsh.
Watkins Glen—R. D. Crum, A. Orr, Jr.
Warsaw—L. E. Walker.
Niagara Falls—Barrett, J. J. Reilly.

225. Zuber, G. L. Mexico. Mazatlan, panorama of the
city, ca. 1876.

226. Brady, M. B. Washington, D.C., street scene with
Treasury Building at left, 1862.

227. Peck Brothers. Connecticut. Yale College,
New Haven, 1862.

228. Kilburn, E. New Hampshire. White Mountains. Tourists
at Crawford House. Littleton, N.H., ca 1863.

229. Soule, John P. Massachusetts. View of Boston Harbor
from Bunker Hill Monument, no. 616. Note imprint
of dealer, Ward & Son. Negative ca. 1863, carte
issued 1868.

230. Anonymous. Maine. Searsport House. An advertising carte distributed by the proprietor, W. H. Matthews, 1873.

231. Warren, G. K. Massachusetts. The Watertown Arsenal. Cambridgeport, 1862.

DAVID WILBER'S HOME, (Crumhorn,) 1845.
Otsego Co.

232. Smith, W. G. New York. "David Wilber's House" near Cooperstown, ca. 1872.

235. Johnson, N. G. Pennsylvania. Oil Creek, Pattersons' Refinery, Boyd Farm, no. 31 in Pennsylvania Oil Region Series, 1864.

233. Chase, W. M. Washington, D.C. The United States Capitol, street car in foreground. Chase & Bachrach, Baltimore, 1872.

Nearly every town had scenic series published by a local photographer. Fine examples include:

Camden—Hinckley.
Castile—A. J. White.
Cooperstown—W. G. Smith.
Ithaca—S. Spencer.
Malone—Fay & Ferris.

Massachusetts and New Hampshire are also well illustrated by cartes de visite. Many small communities

234. Johnson, N. G. Pennsylvania. Titusville and Oil Sheds, no. 1. "Johnson's Photographic Views of the Pennsylvania Oil Region." Erie, Pa., 1864.

are much better covered by cartes than stereos. Boston was so extensively photographed by Soule that he had little competition. In the early 1860s, Horton and Seaver issued some excellent views.

Warren published many scenic cartes of Cambridge, including Mount Auburn Cemetery; Watertown, including superb views of the Arsenal; Concord and Lexington. Butterfield also published fine scenes of buildings in Cambridge.

Typical town series are exemplified by:

Lawrence—Frank Russell, H. R. Robie.
Northampton—Knowlton Brothers.
Orange—J. W. Jones.
Taunton—Battelle & Rankin, Reed.
Ware—C. P. Adams.

New Hampshire. The White Mountains were illustrated by Soule and Bierstadt Brothers. E. Kilburn issued fine cartes before he and his brother established their well-known stereographic publishing business. Many of the images are identical to stereo halves.

Manchester had several photographers who issued local scenic views.

S. Wilkins & Co., Suncook, published an attractive series of the vicinity. H. H. H. Langill produced fine views of Hanover.

Vermont. There is excellent coverage by many small series.

Brattleboro—G. H. Houghton.
Montpelier—S. O. Hersey.
Woodstock—W. P. Kendall, H. Cushing (Skillin Collection).

The following enumeration includes both well-known and hitherto unrecorded photographers who published scenic cartes de visite of their vicinities. The names are arranged by states.

California—T. Houseworth, Lawrence and Houseworth, C. E. Watkins, A. A. Hart, C. C. Weed, E. Muybridge, J. J. Reilly, all of whom were famous for their scenic stereographs.

236. Coonley & Wolfersberger. Pennsylvania. Philadephia, "panorama looking NNE from the Continental Hotel," ca. 1863. Courtesy of Henry Deeks.

Colorado—W. C. Chamberlain, W. H. Jackson, J. Collier, Denver; C. Weitfle, Central City; W. E. Hook, Colorado Springs; J. Thurlow, Manitou.

Connecticut—many, Peck Brothers, New Haven; E. A. Scholfield (W. M. Peterson Collection), Mystic River; Burrows & Bundy, Middletown; S. Parmalee, Windsor Locks.

Dakota Territory—J. Berg, Grand Forks; F. J. Haynes, Fargo; S. J. Morrow, Yankton; W. W. Delong, Yankton.

Florida—Engle & Furlong, Gainesville; George Pierron, St. Augustine.

Georgia—J. N. Wilson, Perry & Leveridge, Savannah.

Illinois—Excellent coverage. J. Carbutt, Lovejoy & Foster, S. M. Fassett, Melander, R. Tresselt, Chicago: T. H. Butler, Decatur; H. H. Cole, Peoria; J. A. W. Pittman, Springfield.

Indiana—D. R. Clark, Indianapolis; Bulla Brothers, South Bend; Wm. Evernden, Lafayette; Mote Brothers, Richmond.

Iowa—J. R. Sayre, Des Moines; I. A. Wetherby, Iowa City; H. R. Buser, Cedar Rapids; Elliott & Hill, Marshalltown. There is a good series of Iowa City, ca. 1870, by an unidentified photographer. The style and mounts differ from the earlier views by Wetherby.

Kansas—E. E. Henry, Leavenworth; Charles T. Smith, Topeka; B. F. Card, Emporia; E. G. Fellows, Marshalltown; and many others.

Kentucky—Carpenter & Mullen, Lexington; J. B. Webster, Louisville.

Louisiana—T. Lilienthal, B. Moses, New Orleans.

Maine—M. F. King, Portland; H. A. Mills, Camden; Dunton, Augusta.

Maryland—W. H. Chase, R. Walzl, Baltimore.

Michigan—Jex Bardwell, a large series "Views of Detroit and Vicinity"; Carson & Graham, Hillsdale; S. C. Baldwin, Kalamazoo; C. B. Brubaker, Houghton.

Minnesota—Many, including B. F. Upton, Joel Whitney, C. A. Zimmerman, St. Paul; R. N. Fearon, Minneapolis; C. G. Edwards, Rushford.

Missouri—D. H. Watts, California; L. Taylor, Carthage; J. C. Macurdy, Boonville; G. H. McConnell, Hoelke & Benecke, St. Louis.

Nevada—H. C. Tandy, Austin & Winnemucca; Noe, Virginia City.

New Jersey—G. K. Marriner, Belvidere; J. E. LaForge, Rahway; J. Good, Trenton; Forster, Union Hill.

237. Wilson, J. N. Georgia. Bonaventura Park, Savannah, 1866.

238. Gerrish, F. A. Alabama. Montgomery, with the State House in the distance, ca. 1867. Courtesy of Henry Deeks.

239. Styles, A. F. Florida. St. Augustine street scene. Burlington, Vt., 1867.

240. Macurdy, J. C. Missouri. Shipping marble by river barge and railroad. Boonville, ca. 1875.

241. Edwards, C. G. Minnesota. Rushford
Public School, ca. 1868.

242. Kendall, R. A. Wisconsin. Panorama of Mineral Point,
1868.

Ohio—E. Crew, Alliance; C. Waldack, E. Mendenhall, Cincinnati; B. F. Battels, Akron; E. Decker, Cleveland; Liebich, Cleveland; W. Oldroyd, Columbus; E. H. Alley, Toledo; and many others.

Oklahoma (Indian Territory)—T. M. Concannon, W. Soule.

Oregon—P. Britt.

Pennsylvania—M. A. Kleckner, Bethlehem; H. Bishop, Chambersburg; Tyson Brothers, W. H. Tipton, L. Mumper, Gettysburg; A. D. Deming,

Oil City; W. H. Lochman, Hamburg; Isaac Lachman, Pottstown; A. M. Allen, Pottsville. There are many views of Philadelphia, most extensively by R. Newell and Cremer.

Rhode Island—A. E. Alden, S. B. Brown, F. Hacker, Manchester Brothers, E. G. Windsor & Co., all of Providence.

South Carolina—Pelot & Cole, Aiken.

Utah—Remarkably well covered by the famous photographers Carter, Savage, and Savage & Ottinger, all of Salt Lake City. Many of the early stereographs by these publishers were also issued as cartes de visite but there are many titles not known in stereo format.

Virginia—Anderson, Seldon & Ennis, Richmond.

Washington D.C.—M. B. Brady issued a fine small series in 1862. Alex Gardner published many fine scenic cartes 1864–1866. Bell & Brother, L. C. Dillon and J. F. Jarvis are also noteworthy. There are many scenes of Washington published by non-resident photographers.

243. Fearon, R. N. Minnesota. Minneapolis, Academy of
Music, 1872.

244. Savage, C. R. Utah. Court House, Salt Lake City, ca. 1870.

245. Savage, C. R. Utah. View of Salt Lake City and Mormon Tabernacle, ca. 1868.

246. Lawrence & Houseworth. California. Calaveras County, "Section of the Original Big Tree," no. 878, 1866.

247. Tandy, H. C. Nevada, Austin, 1868.

248. Britt, Peter. Oregon. "Mount Hood, 11,443 feet high." Jacksonville, Ore., ca. 1863.

Among the best known series are those by Anthony, Soule, Chase, Chase & Bachrach, Ranald Douglas (Livingston, N. J.), and R. Walzl.

Wisconsin—R. D. Kendall, Mineral Point; C. B. Manville, Neenah; W. H. Sherman, Milwaukee; H. S. Harman, Sheboygan; E. R. Curtiss, Madison.

Canada

The principal stereographers, W. Notman, L. P. Vallee, and J. Parks, published comparable scenic cartes de visite. Many other photographers issued series illustrating their vicinities. S. Park, Brantford; H. Henderson, Kingston; J. McClure, St. John; Wm. A. Lyon, Toronto are typical.

The foregoing summary must be considered as only an indicative guide. It is not a checklist. There are hundreds of additional photographers worthy of inclusion. There are also great numbers of scenic cartes identified as to location that bear no photographer's imprint. Some of these are of historical importance because of the scanty coverage of the locations they represent—Texas, Nevada, Florida, Dakota Territory. Even more frustrating are fine views without any title or other identification.

Just as the portraits of celebrities and influential personalities comprise an extraordinarily complete record of people, the scenic cartes de visite present an extraordinary pictorial archive of a historical period undergoing tremendous social change. Nowhere was that change more evident than in the American West.

The chances of finding a photograph of any community in the western world between 1860 and 1880 are virtually sure. Locating a picture of a specific landmark, institution, engineering construction, or building, may involve a painstaking search, but there is a good chance of success.

CHAPTER NINE
REPRODUCTIONS OF WORKS OF ART

For centuries the enjoyment of fine arts was a privilege of the rich and powerful. The great paintings and sculpture were housed in churches and palaces. By 1850 the world's art treasurers, many of which had been acquired by museums, were concentrated in a few cities, Rome, Paris, Berlin, Florence, London, Munich and Dresden.

The gradually developing bourgeois society, the rise of a prosperous middle class, demanded sweeping social reforms, not the least of which involved education and leisure. The United States, having a less rigid social class system and freer opportunities for self-advancement, materialized some of these aspirations more quickly and universally than was possible in the older social orders in Europe.

Various efforts to broaden interest in the masterpieces of painting had been attempted in the early years of the nineteenth century. The main idea was to reproduce. the paintings by engraving or lithography and sell the prints, either singly or bound in albums. The small numbers of prints, their relatively high cost, and inevitable loss of accuracy in copying, limited the success of these ventures.

G. Baxter (ca. 1820) envisioned colored reproductions of oil paintings that would encourage refined taste and intellectual appreciation of art among working people.[1] Lacking a method of truthful reproduction which was at the same time inexpensive, Baxter was unable to carry out his dream.

Meanwhile, the movement for compulsory free universal education had made great strides in the United States, with collateral pressure for high school instruction and increase in the numbers of academies and colleges. Curricula were being modified by the inclusion of new subjects, while new concepts as to what education should do for the individual pupils and for society, kept the whole movement in flux.

Instruction in art appreciation, embracing great paintings, classical sculpture and architecture was introduced into American education about 1850 in private academies, mostly for young women, but did not become general until the 1870s. Even then instruction time was reckoned as a few minutes per week. Emphasis was placed upon drawing rather than appreciation.

The commercialization of photographic reproduction revived the hope that art masterpieces would become familiar to many, not limited to the few. The carte de visite provided the vehicle by which this objective was accomplished.

Just as the likenesses of the world's landmarks and celebrities became well-known, so did the master-

pieces of the fine arts. Not until the twentieth century when inexpensive photographic colored images could be produced were the full benefits of reproduction to be realized.

The photographing of paintings and sculpture involved some differences that determined the formats in which the reproductions were marketed. There was no point in copying a painting stereographically because it was an image on a flat surface. Even so, some photographers, like Moser of Berlin, did produce such stereos, obviously without three-dimensional illusion.

Statuary, on the other hand, could be stereographed with stunning effects, far superior to anything achievable in a single image format.

In less than ten years knowledge of the world's art treasures expanded from the exhibition halls of museums to the entire domain of western culture. Once that expansion occurred, the demand for better and better reproductions has continued undiminished. How quickly Da Vinci's *Mona Lisa*, Raphael's *Sistine Madonna*, the *Venus de Milo*, the bust of Julius Caesar, the bronze Romulus and Remus and the Wolf, and the *Pieta* became familiar to millions, through cartes de visite!

It is curious that these cartes de visite of art reproductions are today misunderstood. They were not cheap publishers' ventures. These reproductions were a deliberate attempt to educate, however we may wish to temper the ideal by the obvious commercialism involved in their mass production.

There were some ludicrous examples of publisher's greed. At the bottom of Raphael's Sistine Madonna, two winged cherubs gaze with childish wonderment upon the Mother and Child above them. Some publisher, who chose not to imprint his cartes, made a copy negative of the entire painting, a copy of the two cherubs, and copies of each cherub—obtaining four titles for his series, hopefully to multiply his profit accordingly.

The works of art reproduced in carte de visite format are of two main types: (1) paintings and engravings; (2) sculpture, including bronze, woodcarving and ceramic. The paintings and engravings are, in turn, of two types: masterpieces in museums and private collections and paintings and drawings made specifically for cartes de visite. The latter will be discussed later.

Reproductions of Paintings

The largest publishers of these cartes (ca. 1863–1870) were Giocomo Brogi, the German Photographic Company, F. & O. Brockmann, and unidentified French companies, although there were many prolific photographers. Gouptil & Co., late 1860s and 1870s sold their issues worldwide. Brogi advertised "a gradiose

[1]Bland, David, 1969, *A History of Book Illustration*, 2nd ed., p. 255.

249. Brogi, Giacomo. *Madonna Addolorata*, by Carlo Dolci, no. 357. Florence, ca. 1865.

251. Brockmann, F. & O. *Madonna and Child*, by Hans Holbein, no. 29. Dresden, 1863.

250. Brockmann, F. & O. *Lavinia*, Titian's daughter, by Titian, no. 114. Dresden, ca. 1863.

252. Tessaro, F. *Descent from the Cross*, by Rubens Antwerp Cathedral, Antwerp, 1863.

collection of the principal paintings in the galleries of Europe." He was especially interested in copying the works of the Italian masters preserved in foreign countries. Each carte was identified by artist, title of painting, and collection. For examples, Raphael's, *Cardellino Madonna*, Florence, no. 315 and *Madonna of the Palms.* Lord Egerton Collection, London, no. 317.

The Brockmann series also covered classical paintings but included a wide range of contemporary works such as by C. L. Vogel, Dolce, Ribera, Romano, and other painters almost forgotten today.

The Brockmanns issued a notable subseries of beautiful vignetted heads isolated from the pictures in which they were painted, including *John the Baptist* by Raphael, *A Venetian Girl* by Titian, *Madonna of St. George* by Corregio, and *Herodia's Daughter* by Carlo Dolce.

A fine varied series was published by Gustav Schauer under the imprint, Photographic Art Publishing Institute, Berlin, mid 1860s. Quite different in content, was the large series published by the Art Press of the German Photographic Company (1860s) which included many paintings of the 18th and early 19th centuries, such as Leopold Robert's *The Neopolitan Improvisator* (458), P. Craig's *"Persuasion"* (819), R. Ansdell *"Waiting for Help"* (610).

A very similar series published in Germany (ca. 1867–1873) bears no imprint. The numbered titles do not correspond with those in the Photographic Company's series. These three German issues have the titles in three languages—German, French and English—indicating that they were intended for an international market.

The earliest commercially published series were issued by Italian and French photographers, Alinari Brothers, Florence; L. Powers, Florence; Emilia, Bologna; Spithover, Rome; E. Desmaisons, Paris; and Neurdein, Paris.

In 1867 Braun, who until then had published few art reproductions in carte de visite format, began the systematic large-scale manufacture of art repro-

ductions but generally in sizes larger than carte, most popularly 8 × 10 and 11 × 14 inches. When Braun died in 1877 the business passed to his sons. With a file of 500,000 negatives of notable paintings, the Braun Company became the world's largest publisher of art reproductions.

In all cities with famous art galleries, local photographers published series of reproductions. A. Jager issued a beautiful series of the paintings by the Dutch masters (early 1860s). Tessaro, Antwerp, produced fine cartes of Ruben's masterpieces in that city. Another fine extensive series was published by Carpentier & Ebeling of Vienna, the photographic work being done by Oprawil & Co. (late 1860s and 1870s).

Few American photographers published large series of art reproductions no doubt because there were no great art galleries in the United States and in 1860 no great native tradition. Nevertheless, there was extensive trade in imported cartes beginning about 1861. Many of these bear the imprints of American dealers, not only of the wholesalers, such as Joseph Ward, Boston; Charles Taber & Co., New Bedford; and the New York Photograph Company, but also by individual photographers like Carbutt, Chicago; Whitney, St. Paul; and Bradley & Rulofson, San Francisco.

Taber was a publisher as well as an importer. He issued a considerable number of reproductions of American paintings, including portraits, but he also pirated extensively, including foreign issues. Thus Taber's output included imported cartes, images from his own copy negatives, and from pirated copy negatives. The imported images probably were produced in France (most English paintings have titles in French) and were purchased unmounted because these were less expensive and could be mounted on his own standard cards, a circumstance that sometimes makes it difficult to recognize a pirated copy.

J. O'Kane (New York, 1862–1865) issued at least a hundred, possibly many more, reproductions of paint-

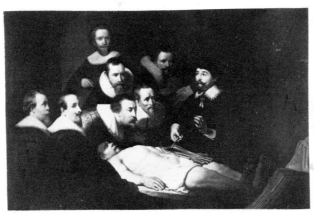

253. Jager, A. *The Anatomy Lesson*, by Rembrandt. Amsterdam, ca. 1865.

254. German Photographic Co. *The Neopolitan Improvisitor*, by Robert Leopold. Berlin, ca. 1867.

255. Brockman, F. & O. *Children* by C. L. Vogel. Dresden, ca. 1862.

256. Taber, Charles. *Heavenly Consolation* by Thomas Brooks. New Bedford, Mass., ca. 1863.

257. O'Kane, J. *The Horse Fair* by Rosa Bonheur
(Landseer Collection). Carte purchased at Saratoga,
August 10, 1863, New York.

ings held in American collections. Rosa Bonheur's *The Horse Fair*, Landseer Collection (now in the Metropolitan Museum of Art), is a fine example of O'Kane's series.

Identical typography on some Taber and O'Kane mounts suggests that the reproductions were made by another publisher, probably French or by an unrecognized American wholesale importer-publisher.

There are paintings, including many of American origin, signed or initialed and dated 1859 to 1865, which may have been done for reproduction in carte format. Probably the sets of initials can be identified. The subjects and realistic styles are typical of the period.

Among the American photographers who published reproductions are J. E. Tilton & Co., Boston; Maurice Stadtfeld, New York; Geo. Stinson & Co., Portland, Maine; H. R. Lindsly, Auburn, New York; G. W. Tomlinson, Boston; F. Gutekunst, Philadelphia; and Christ Siebert, Thomaston, Conn., all issuing them in the early and mid-1860s.

Some well-known photographers occasionally published similar cartes which are seldom seen, e.g., Allen & Horton, Boston, early 1860s.

John P. Soule, like A. Braun, developed a specialized art reproduction business. Soule began his career in Boston, 1857–1858, as a print seller in partnership with John Rogers. In 1859 Soule established a photographic gallery which prospered because of his consistently excellent images and skillful merchandising. His work covered the whole range of glass negative-albumen print formats, but specializing in the publication of stereos and cartes. In 1866 he reorganized as John P. Soule, Publisher of Photographs, relying largely however upon his own negatives. He did limited custom work into the mid-1870s, including copying lithographs and engravings for other publishers (Bufford, Tomlinson, et al. in the early 1860s).

In 1873 he abandoned photography as such, to engage in the manufacture of reproductions of paintings and engravings, ultimately accumulating more than 25,000 different negatives. The Soule Photographic Art Company produced prints by various photo-mechanical processes, in many sizes, ranging from 2 × 2 inches to 18 × 24 inches for school instruction. The prints were usually sold unmounted by the dozen. Children could mount their own or use them as a teacher directed. Soule also devised card games for the pupil to match pictures with artists, various sets and selections to illustrate periods, styles, and painters.[2] Upon Soule's retirement, the business was sold to his brother William, senior partner of Everett & Soule.

Photomechanical reproductions, especially fine if collotypes and photogravures, in large sizes quickly displaced the carte de visite reproduction after 1873. These larger images paved the way for the thousands of illustrated art books which have enriched our common cultural heritage.

Sculpture

What has been narrated about cartes de visite of paintings applies generally to photographs of sculpture. Virtually all of the notable pieces in museums and private collections in Europe were stereographed between 1851 and 1863. By 1865 pictures of nearly all of them were available also in carte format.

Brogi again led the field with about three hundred titles, mostly of works preserved in Florence. Georgio Sommer, Naples; Spithover, Rome; and Alfredo Noack, Genoa, produced fine series. Altobelli & Molins issued a superb series in the treasures in the Vatican. Alfredo Noack published a series of sculptures by Canova.

F. & O. Brockman, Dresden, published a large series of classic and contemporary sculpture, such as *Night* by Johann Schilling.

Among the unusual series is that of L. Powers (also Powers Brothers), Florence, illustrating the works of his father, Hiram Powers, and students. Hiram Powers

[2]For example, a card game, "Old Masters and their Works."

111

258. Spithover, Joseph. Statue of Charlemagne, St. Peters, Rome, ca. 1864.

260. Powers Brothers, Bust by Pierce F. Connelly, a student of Hiram Powers. Florence, ca. 1864.

259. Noack, Alfredo. *Love's Embrace* by Canova. Genoa, Italy, ca. 1866.

261. Douglas, T. H. Lighting effects in photographing statuary. Edinburgh, Scotland, ca. 1872.

(1805-1873), an American, established a studio in Florence and there produced his most famous works such as *The Greek Slave, America* and *Last of the Tribes* (no. 200).

In the United States there were few recognized sculptors. The popular works of John Rogers, which were sold widely as plaster casts, enjoyed a tremendous demand for both stereo and carte photographs. A. Sonrel, Boston, produced a beautiful series of "Palmer's Marbles." Figure 262.

During the period of the carte de visite, cemeteries in America were undergoing a great change, being transformed from simple burying grounds to landscaped parks with carriage ways lined with elaborate memorials and fine statuary. Mount Auburn, Cambridge, Mass. and Greenwood, New York City, became showplaces of some of the finest sculpture being done in the United States. Many of these pieces were photographed for cartes de visite, commercially as well as for the families who commissioned them.

T. H. Douglas, Edinburgh, ca. 1872, published some of the most striking views of sculpture produced in this format. Some of the images were done with full lighting on all sides achieving a remarkable roundess, while others were done by subdued lighting with beautiful shadow effects. Figure 261.

John Titterton, Ely, England, issued several dozen photographs of the wood and stone carvings in the Ely Cathedral.

About 1872-1874 a series of approximately a hundred works of sculpture preserved in the Vatican and Rome was issued on buff cards without a photographer's imprint but with a sketch of Saint Peter's Square printed on the backs. This is probably a copied series.

* * *

The idea of publishing copies of paintings and engravings in inexpensive small card formats did not originate with the carte de visite. What photography did was to take over a field that had been developing slowly since the early years of the nineteenth century. By the 1840s and 1850s monochrome portraits printed from wood engravings and engravings and scenes of many lands, from lithographs and engravings, often tinted, were sold widely in print shops and novelty stores. Such attractive pictures were collected by children and commonly placed in scrap albums.

The subjects were drawn or copied to fit the card size. Generally these were not reproductions of classical works of art, nor of pictures available in any other printed formats.

Drawings and Paintings Made for Cartes de Visite: Popular Art

It might at first glance seem to be inappropriate to include drawings intended for publication as cartes with reproductions of works of art. Although convenience is a consideration, the main reason is the role of popular art in the transition from the independent artist to the artist in the employ of a publisher of magazines and newspapers to meet the accelerating

262. Williams, J. H., Jr. Rogers' Groups: *The Slave Auction.* New York, 1864.

demand for illustrations for fashion apparel, humorous sketches, artist's conceptions, etc. The commercialization of art involved much more than photography.

John Soule seems to have been the first to recognize the potential market for a series of sentimental cartes intended for the amusement of children. G. G. Fish, a locally well-known artist was engaged to draw a series of sketches illustrating several semi-serious themes. The drawings were not published in any other format. Soule himself drew about three dozen titles for the series which was begun in the summer of 1863.

Almost immediately the New York Photograph Company commenced a similar series, obviously imitating Soule's novelty. E. P. Barney drew the sketches for this series. In 1864, G. W. Tomlinson, Boston, entered the field by issuing a similar series, including several thinly disguised piracies of Soule's pictures.

These three series have so much in common that Soule's, the most extensive, can be used to illustrate the genre. Figures 263-266.

The treatment of the subjects is reminiscent of the famous *McGuffy Eclectic Readers* (1836-1857) and probably reflects their influence. Many of the pictures teach or preach a moral sentiment. The prevailing American values, busy hands, obedience, family love, patriotism, learning, kindness to animals, and piety, are shown in simple direct illustration or in allegorical symbols. Some titles are humorous. Occasionally the subject seems far-fetched, such as the twelve titles in *Animated Flowers*, in which various flowers are drawn as humanized figures (Harebell, Thistle, Ivy, etc.).

263. Soule, John P. Sentimental Series: *Shadow*. Boston, 1864.

265. Soule, John P. Sentimental series: *Practicing*. Boston, 1865.

264. Soule, John P. Sentimental Series: *The Bird Catchers*. Boston, 1865.

266. New York Photographic Co. Sentimental Series: *The First Lesson*. New York, 1864.

There are other sub-sets, such as *The Four Seasons*, six periods of the day, etc. Soule's series was continued into 1868 at which time more than 250 titles had been published. During the early years the cards were sold tinted and untinted, but after 1865 nearly all were untinted. The collector should be cautioned that many of the colored pictures found today were done by children. These were nearly always painted over with opaque pigments whereas the original tinting was done with transparent or translucent colors.

According to the imprint on "Autumn Leaves," the proceeds from the sale of this carte were donated to the "Artist's Fund for 1863."

The New York Photograph Company's series contains some interesting original artist's conceptions, such as *Salem - 1690*, a haunting witchcraft scene.

In addition to these well-defined series, there are many scattered copies of drawings and paintings which seem to have been made for carte de visite reproduction. There were also paintings which received local acclaim and were considered worthy of commercial publication in carte format. As novelties, such reproductions occur among the issues of a great number of American photographers, for example, W. L. Germon, Philadelphia; E. L. Brand, Chicago, Melander & Copelin, Chicago; W. G. Smith, Cooperstown, N. Y.; and M. F. King, Portland, Maine.

The assassination of Lincoln prompted several publishers to issue sentimental paintings and drawings mourning the President. These range from Lincoln's sarcophagus with America weeping, to paintings of the Lincoln family.

There are also many paintings produced as single titles, probably for cartes de visite, for the amusement of children: *The First Lie*. These are of great variety including scenes illustrating fairy stories and legends (French, German, and American) and religious topics very likely intended for use by Sunday Schools. Names of the artists are rarely given.

There are cartes of religious paintings done by local artists, the majority of the Virgin Mary, Christ on the Cross, The Sacred Heart, and various symbolic designs. Several fine cartes, without photographers imprints, were distributed by Roman Catholic churches in the Province of Quebec, ca. 1868–1873.

Humorous paintings of adult interest were issued by von Bohr (Vienna).

Cartoons, Comic Art

It is a short step from the sentimental and educational drawing to the comical and satirical. The variety of such cartoons, drawn for or reproduced as cartes de visite, is enormous. Some are simply poking fun, such as a fat lady squeezing through a narrow gate, or the recent Irish immigrant bewildered by his new surroundings. Some are funny pictorial jokes, while others are shamelessly malicious.

The relative rarity of surviving cartoons is probably the result of a combination of factors: their ephemeral nature, cheap card stock, and trivial subject matter. Excepting the malicious and scornful, the cartoons are very similar to those found in the comic section of a modern newspaper or magazine.

Other Types of Photographic Reproductions of Drawing and Lettering

There are many lithographs and engravings which were copied for publication in the carte format. The variety is so great they defy classification. Eight examples will be described to suggest their diversity and the purposes for which they were produced.

1. *The Lord's Prayer*, published by L. Cowles, ca. 1865, photographed by A. Morand from a picture drawn by D. F. Brown. The prayer, in ornate letters of different sizes, is surrounded by the portraits of the twelve apostles and the portrait of Jesus in the center, ten scenes from his life from the Nativity to the Ascension, all copied by hand from paintings of the old masters, and a young boy and girl drawn from life. The back of the card bears a printed description of the painting, an advertisement for large photographic copies of the originals, and an impressive list of endorsements by prominent clergymen. Late issues of this carte, ca. 1868, do not have the promotional information on the back. Although obviously issued as an advertisement for the panel, the cartes were sold widely as a religious keepsake. Figure 272.

There is another presentation of the Lord's Prayer, a rather similar lettered panel with a vignette of Jesus in the center, surrounded by small vignettes (25) arranged as an oval frame and with small vignettes in the four

267. Benedict, W. C. Copy of a sentimental painting (amateur?) for carte reproduction. New Boston, Ill., ca. 1868.

ANGEL OF PEACE.

268. Stinson, Geo. & Co. Sentimental, painted for carte de visite reproduction: *Angel of Peace*, death of a child. Portland, Maine, 1866.

269. Anonymous. Cartoon. "Does Paddy Want to Return To Ireland?" Original drawn by Nicol, 1854. Carte ca. 1863.

corners. It was reproduced under the imprint of S. B. Brown (Providence) in 1865.

A reproduction panel of the Ten Commandments was also reproduced in carte format. The examples I have seen have no publisher's imprint.

The Prayer of St. Francis, a large panel, beautifully lettered by hand, was copied and sold by Coddington, New York in the mid-1860s. This carte may have been inspired by the foregoing *Lord's Prayer*.

2. *Information and Instructions*. There are some curious examples. Fernando Dessaur (New York) issued, ca. 1863, a carte of about 25 Masonic Symbols, reproduced from a chart which appears to have been drawn for a local Lodge. The various symbols are neither identified nor explained.

3. *Poems*. The example selected here is known in several issues by different publishers. It describes the purpose of the carte album and invites contributions to

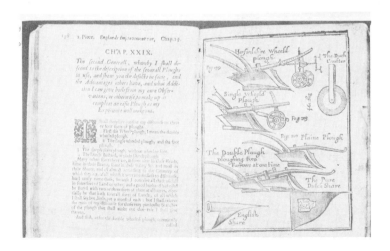

270. Gade, R. "Photographed from a print in an old book, *England's Improvement*, by Captain Walter Blith. A double plow, time of Cromwell." Ipswich, England, 1872.

116

271. Ashford Bros. & Co. A carte inviting contributions to the album. London, ca. 1864.

272. Morand, A. *The Lord's Prayer*, reproduction of a pen drawing, 14 × 22 inches, by D. R. Brown, New York, 1866.

it. The poem was sometimes placed in the first window of an album by the manufacturer to greet the purchaser upon opening it. The most attractive issue was produced by Ashford Brothers & Co., London, ca. 1864. Most of the poems lettered for publication of cartes are of a sentimental nature. Figure 271.

4. *Old Books and Manuscripts.* The carte shown here is the copy of two pages of an open antiquarian book, in this instance, *England's Improvement* by Captain Walter Blith, "Time of Cromwell." The image shows the double plow of 200 (now 300) years ago. The carte, distributed in January, 1872 by the company of Ransomes, Sims, and Head, was photographed by R. Cade, Ipswich. Figure 270.

5. Weekly lists of marriages, births and deaths, which appear to be copied from published lists. Sometimes the three categories appear on the same carte, more often, in large communities separately. Possibly these were copied from official announcements or newspapers. I have seen eight examples, seven English, one German, all of the 1880s. The cartes were probably purchased by those families whose names appeared in the lists.

6. Patent sketches. These are relatively frequent. Typically the image includes the design and an explanatory key to the parts of the device and their functions. The patentee probably distributed copies among prospective purchasers of his design or product. Some cartes bear a photographer's imprint, but many do not.

7. Maps and plats. These rare cartes de visite show

the plans for townsites and farmlands for division and sale in the American mid-west in the 1880s, chiefly in Iowa, Kansas, and Nebraska. These were distributed by land companies.

8. Newspapers and magazines, microprinting. Cartes de visite copies of the front or title page of such publications as newspapers, magazines, or books are a curious type of reproduction. Some were produced to advertise the publication but others may have been issued to display the skill of the typographer or photographer. The best-known example is F. Gutekunst's copy of the Philadelphia Public Ledger (1874), known in two carte images and as a victoria card. One carte is a view of the front page and the other of a two-page spread, which was also issued in victoria format. The printing of the one-page carte and the double page victoria can be read easily without a magnifying glass. The double-page carte, although requiring magnification, is perfectly legible. The two-page image, carte and victoria card, was distributed with the compliments of George W. Childs, publisher of *The Public Ledger.*

* * *

To a remarkable degree the foregoing types of carte de visite reproductions illustrate the versatility of the camera as a copying machine.

Unquestionably the most far-reaching and important effect was the phenomenal expansion of art appreciation, in a sense removing the masterpiece from its isolation in a museum and making it available to all who might find interest and beauty in it.

While other uses might seem to be unimportant in comparison, certainly the carte de visite cartoon was a precursor of the comic page of the modern newspaper and weekly magazine.

Overall, the commercial photographer was feeling his way, exploring the usefulness of his skills, and applying them to new fields of human endeavor. Paramount in all of these efforts was the dissemination of information.

o o o

EPILOGUE TO PART ONE

The accumulated experience of photographers working in studios and laboratories had, by the close of the carte de visite period, resulted in a new synthesis of the art of photographic communication.

Collodion proved to be the material from which celluloid could be produced. Celluloid made possible flexible, translucent, rollfilm. Early experiments in photographing animal motion led to the development of motion picture cameras which, in turn, were dependent upon reliable roll film. Over the years, the camera had proven itself as a recording instrument, a printing machine, and a projector of images.

Last but not least, studio photographers interested in creating humorous and sentimental pictures had devised a wide range of illusory and trick techniques: ghost figures, double exposures, table top photography with scaled models, and ingenious sets. The array of props at their disposal was incredible: painted scenery; cardboard sets, balconies, balustrades, doorways; artificial flowers; papier mache rocks, walls, mantle pieces; and whatever genuine articles added to the authenticity or spirit of the scene. The photographer enjoyed great leeway in creating pictures to tell a story.

The converging of these lines of development culminated in the rise of the motion picture industry in the period 1895–1920.

PART TWO:

A SUBJECT GUIDE TO CARTES de VISITE

This encyclopedic section summarizes approximately seventy subjects that are richly illustrated by cartes de visite. These notes provide information for collectors who may want leads in the search for cartes related to specific interests and as a guide for historians and archivists who are seeking iconographic information.

Less than one percent of cartes de visite are of subjects other than portraits. The reader should not lose sight of this relationship.

The points considered under each heading include types of images available, comprehensive series, the photographers who produced them, and typical examples. Cross references to related topics are given when helpful.

The limitations of these summaries must be emphasized. This is a first attempt to survey cartes de visite. The notes are based upon personal observations and experience. Undoubtedly there are many series, unknown to me, that are equally or more important than those mentioned here. As yet there are no comprehensive systematic reference collections in any public institution in the United States, nor so far as I know anywhere in the world. Much work must be done before a definitive survey of the carte de visite will be possible.

The arrangement is alphabetic by subject.

Advertising
Advertising Art
Agriculture
Allegory
Anthropology
Architecture
Astronomy
Autographica
Botanical
Bridges
Circus & Circus Performers
Costume
Disasters
Engineering
Exhibitions & Expositions
Expeditions
Fashion Photography
Fraternal
Furniture in Portraiture
Geology
Hair and Hair Styling
Horses & Horse-drawn vehicles
Human Oddities
Humor
Identification cartes
Indians
Industrial Archaeology
Jewelry
Landscaping
Literary
Machinery
Markets
Medicine
Military
Mills & Factories
Mines & Mining
Montages, Composites
Monuments
Mortuary, Mourning
Mug Shots
Music & Musicians
Naval
Negro, Black Culture
Novelties
Occupations
Pastimes
Petroleum
Pets
Philately
Photographica
Politics
Presidents
Propaganda
Railroads
Religions
Resorts
Schools & Colleges
Sculpture
Sentimental
Ships & Shipping
Sports
Theatrical
Tintypes
Toys
Transportation
Wars
Zoology

The reader should also check the index for subjects not listed above.

Advertising

From its beginning, the carte de visite was recognized as an effective, versatile medium for advertising.

The most extensive use was advertisement by the photographer himself. The imprint or logo was usually accompanied by supplementary information, providing an almost unbelievable detailed record of the photographic profession from 1860–1890.

Many types of business and professional enterprises used the services of photographers for promotional purposes. The most common were hotels and resorts, tourist attractions, schools and colleges, retail stores, factories, and real estate offered for sale. Most of such custom made cards bear a photographer's imprint, although many advertisers insisted that only their own names appeared on the mount.

Among the more unusual cartes were illustrations of products for which traveling salesmen were soliciting business. Sometimes the cartes were sent by mail to prospective buyers. Furniture, glass, pottery, clothing, machinery and jewelry were advertised in this manner.

John Seckler, "The Popular One Price Clothier," Leavenworth, Kansas, advertised himself. He distributed his full-length portrait by E. E. Henry on a carte with his address and specialties, ca. 1872.

Many architects and building contractors distributed cartes of their designs, plans and constructions to promote their reputations.

Another common promotion use of cartes was as premiums, being given free or at slight cost, with

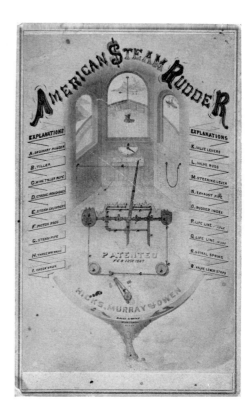

274. Advertising. Patented steam rudder. Ricks, Murray & Owen, February 1867. L. Moulton, photo., Muskegan, Mich.

273. Advertising. Highland House, Martha's Vineyard, Mass. June, 1871. Unidentified photographer.

275. Advertising. What-Not shelves; carte mailed to prospective customers and distributed by salesmen. Photographer not identified. Leominster, Mass., ca. 1864.

120

276. Advertising. Promotion of a sale. Notman Photograph
Co., Boston, 1876.

purchases of goods. Often a minimum purchase amount such as "this card with a purchase from our 99 cents display" is printed on the card. The subject of the image can be of any subject, but humorous and sentimental being most frequent. Sometimes the merchant simply printed a message on the back and passed the cards among his fellow townsmen.

Promotional cartes de visite of propagandistic, religious or self aggrandizement nature are discussed separately. See also: Fashion Photography, Propaganda, Religions.

Advertising Art

The embellishment of the card mount comprises the most extensive record of the commercial art of a specific business or occupation in the nineteenth century. At first the image was mounted on a plain white card. The carte de visite mount rapidly underwent a process of elaborate ornamentation, that embraced the card front, card color, background, pictorial vignettes and a diverse variety of designs ranging from geometric to conventionalized plants and animals and ingenious symbolism. Such symbols as camera, sun, sun

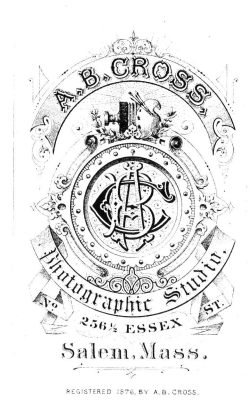

277. Advertising Art. Imprint of A. B. Cross, Salem, Mass.,
1876.

278. Advertising Art. Imprint of C. D. Mosher, Chicago,
1875.

rays, cherubs, chemical apparatus were used in countless ways.

Card manufacturers offered hundreds of stock designs from which the photographer could choose one he liked. On the other hand, many photographers devised highly individualistic logos or sought the services of an artist to draw one. Occasionally the delineator's name appears on the card.

There was a remarkable chronologic sequence of styles and fads which will be illustrated fully in the section on Documentation of cartes de visite, pages 172–182.

279. Agriculture. Hawaii. Vendor selling taro. A. A. Montano, Honolulu, 1883.

Agriculture

Cartes de visite of agricultural subjects are much rarer than stereographs. Those depicting farming practices are seldom seen. On the other hand, photographs of farm houses, buildings and equipment are more common. Newly patented farming machines were often advertised by the carte view.

European cartes of rural settings often show peasants hay making, farm yards, milk cows, goat herds, etc.

Crops and farm products characteristic of different countries in various parts of the world were always photographed in travel series, along with natives using farming tools. Europeans were especially fascinated by rice cultivation under the paddy system. The native Hawaiian vendor of taro, a plant which supports a hundred million people, is shown in figure 279.

A typical plant nursery was recorded in several fine cartes produced by H. N. Robinson, Reading, Massachusetts, for advertising cartes distributed by J. W. Manning, the proprietor. Figure 280.

There are many cartes of country and state agricultural fairs and of prize-winning farm animals. A fine series of the Worcester (Mass.) fair of 1873 was issued by H. J. Reed. Agricultural exhibits of the International Exhibitions of 1867, Paris, and 1877, Vienna, were also photographed in carte format.

The various agricultural colleges in the United States were photographed in the 1870s.

See also: Botany.

Allegory

One of the curious uses of the carte de visite was to teach, preach, and indoctrinate. Especially in the United States there was a conscious effort among intellectual leaders to encourage what had already become the American tradition, the work-thrift-success-patriotism ethic, which also involved moral values of conduct. Many of the drawings published as sentimentals by Soule and others, carry these messages.

But there were many others, ranging from patriotic to the acceptance of death, that are more subtle. The scene may be a drawing or painting or posed models.

280. Agriculture. Plant nursery of J. W. Manning, Reading, Mass. H. N. Robinson, 1877.

One subject, known in at least a half dozen treatments, was the woman's life, generally titled, "Past, Present, Future." One version shows three figures, back to back, a teen-age girl, a bride, and an older, but not yet middle-aged woman. Another version shows young bride dressed in white; a mature woman, and a widow in black.

Bogardus published a picture of a mounted soldier riding into battle with two guardian angels hovering behind him.

Among religious cartes there are many examples of symbolism and allegory including ghost figures, the widow's mite, the Rock of Ages and the Crown of Thorns.

The significance of these images is their preservation of contemporary values and methods of pictorializing them.

Anthropology

The scientific study of man is commonly considered to be anthropology, divisable as physical and cultural anthropology. There are actually many specialized sciences of man, including psychology, human genetics, etc. The nineteenth century, however, adopted the simple view.

It has been noted earlier (page 60) that interest in the races of man had developed prior to the introduction of the carte de visite. Publication of Darwin's evolution theories *Origin of Species* (1859) and *The Descent of Man* (1871) strongly influenced scientific and popular interest in the so-called primitive peoples of New Zealand, Australia, Africa and North and South America—those peoples who had not developed sophisticated material cultures.

The thousands of photographers who scattered over the world, recorded all of the native people's before 1880. Although no organized or systematic approach was attempted, there were a few attempts to encourage a complete country-wide coverage. For example, in the 1850s, Lord Canning, while Governor General of India,

planned for a photographic survey of native types, but this was not accomplished during his lifetime.

The cartes de visite illustrate the following:
1. Physical features and costumes
2. Typical tools and occupations
3. Family, community and tribal life
4. Homes and shelters
5. Ceremonies
6. Leaders

See: Chapter Six.

Architecture

There are carte de visite images of virtually all of the well-known buildings of the world, including Egyptian, Greek, and Roman antiquities. Especially noteworthy are the cathedrals and castles of Europe. The great temples of Asia were also illustrated. Most of these were photographed as points of interest to tourists.

In the United States, the principal public buildings and churches were similarly recorded. Victorian enthusiasm for architecture contributed to the thorough coverage, and indeed increased the fame of many structures. In keeping with the influence of Ruskin, many cartes illustrate architectural detail.

The accumulation of wealth in America enabled some families to build handsome mansions and fine dwellings, even in small, "one-industry" towns, where the proprietors of the factory lived "on the hill." Few of these homes survive today, but hundreds of them are known by the cartes photographed more than a century ago.

In the United States, the early trend toward plain functional design and construction of schools, factories, and even churches, is well illustrated by contemporary photographs. The common row houses and business blocks became a monotonous, yet striking, feature in the city landscape.

The designer of the Mercantile Library Building in Brooklyn circulated cartes of the completed structure

281. Architecture. American Early Victorian home and stable. Family carriage and baby carriage in foreground. Buchholz & Hendricks, Springfield, Mass., 1866.

J. H. Schönscheidt   Cöln a. Rh.

282. Architecture. Cathedral interior, Koln, Germany. J. H. Schoenscheidt, ca. 1870.

with his name, P. B. Wright—Architect, stamped on the back (Cauthen collection).

Architects' advertising in cartes de visite provides an extensive variety of designs and renderings. Copies were often distributed among members of building committees and prospective clients.

Real estate brokers gave cartes of homes and business properties for sale to their prospective buyers often mailing them to parties residing at a distance. There are many cartes of newly constructed summer cottages offered for sale.

Astronomy

Astronomical cartes are scarce. There are several views of the moon. A Warren de la Rue image was issued in carte format in England about 1862. L. M. Rutherford's well-known negatives of the phases of the moon were copied by Bierstadt Brothers and Beer Brothers and published in carte, as well as in stereo format.

Collateral to actual astronomical images are cards that record activities of the photographers who participated in various expeditions to photograph solar eclipses and the Transits of Venus on December 9, 1874 and December 6, 1882. Small parties, including astronomers and photographers, were dispatched to predetermined stations in various parts of the world. The imprint of Augustus Story (1883) illustrates the relevance of such information. Figure 284.

Autographica

There are two main types of autographic cartes de visite: portraits signed by the subject and the cards or images signed by the photographer.

Most common are the signed portraits. The more famous the subject, the more prized the autographed print.

In many cases the signature is accompanied by an inscription to a friend or admirer. Some photographers enticed the subject to sign a quantity of cards which were then sold at a premium. Theatrical personalities were the more common of this type.

The collector should be warned that facsimile signatures were occasionally printed on the bottom front or on the back of the mount—A. Lincoln, Charles Stratton (Tom Thumb), Lavinia Warren, and many others. These are not autographs.

Great numbers of ordinary portraits bear signatures, with or without other inscriptions. Although these hold little interest to the autograph collector, local historians should not neglect them.

Many photographers produced self-portraits which were usually autographed. Many of these were exchanged with fellow photographers.

283. Architecture. American modified Georgian-Neo-Classical mansion. Home of George H. Gilbert, Ware, Mass. C. P. Adams, Pittsfield, ca. 1864.

284. Astronomy. Imprint of Augustus Story, Chief photographer, U.S. Expedition to New Zealand to study the Transit of Venus, 1882. East Boston, Mass., 1883.

285. Botany. Fan Palm. Quinby & Co., Charleston, S. C., ca. 1868.

Mounts or images signed by the photographer are relatively scarce, although thousands of cartes bear manuscript titles written by the photographer. Handwriting samples are indispensable in documenting early images, authenticating cards without imprints, and identifying the various titles in a series.

Attention is called to the autographed cancellation of revenue stamps.

Botany

The types of images illustrating the plant kingdom and vegetation are quite limited. There are four main types: specimen plants, crop plants, gardens, and natural vegetation. Views of specimen plants and gardens, especially formal, were usually photographed carefully to illustrate essential features. Those of crop plants and vegetation were usually incidental to the landscape.

There are several excellent series illustrating cultivated flowering plants, two German and one French, published in the period 1866–1873, being the most important. These were sold tinted. Typically two or three stalks are shown in full flower. The largest series, by E. Linde & Co., exceeds 150 titles, identified by genus and vernacular names, includes many fine examples (44 *Rhododendron*, 76 *Pelargonium*). Copies intended for sale in England had the common names in English, instead of German.

J. E. Tilton, early 1860s, published a series, the number of titles of which is unknown. The emphasis

286. Botany. Rhododendron, no. 44, Linde & Co., series, Berlin, ca. 1870.

125

was on native American plants, magnolia, yellow water lily, cat-of-nine-tails, etc. These views were sold untinted.

There are cartes of flower arrangements, such as a cluster of calla lilies photographed by Lucelia Carpenter (Parkersburg, Iowa, ca. 1880).

Tomlinson published (or imported) various series of botanical and other types of natural history cartes. One set was titled "Album Flowers," most of which were showy, cultivated plants. Another small set, "Fruits and Flowers of the Holy Land," illustrated plants mentioned in the Bible.

Davis & Co., Andrews photographer, Boston, also published some excellent cartes of native plants, including some in still-life arrangements.

There are many close-up pictures of such economic plants as cotton, coffee, date palm, taro, sugar cane, etc. These are to be found among the travel series of countries in which the crops are grown. Crops under cultivation and being harvested are usually included in the series.

Scenes of home gardens are uncommon except as incidental to the landscape. Formal gardens, especially famous ones, were more frequently photographed. Pollock (Boston), produced a fine series of the gardens around Boston and Wellesley photographed by C. Seaver, in both carte and stereo formats.

Public botanical gardens were usually photographed. Among the beautiful examples are Kew Gardens by Chappius, Rio de Janeiro by Photographia Brasiliera, and the Smithsonian (United States National) Garden by Gardner, Bell & Brother, and Smillie.

Native vegetation is well illustrated by great numbers of cartes. The forests of Maine, New Hampshire, Michigan, Oregon and California—including the Sequoia and Redwood—were photographed many times. Tropical palms and tree ferns, cactus and other desert plants are frequently found. Some of A. Beato's views show oases in the Saharan desert.

The botanist can recognize many details not evident in a casual examination of a landscape.

Bridges

Cartes of bridges may be classed in six categories.
1. The great engineering triumphs, such as the Victoria Tubular Bridge over the St. Lawrence River, The Cincinnati Ohio River Suspension Bridge, and the Britannia Bridge in Wales.
2. New bridges, photographed to document completion of construction or as a newsworthy event.
3. To illustrate engineering construction, often as an advertisement of the engineering company, the builder, the commissioners who authorized construction. Such cartes often have names and specifications, etc., printed on the back.
4. As an incidental feature in a scene or landscape, especially in cityscapes.
5. As a picturesque object in a scene. Most commonly these are stone or wooden rustic bridges.
6. As a disaster, a bridge collapsed, burned, or otherwise destroyed.

Categorically every notable bridge standing between 1860 and 1880 was photographed for the carte de visite. Rockwood, for example, about 1861, issued a view of the greatly admired wooden trestle bridge over the Genesee River at Portage, N.Y., 235 feet high and 1600 feet long.

Circus and Circus Performers

Traveling circuses toured the settled portions of the United States regularly from the 1850s well into the twentieth century. Large companies concentrated upon populous areas but smaller circuses performed in many rural villages.

There were three parts of the circus performance, the street parade, the tent show or ring, and the side show, with a retinue of hawkers and concessioners who sold refreshments, balloons, flags and other souvenirs.

The dangerous animals were displayed in cages while trained animals such as dogs, horses and elephants performed in the ring. Clowns, acrobats, jug-

287. Bridges. Rochester, England, Cathedral and castle in the background. Charles Deana, 1865.

288. Circus. "Zula Zingarra, the Circassian Queen," sideshow and stage performer. A. J. Fox, St. Louis, ca. 1874.

289. Costume. Velvet cape. C. D. Fredricks, New York, 1864.

glers, and trick riders were the principal ring entertainers.

Most important to the carte de visite trade were the side show performers, the human oddities—bearded ladies, human skeletons, wild man, and fat ladies.

Eisenmann was the world's leader in photographing these unusual people and other performers like contortionists, aerialists, jugglers, etc.

Generally the cartes of circus animals, tents and wagons are scarce.

See also: Human Oddities.

Costume

No other medium can approach the carte de visite as a documentary record of costumes worn between 1860 and 1895. The millions of different portraits preserve basic styles, variations, and details of clothing worn by all social classes, with unquestionable authenticity.

There are three major aspects which should be distinguished:

1. Characteristic native costume such as Ukranian, Palestinian, or Plains Indian.
2. Dress related to occupation or condition: clergymen, cowboy, soldier, jail prisoner, etc.
3. Fashion.

The first two require no explanation. The third, fashion, is the important aspect to be considered here. Most women sitting for a portrait were dressed in their finest garments. The voluminous silk, taffeta, tight-waist dresses characteristic of the early and mid-1860s show the skill of seamstresses. The rapidity with which

290. Costume. Lace mantilla. S. C. Hamilton, Nashua, N. H., 1872.

127

291. Costume. Hat and muff. Dana, New York, ca. 1893.

292. Costume. Top hat and short overcoat. J. Loveridge, Newark, Ohio, 1867.

"the latest style" moved across the western world is thoroughly documented.

Hats, gloves, shawls, lace, muffs and coats are shown in thousands of portraits.

No less socially important were the homemade dresses for the children and female members of the family. The range is complete, from skillfully sewn dresses of quality to pathetic attempts to decorate a plain garment.

The sewing machine was entirely an American invention (Howe, 1846; Singer, 1851; Miller, 1854; Wilson, 1854) which within a decade transformed the manufacture of clothing, both industrially and home made. By 1860 a hundred thousand machines had been sold, two-thirds of them for home use. See page 39. In 1858 the sewing machine was adapted to the shoemaking industry.[1]

The contrast between hand sewn and machine sewn dresses and childrens garments is strikingly evident in many portraits of rural America in the 1860s and early 1870s. The first practical paper patterns for dresses and other garments were introduced by Ebenezer Butterick in 1863. The Butterick Company is still in existence.

Male attire was also a matter of fashion but not so obviously. The chief features were coat lapels, vests, neckties, shirts, and hats.

Children's clothing was also subject to fashion and changing styles. Boys until the age of five wore dresses like their sisters. Many cartes show "Willie's First Pair of Pants." The suits were often ornamented with cording, fancy buttons, stripes, etc. Little girls commonly displayed their lace bordered pantalets below the hemline. Infants were usually photographed in long dresses, often with lace or crocheted borders. Commonly the child's first portrait was in its christening dress.

There are also many examples of special costumes such as religious habits, non-military uniforms (firemen, policemen, musical bands, fraternal organizations), riding costumes, etc.

The shift from tailor made to factory made suits, shirts, and collars can be recognized in the cartes of the latter 1860s and 1870s.

The person who examines a number of cartes de visite for the first time is in for a surprising treat.

See also: Hair Styling, Jewelry.

Disasters

Stereographs of disasters are varied and abundant whereas cartes de visite are scarce, probably because the three-dimensional illusion gave a more spectacular image. Such events as the Johnstown Flood, San Francisco Earthquake, and eruption of Mont Pelee, of course, occurred after the carte de visite had declined.

Cartes of the Chicago Fire, 1871, and the Boston Fire, 1872, were produced by some of the well-known stereographers: P. B. Greene, Lovejoy & Foster, Soule, R. A. Miller.

Large-scale disasters, especially fires and floods,

[1]Oliver, J. W., 1956, *History of American Technology*, pp. 269-271, 281-282.

293. Costume. A young boy wearing a dress and pantalets. M. Smith, New Bedford, Mass., 1864.

294. Costume. Scotchman in traditional dress. Douglas, Edinburgh, ca. 1865.

reported in newspapers were usually photographed in both formats.

There were, however, many local occurrences such as explosions, floods, fires, blizzards, and train wrecks known in carte format, but not in stereo. These were apparently of regional interest only.

Victims of Disasters. There are many carte de visite portraits of the survivors of disasters, especially of shipwrecks. The example illustrated here shows life-saving equipment. Figure 296.

Occasionally a dead victim is memorialized by publishing a portrait of the person, as for example, Mrs. P. B. Bliss, killed in the Ashtabula (Ohio) train wreck, December, 1876, photographed by Copelin, Chicago.

Engineering
The latter half of the nineteenth century witnessed the development and specialization of the engineering profession and many feats of historical importance. Among the triumphs were the great railroads, tunnels

295. Disaster. Fire ruins, Greenfield, Mass. B. F. Popkins, 1877.

296. Disaster victims. "Fletcher and Cuddiford, sole survivors of *H.M.S. Euridice*," capsized in a snowstorm, March 24, 1878. Note life preservers. Geo. Simco, Landport, Australia.

and bridges, all of which were interrelated. The evolution of large-scale machinery for mining and manufacturing and the organization of operations were other aspects of technological change.

The old windmills of continental Europe and the small iron furnaces were frequently photographed, often for their picturesque appeal.

Construction of the Hoosac and Mt. Ctenis tunnels

was photographed in both stereo and carte formats, but the latter are much scarcer.

Digging of the Suez Canal was begun with convict forced labor but beginning in 1866 special dredging machines were used. Figure 297.

Methods of building construction and repair are well illustrated. The use of cranes, lifts and scaffolding in both new buildings and in restoration of large structures such as cathedrals. The use of manpower for earthmoving and in heavy industry is also documented.

Among the striking subjects in carte format are the sluices and wheels used in hydraulic gold mining in California and the Dakota Territory.

The application of electric lighting to photography is noted in the imprints on the backs of many cartes issued after 1883.

There are many fine portraits of the great engineers, especially those of France and England.

See also: Mills & Factories; Mines & Mining; Petroleum; Railroads; Transportation.

Exhibitions and Expositions

The carte de visite had not yet been introduced at the time of the Great Exhibition of 1851 and the Paris Exhibition of 1855. The Crystal Palace was dissembled and rebuilt in Sydenham. Many fine cartes of this remarkable structure and its exhibits were published. In 1860 Negretti & Zambra issued an attractively tinted series. The London Stereoscopic Company also produced a fine series of the Crystal Palace, ca. 1862.

The Paris Exposition of 1867, so richly stereographed, was also photographed for cartes de visite by Leon & Levy. The cartes, however, seem to be scarce.

Cartes de visite and victoria cards of the Vienna Exhibition of 1877 were published by the Vienna Photographic Society.

The Centennial Photograph Company produced some cartes of the Philadelphia exhibition of 1876, but these too are rare.

In all these series the images cover the buildings,

297. Engineering. Suez Canal construction, Lavalley trough dredgers. Nicholas Koumianos, Port Said, Egypt, 1867.

298. Engineering. Engineer Corps, Western Kansas City
and Northwest Railroad. Chief engineer, J. M. Mitchell,
with top hat. Winans, Independence, Mo., ca. 1872.
Courtesy of Henry Deeks.

299. Engineering. Masonry Dam near Bombay, India. Hurrychund Chintamon, Bombay, ca. 1868.

300. Exhibitions. International Exhibition, 1873, London.
Statuary series, Marble by L. Pagani. William England,
London.

grounds and exhibits, including statuary, machinery and colonial products.

Local and special exhibitions were often photographed in carte format. The various Civil War Sanitary Commission Fairs held to raise funds for the care of Union soldiers were very well documented. Views of many agricultural and mercantile fairs are known.

Attention is directed to the many photographer's imprints that include reproductions of medals received at exhibitions and statements about other premiums and awards earned at local fairs and international exhibitions.

See also: Identification cartes.

Expeditions and Explorations

This category, so well documented by stereographs, is rarely found in cartes de visite. One of the earliest series was published by Bisson Brothers recording their famous expedition to climb and photograph Mont Blanc. The imprint of a card in this series is illustrated in Figure 209.

No cartes of the several federal geological and geographic surveys of the American West (King, Hayden, Wheeler, Powell, 1867–1877) were commercially published. In contrast, there were hundreds of titles of stereos published by each survey.

W. Burger (1870–1872), photographer for the Royal East Asian Expedition, produced in carte format fine scenic views similar to his stereographs. He also produced portraits of native peoples, including their leaders, which were probably not issued in stereo format.

The Norton Collection includes two cartes of *Dr. Ridgeway's Arctic Series,* one showing eskimos and the other an iceberg. The imprint reads "Dr. Ridgeway—Brig. Gen. Frank E. Patterson, copyright by P. F. Cooper, 1862."

Astronomical expeditions included one or more photographers. Cartes of members of the parties are more frequent than of astronomical subjects which are very rare.

See also: Astronomy.

Fashion Photography

This category refers to carte images of modeled clothing or of drawings by commercial artists for reproduction as cartes de visite. These seem to be relatively rare although garments and shoes for women, men, and children were advertised in this medium. Sarony photographed a boy modeling the "Lorne Suite," a new style introduced by Devlin & Co., New York, in the Spring of 1871 (Rosenthal Collection).

John C. Lewis Co., Louisville, Kentucky, ca. 1873, distributed a line cut of a ladies' Duck suit, available in several colors, with a "skirt four yards round, full sleeves, and a jaunty coat" for $1.49, adding that the regular value was $2.75 (Guglielmi Collection).

Fraternal Organizations

The activities of many fraternal organizations and portraits of members, singly and in groups, are shown in a great variety of cartes de visite.

Most numerous are those of Masonic bodies: Masonic Temples, cornerstone laying ceremonies, parades; Knights Templar in uniform; Masons with aprons and other symbolic regalia. Less conspicuous are hundreds of portraits of men wearing Masonic jewelry. Figure 301.

Images of members of the Independent Order of Odd Fellows and the Grange and Grange Halls are occasionally found.

Groups of members of College fraternities and Greek letter societies are fairly common among the cartes produced by photographers in college towns. Sorority groups are more rare, largely because education of women was more limited.

The Phi Beta Kappa key can sometimes be recognized on a watch chain. This famous honorary academic society was founded in 1776.

Hundreds of photographers in the United States and England include Masonic symbols with their logos, most frequently the compass and square. The Odd Fellows symbol is occasionally encountered in photographers imprints.

Furniture in studio portraiture.

The great majority of seated and standing portraits made in the 1860s have the subject posed on a chair, commonly also with a table or desk. Many photographers had several handsome carved chairs or with needlepoint upholstering covers. Fine studios, prior to 1865 had selections of fashionable expensive chairs for

301. Fraternal. Knight Templar in dress uniform. Staniford, Salem, Mass., ca. 1880.

posing. In more humble studios ordinary household furniture was used. Figures 302, 303.

This individuality rapidly yielded to the adoption of special studio furniture: posing chairs, pedestals, columns, tables. Famous photographers patented their designs and manufacturers mass-produced them: "Sarony's chair," "Bowdish's chair," "Reutlinger's pedestal," "Salomon's column," etc. Some manufacturers named their chair models "Scovill," "Phenix," "Pharoah," etc. Thousands of each of these were sold between 1863 and 1875.

The Phenix chairs had removable arms which were adjustable for height and a child's chair attachment. Posing chairs, with fringe or curved back and tassels were displaced when the standing pose became more popular and staging involved papier mache, cardboard and other props in the latter 1870s.

Geology

Geological features recorded in carte de visite images are generally incidental to the landscape rather than photographed deliberately to illustrate a structure or phenomenon. Figure 304.

Such land forms as glaciers, moraines, deserts and forested mountains were photographed for their scenic beauty or characteristic features. The many types of physical environments are, of course, well illustrated.

There are many images of volcanoes and lava flows in Italy, Sicily, and Nicaragua. The well known scenes of Fingal's Cave and The Giants Causeway are classic illustrations of columnar basalt.

303. Furniture. Chair with needlepoint cover. J. Byron Jewell, Nashua, N.H., 1864.

302. Furniture. Fine furniture, especially chairs, was used in studio posing in the early 1860s. W. R. Rolfe, Newark, N.J., 1863.

Published by Whitney's Gallery, St. Paul, Minn.

Pulpit Rock,
Sand Stone, Forty feet high, Saint Croix Co., Wis.

304. Geology. Erosion of Sandstone. Pulpit Rock, St. Croix County, Minn. Whitney, St. Paul, ca. 1863.

305. Hair Styling. 1863. Note uniformity of styling, middle parting, pulled back, bridal party. Mead Bros., New York.

The exposures of rock strata in excavations, railroad construction, and tunneling were recorded in many cartes.

Various aspects of quarrying and mining are well recorded. Among the best examples are granite quarrying in Rhode Island and Massachusetts and marble in Vermont. The alluvial deposits mined by hydraulics in California and the Dakota Territory are graphically shown in fine carte images. Among the most striking are those by Lawrence and Houseworth.

Fossils of vertebrate animals were photographed in the rock deposits and after removal by Cross, Niobrara, Nebraska, ca. 1878–1880. Mounted skeletons in museums at Yale University, the Smithsonian Institution, and the British Museum were photographed for cartes.

See also: Mining.

Hair Styling

The freedom of women today in Europe and North America to choose a personal coiffure has resulted in an almost endless variety of hair styles. While certain styles and fads predominate for a time, the range from long or short hair, straight or curled, fluffed or swept up, presents a degree of individuality not to be found in the nineteenth century. Styles were then more rigidly followed. Commonly a group of five or six women will show almost identical hair styling. Figure 305.

The typical style in the 1860s was long hair, parted in the middle, combed straight, tightly gathered, and tied in back. In the 1870s, tight ringlets, waved hair, curls, knots, and buns were fashionable. Figure 306.

Hairstyling of men generally involved the manner of cutting but combing was also subject to fads, especially in the 1890s.

Many styles of beards and moustaches can be found readily.

The use of hair ornaments by women such as combs, pins, ribbons and jewelry and such pieces as lace, bands, and snoods, were strikingly recorded.

The conventional hair stylings of non-European and American cultures are shown in the cartes of the native peoples of the world. There are interesting scenes showing barbers and hairdressers.

Horses and Horse Drawn Vehicles

The horse was not only the main means of hard labor and transportation in Europe and America but also a source of enjoyment and pride. Many breeds of horses were developed to perform in a special way, as draft horses, endurance runners, thoroughbred racers, farm

306. Hair Styling. 1876. Tight curls, ringlets, and long curls. Joshua Hough, Chicago.

134

307. Horsedrawn. "Joseph Wilkins' family carriage."
J. Wilkins & Co., Suncook, N.H., 1864.

animals, pleasure riding, and docile animals to pull family carriages.

Great lorries moved bulk goods over the cobblestone streets of London, Paris, Berlin and New York while thousands of merchant's wagons and private carriages plied the side streets and boulevards. Interurban and remote areas were linked by lines of stage coaches, supplementing the railroads which were rapidly displacing the horse for long hauls.

Street scenes, when photographed on a week-day (many photographers preferred to work Sunday when there was little activity and the streets were clear), usually show the importance of the horse-drawn vehicle.

Schreiber & Son, Philadelphia, famous photographers of domesticated animals, published two series of horses, one a series of champions in various breeds of work horses, and the other of fine racers identified with their names and their owners. Schreiber also produced many photographs of family horses as sentimental

mementos. Many of these cartes are simply titled "Mr. Biddle's Horse," "Bessie," or the like.

The variety of scenes in which the horse was an integral detail is endless: wagon trains, tread-mills, sleighs, logging, military cavalry, hearses, cowboys, mounted Indians and pleasure riding, to name only a few.

Attention is called to the horse-drawn photographers' vans with the operators name and address painted on the sides.

Human Oddities

Human oddities have fascinated mankind for centuries. Modern medical science recognizes that many of the anomalies were genetic, i.e., congenital, while others were endocrinological. There is an extensive medical and popular literature concerning famous individual personalities of the past and types of anomalies.

308. Horsedrawn. Fire engine, Metropolitan Company 15,
New York City, Walker & Boyles, ca. 1867. Courtesy
of Henry Deeks.

135

309. Horsedrawn. Milk wagon. Hamburg, Germany,
E. Hattorff, ca. 1870.

310. Horsedrawn. Hackney carriage, Singapore.
G. R. Lambert & Co., ca. 1868.

The development of the circus and carnival side show in the nineteenth century provided promoters like P. T. Barnum opportunities to exploit unusual people—dwarfs, giants, Siamese twins, and many others.[2]

Many of these characters earned a livelihood appearing in circus side shows or on the stage, usually vaudeville, as oddities or performers. Brady, Fredricks, Appleton, Anthony, Gurney, and Scholten published many cartes of the more famous but hundreds of photographers contributed to an incredible gallery of these people. Figure 311.

Charles Eisenmann who made a specialty of portraits and poses of every conceivable type of unusual people, establishing himself as the foremost publisher of such cartes in the world. Wendt, who published in the 1880s and 1890s, issued most of his portraits in cabinet card format although he produced many cartes. Another

important publisher in this field was Swords Brothers (York, Pa.) in the latter 1880s and 1890s. There is very little duplication in these three series.

See also: Chapter Five, page 52; Circus.

Humor

The carte de visite was extensively used for humorous subjects. There are two main types: posed individuals or groups in an amusing situation or illustrating a jocular circumstance, and copies of drawings and sketches intended to be comical. To this latter group belong cartoons and the many issues of subjects considered to be funny.

Posed groups are uncommon and are quite varied. They range from mischievous children, accidents such as "spilled milk," "the broken pitcher," to "the absent-minded professor" and "marital strife." There are also groups depicting "Puss in Boots," "Little Red Riding Hood," "Prince Charming," and "Hansel and Gretel," and other fairy tales. Many of these issues were hand

[2]Drimmer, Frederick, 1973, *Very Special People*, an introduction to the lives of some of the more celebrated.

BEARDED GIRL AND MOTHER.

311. Human Oddities. Annie Jones, the Bearded Girl, age 7. Copy issue, 1873.

colored. Some of these poses were produced by well-known photographers as occasional titles in their trade lists.

Cartes of cartoons and drawings are much more common than of staged groups. The subjects are often slap stick, ridiculous, or puns. The butt of a joke is commonly a country rube, a drunkard, an Irishman, or occasionally a blackman.

Many of these cartes, especially the cartoons, were printed on cheap card stock so that they could be sold for a few cents. They were, as a result, more or less ephemeral.

Identification Cartes

The use of portrait cartes bearing the individual's signature and physical description were used to identify officials and workmen as passes for admission to exhibitions, restricted areas, etc. See page 40., Figure 84.

I have seen examples from the following international exhibitions: Paris, 1867; Philadelphia, Centennial 1876; Vienna, 1877; Antwerp, 1884; and the International Cotton Exposition, Atlanta, 1881.

Identification cartes were also issued by railroad companies for employees, courtesy passes, and holders of season tickets. Traveling salesmen sometimes carried a portrait carte, identifying them as representatives of a business firm.

Indians, The American Indians.

The splendid carte de visite iconography of the American Indians has been summarized in Chapter Six, but a brief synopsis with some additional notes is included here for convenience.

There are hundreds of fine studio portraits by literally several hundred photographers taken over a period of more than twenty-five years and embracing the great majority of tribes including those in New England. The range of outdoor scenes is tremendous, the more important of which are:

1. encampments and meetings
2. receiving government issues
3. families and group portraits
4. mothers with papoose
5. dwellings, such as tepees, wickiups, adobe
6. hunters and their kill
7. prisoners
8. Indian troops in the Civil War
9. The Modoc War
10. Burial customs

The white victims of Indian depradations and atrocities in Minnesota in the 1860s were photographed by Upton and Whitney.

The most important tribes documented by cartes and the photographers who published the images are listed in Chapter Six.

Industrial Archeology

Both cartes de visite and stereographs offer extensive documentation of nineteenth century technology. Processes and products as well as mines, mills, and factories were photographed. Scenes of people at work using typical tools are relatively common. There are fine views of factory and ghost towns, company housing, shipping facilities, etc. There are also views of earlier grist mills, iron furnaces, mine pits, and industrial artifacts. The transportation of raw materials and finished manufactured goods was recorded in great numbers of cartes.

See also: Engineering, Machinery, Mills and Factories, Mines and Mining, Petroleum, Railroads, Ships and Shipping, Transportation.

Jewelry

The wearing of jewelry, especially by women, has been a symbol of wealth and position since ancient times. Along with other aspects of democritization, the possession of adornments, inexpensive costume jewerly, became available to anyone who wanted to wear it.

The majority of portraits of women show some type of jewelry, most commonly a pin, a necklace, and earrings. Often there are more ornate pieces: brooches, combs, half-crowns, bracelets, and clusters of gemstones. The wedding band is common.

One of the curious features in portraits taken in the 1870s, especially in the United States, was a conspicuous Christian cross, often carved of jet. Larger crosses, often measuring three or five inches in length hung on coarse linked chains, were studio props placed around the sitter's neck by the photographer. A studio

312. Jewelry. Necklace of sea shells. Notman & Sandham, Montreal, ca. 1876.

313. Jewelry. Cross, brooch, and pendant earrings. Sherman Gregg, Rochester, N.Y., 1873.

usually owned several sizes of such crosses from which a suitable piece could be selected for the subject. Figure 313.

Earrings were of many remarkable designs, ranging from single pearls to huge pendants.

Careful examination of images may reveal fine cameos, miniatures, complex garnet clusters in geometric settings, fraternal emblems, watch charms, and various identifiable insignia.

Occasionally photographic jewelry, especially portraits mounted in lockets, can be recognized. Figure 352.

Landscape Architecture

Landscape architecture in the western world has had a venerable history. In France and England the manorial estate included lawns, terraces and gardens laid out in traditional patterns, yet with remarkable conformity to the contours of the land. The hermitage or retreat was a jewel in this setting. The rising middle class had neither the land nor the wealth to imitate the baronial manor, but many newly rich families were able to build fine residences surrounded by spacious grounds. Many of these became show places which were periodically opened to the public, especially when the flower gardens were most spectacular.

The more common commercially published cartes illustrating landscape architecture are related to the great public parks and the developing cemetery movement in the United States. Central Park in New York City, the Public Gardens in Boston, and Druid Hill in Baltimore are fine examples. There are beautiful views of the Bois de Boulogne in Paris and the grounds of Windsor Castle.

See also: Botany—Botanical Gardens.

Literary

The portraits of literary figures are among the more common cartes of celebrities. Few well-known writers were overlooked by enterprising photographers. The likenesses of authors, illustrated in biographical dictionaries and in books 1865–1900, were in most cases reproduced from carte de visite portraits.

The more famous the individual, the more likely he was photographed by one of the masters—Reutlinger, Disderi, Kilburn, Mayall, Fredricks, Gurney, and many more.

Novelists and poets were the most frequently photographed, but historians, biographers, translators of the Greek classics, scientists, and playwriters were included. Not only those literary figures living at the time were illustrated in carte format, but also copies of every known writer of historical times from the legendary bust of Homer to John Bunyan.

The homes of great authors were commonly photographed—especially of Shakespeare, Dickens, Longfellow and James Fenimore Cooper. Public sympathy aroused by the tragic death of Mrs. Longfellow created a demand for the group portrait of their children (there are many pirated issues, usually without an imprint).

Quite commonly scenes made famous by novels and poems, or associated with the author, were photo-

138

graphed for cartes, for example Sleepy Hollow, near Tarrytown, N.Y.

There are posed groups illustrating memorable scenes from plays, operas, and children's stories, portraits of actors and actresses in the costumes of favorite roles are quite common.

Machinery

Cartes de visite of machinery and mechanical devices may be considered in six groups:
1. machinery used in industry, including steam engines of all kinds.
2. models for newly patented devices.
3. household machines
4. military weapons, machines for war
5. compound optical and scientific instruments
6. historical clock mechanisms.

The term machine is here used in both its proper technical sense and popular connotations. A machine is any device constructed of two or more parts which transmit force and motion to perform work. The simple machines or mechanisms such as lever, wheel and axle, pulley and screw were linked in various ways to achieve power, speed, or accuracy beyond the capability of human skill. (Modern technology with chemical and electronic sensors has rendered obsolete this nineteenth century simplistic concept of the machine as a compound of simple machines.) At any rate, the sewing machine and the railroad locomotive were ingenious combinations of simple mechanisms.

Industrial machinery used in manufacturing, pumping water and steam, transportation, railroading and shipping, was extensively photographed in both carte and stereo formats. Mine hoists, derricks, and booms were commonly illustrated, sometimes incidentally in a view of quarrying or building construction.

Views of the interiors of machine shops and factories with operating machines were occasionally taken.

Working models of newly patented devices and engineering drawings of them are fairly frequently encountered. Most common are designs for farm machinery but the variety is considerable.

Household machines are especially remarkable. Sewing machines, "the magic needle" with their proud owners, are fascinating (see page 128). Views of kitchens, although rare, show such devices as flour sifters, apple peelers, cheese presses, washing machines, etc. Figure 314.

The greatest variety of military machines, from gun mounts to armored ships are to be found among the cartes of the Civil War. Exhibits of military weapons at international expositions were commonly photographed. Krupp's distributed cartes of their great guns in the 1870s.

Compound optical and scientific instruments, especially those with movable parts are among the great precision machines developed in the nineteenth century. Typical examples include the microscope, telescope, theodolites and other surveying instruments. The camera is a machine as is its counterpart the projector (the microscope is actually a projector of an image). Figure 339.

314. Machinery. Woman with sewing machine, "The Magic Needle." DeLoss Barnum, Cortland, N.Y., ca. 1867.

The evolution of precision tools and measuring devices progressed rapidly as an adjunct to scientific technology. Occasionally portraits of scientists, physicians, and engineers have a symbolic instrument on a table indicating the profession of the subject.

Historical horological machines were popular subjects for cartes and stereos. The famous town clocks of Europe were repeatedly photographed. Construction of complex astronomical clocks was an avocation of many people. The example illustrated here is typical. Figure 315.

See also: Mills and Factories.

Markets and Street Vendors

The market place is so universal that every travel series included one or more typical examples.

In European scenes, the market squares are teaming with vendors and customers. Commonly the city markets were specialized for cheese, vegetables, flowers, clothing, etc. In Latin America, the vendors squat alongside their produce.

In the United States in larger towns the farmers' markets were housed in buildings before 1870, as protection against inclement weather. Fanueil Hall had its indoor shops but, in season, scores of farmers and fruit sellers wagons surrounded it. Many Boston photographers published cartes of this busy famous landmark.

Many street scenes in the larger cities of the world show vendors of various products from bread to hats.

139

315. Machinery. Astronomical clock, constructed by a local model maker. S. S. Hull, Carbondale, Pa., ca. 1872. Courtesy of Robert Cauthen.

In rural United States the "general store" was a conspicuous business place, a remarkable combination of barter trade, public market, and varied inventory of manufactured goods. Every village had one.

Medicine

There are four major categories of cartes de visite of medical interest:

1. portraits of physicians and surgeons
2. medical cases, the patients
3. medical care, including hospitals
4. medical education

The most extensive coverage was portraiture of physicians. Many of the great figures in medical history including Rudolf Virchow, Joseph Lister, Claude Bernard, Jean M. Charcot, John C. Warren, and Ignaz Semmelweis, were well known to their contemporaires Reutlinger, Nadar, and Disderi photographed the great French physicians. In other countries, local photographers issued these portraits.

Women famous as medical reformers like Florence Nightengale and Dorothea Dix were photographed several times. Roman Catholic sisters assigned to hospitals were recorded in Canadian, French and American views.

The most incredible, however, are the cartes illustrating the medical history of the Civil War. The War Department ordered a photographic record of wounds, their treatment, and recovery. Thus there are detailed views of amputations and operations, particularly of the patient after recovery, but often shortly after admittance to an army hospital.

Medical care is best illustrated by the views of hospital interiors, from which prevailing views of space and arrangement of beds are evident. There are images of army hospitals in the Civil War, also of temporary field tent hospitals, as at Gettysburg. Portraits of patients occasionally show severe wasting, blindness, hunchback, artificial limbs, amputations and ugly scars.

Medical schools and groups of medical students are fairly common, those of Edinburgh the most frequent.

Mention should be made of the occasional medical doctor or dentist residing in a small town who doubled as the local photographer, his logo announcing both professions. Examples: J. C. Mills, M.D., Pen Yan, N.Y., Dr. G. W. Tainter, Linn, Mo., "Dentist and Photograph Artist," and Dr. Higgins, Wenona, Ill., dentist.

Military

This category embraces military subjects exclusive of Wars, q.v.

Every country in Europe and the Americas in peacetime maintained a standing army, usually of modest size. Required military service of young males varied from country to country and from period to period.

Portraits of soldiers in their uniforms were a source of family pride. Such portraits are common in every European country, even among the most peaceful Scandinavians. Excepting during the Civil War and for a few years after in western garrisons, American soldier portraits are rare.

The poses are quite conventional, the soldier standing at attention or assuming a stern manner. Occasionally he is at ease, usually with hat by his side and his hand resting on a dress sword or other object. Figure 316.

Somewhat more rare are groups of soldiers assigned to special peacetime duty, such as the contingent present at Promontory Point in Utah in 1869 at the driving of the golden spike linking the Union Pacific and Central Pacific railroads (C. R. Savage).

The students and graduates of military academies were often photographed, individually and in groups, U.S. Military Academy, U.S. Naval Academy, Aldershot, etc.

There are cartes of Army forts and posts in the American West, mostly in the 1870s, also of soldiers assigned to them.

Arsenals, navy yards, warships, gun parks, etc., have been frequently photographed for the carte de visite.

Encampments of the Grand Army of the Republic and of military units in parades, such as presidential inaugurals, are occasionally found.

There are great numbers of scenic cartes of the battlefields of the world, Waterloo, Lexington, Concord, Valley Forge, Gettysburg, generally with emphasis on the memorials erected on them.

See also: Civil War, Naval, Wars.

Mills & Factories

A curious feature of the iconography of mills and factories and other industrial establishments is the

316. Military. Soldier portrait; Denmark. Chr. Sorensen, Copenhagen, ca. 1872.

by the living standards of American workmen, the social level of young women employed in factories, and the opportunities for personal advancement. Some of the factory systems, like the Boston Manufacturing Company, were world famous.

Factories of every description were photographed for cartes: furniture, wagons, plows, clothing, shoes, watches, pottery, and weaving cotton, linen and silk. There are four types of factory views:
1. panoramic, of the mills and related buildings;
2. the main building often with the employees lined up in front of the main entrance;
3. products of the factory so placed in front of or beneath the company's name as to prominently advertise the firm; and
4. interior views to show machinery and people at work. Figure 317.

Occasionally the source of water power or the boiler plant for producing steam is photographed. Water power usually involved a mill pond or diversion conduit in a river, through a mill race to the water wheels.

Other types of mills included iron and steel furnaces and fabricating shops, ore-smelting plants, sawmills, etc., all of which were occasionally photographed for cartes.

preponderance of images of American enterprises. Factories are rarely included among the subjects in a European travel series. They were avoided. In the United States, contrarily, they were regarded highly by rich and poor alike. The factory was a symbol of work, stability, prosperity and progress. Many European visitors, among them Lyell[3] and Peto[4], were impressed

[3]Lyell, Charles, 1845, *Travels in North America*, Vol. 1, pp. 93-95.
[4]Peto, Sir Morton, 1866, *Resources and Prospects of America*, p. 364ff.

Mines & Mining, including quarrying.

Cartes de visite showing mining are much less common than stereographs. The best covered industry was placer gold mining, i.e., hydraulic mining, washing the gold from gravel and sand. There is an early series of California scenes not later than 1861 without a photographer's imprint. A few years later Lawrence and Houseworth and Watkins produced fine views.

The silver and gold mines of Nevada, Colorado, Idaho and Utah were photographed many times, notably by Savage, Carter, Chamberlain, and Weitfle. Many of the scenes of mining towns and camps show sluices, piles of tailings, and loaded railroad cars, others show smelters, assaying offices, etc.

317. Mills and Factories. Sleigh factory, Keene, N.H.
French & Sawyer, 1872.

There are scattered cartes of other types of mining, such as iron ore at Cornwall, Pa. (John Daily, Lebanon), lead near Joplin, Mo. (Taylor & Vohringer, Carthage), and copper in Michigan (Carbutt).

Views of coal mining are rare. Schurch and Johnson published cartes of anthracite mines and breakers in the vicinity of Wilkes Barre and Scranton, also Bretz of Pottsville.

Scenes of marble and granite quarries are occasionally found among the issues of local photographers. Images of slate and limestone quarries are more scarce.

See also: Petroleum.

Montages

The composition photograph has been mentioned in several connections, including portraits of the British Royal Family, Abraham Lincoln and his cabinet, college faculties, etc., but its uses were much more varied.

The technique is basically very simple: to cut out two or more portraits, or other images, arrange them as desired, paste them on a board, and then photograph the composition. The terms composition, composed photograph, and montage are used interchangeably to identify the resulting image. As used in cartes de visite, the montage differs in important respects from the famous examples of artistic compositions typified by H. P. Robinson who sought to create pictures. The carte de visite montage is a poor relative. Nevertheless, it was an important member of the photographer's productions.

Typically, the carte montage is a group of portraits of persons in some association: members of a family, a prime minister's or president's cabinet officers, members of a college faculty, a team of foreign religious missionaries, a group of Union generals, of Confederate naval commanders, a college graduating class, a state legislature, and many, many more.

The possibilities of the montage seem to have delighted many photographers. Disderi, ca. 1862, produced several montages of popular actors and actresses: *Theatre Francaise, Theatre Angleterre,* and *Theatre Italienne.* The Lutheran church in Sweden distributed montages of groups of foreign missionaries, 1869–1872.

Many publishers of scenic cartes issued montages of 6, 9, or 12 of their choice views, as novelties and advertisements. Figure 319.

Aside from these informational images, there are many more or less experimental montages in which the photographer tried to include as many human heads as can be clearly identified with a hand magnifying glass. There are such montages with as many as 600 to 1700 heads.

In England in the latter 1860s the so-called diamond carte enjoyed brief popularity. Four exposures of the sitter were taken from different positions with the four lens camera and mounted as one print with a top, bottom, and two-side images.

A humorous trick occasionally produced for college students and club groups was the placement of enlargements of the heads on the small bodies of the posers.

318. Montage. "State Government of Massachusetts" B. B. Russell & Co., publisher, Boston, 1865.

319. Montage. Views of Venice, Italy. A. Perini, ca. 1863.

The grotesque effect is sometimes further exaggerated by wearing comical hats, holding toy swords or toy musical instruments, etc.

In the montage medium there were also scandalous attempts to ridicule public figures. By cutting half figures, heads, and background, fake pictures could be easily made readily. Among the notorious examples were Empress Eugenie (her head on another body) swimming nude, the Pope wearing Masonic emblem,[5] and Henry Ward Beecher and Mrs. Tilton facing each other but with a board fence between them.

Monuments

Included in this category are memorials to famous persons and historical events. Excluded are grave markers in cemeteries, no matter how impressive or ornate they may be.

The great landmarks such as the triumphal arches of Rome, Paris and Berlin have been photographed many times for carte images. Such structures as the great obelisks, the Washington and Bunker Hill monuments, and the Prince Albert and Robert Burns memorials were exceptionally popular subjects.

Following the Civil War, hundreds of towns erected monuments commemorating the men who served in the war. Most of the familiar cast iron or bronze soldier figures were mass-produced, but there were also many fine works of sculpture. (See page 87.)

[5]See Braive, M., 1966. A Social History of the Photograph, p. 66.

321. Monument. Civil War, Michigan State Memorial. Full description including symbolism, on back. Randall, Detroit, 1867.

Sir Walter Scott's Monument, Edinburgh.
G. W. Wilson   No 115   Aberdeen

320. Monument. Sir Walter Scott Memorial, Edinburgh, Scotland. G. W. Wilson, Aberdeen, ca. 1870.

BATTLES
in which the
77th Reg't, N. Y. S. V.,
WAS ENGAGED.

Lee's Mills; April 5th, 1862.
Williamsburgh, May 5th, 1862.
Mechanicville, May 24th, 1862.
Golding's Farm, June 27, 1862.
Garnett's Hill, June 28th, 1862.
Savage Station, June 29th, 1862.
White Oak Swamp, June 30th, 1862.
Malvern Hill, July 1st, 1862.
Crampton Gap, Sept. 14th, 1862.
Antietam, Sept. 17th, 1862.
Fredericksburgh, Dec. 13th, 1862.
Marye's Heights, May 3d, 1863.
Fredericksburgh, May 4th, 1863.
Franklin's Crossing, June 5th, 1863.
Gettysburgh, July 2d, 3d, 1863.
Chantilly Picket Fight, Oct. 17th, 1863.
Rappahannock Station, Nov. 7th, 1863.
Mine Run, Nov. 30th, 1863.
Wilderness, from May 5th to May 9th, 1864.
Spottsylvania, from May 9th to May 18th, 1864.
Cold Harbor, from June 1st to June 12th, 1864.
Petersburgh, June 20th and 21st, 1864.
Reames Station, June 28, 1864.
Fort Stevens, July 12th, 1864.
Charleston, August 21st, 1864.
Winchester, Sept. 19th, 1864.
Fisher's Hill, Sept. 22d, 1864.
Newmarket, Sept. 24th, 1864.
Mt. Crawford, Sept. 29th, 1864.
Cedar Creek, Oct. 19th, 1864.
Petersburgh, March 25th and 26th, 1865.
Petersburgh, April 2d and 3d, 1865.
Sailor's Creek, April 7th, 1865.

322. Monument. Civil War. Reverse of mount, giving the regimental history, 77th Reg., New York State Volunteers. Photographer not identified.

The dedicatory ceremonies were often photographed for cartes, more frequently than for stereographs. There are also scenes of Fourth of July and Memorial Day exercises.

There are hundreds of historical sites, little known as well as famous, throughout the world that are marked by monuments. A few examples, well-known in carte photographs, will suggest the range: The Bastille column, Plymouth Rock canopy, "The Minute Man" at Concord, the shaft at the scene of the Wyoming (Pennsylvania) Indian massacre of white settlers.

The homes of many celebrated persons have been preserved as monuments, usually with a marker to identify the site. Similarly, many communities have restored their "oldest house" or some other landmark, a practice already prevalent before the Civil War. Among the cartes documenting these houses are: the birthplace of Paul Revere, The Salem "Witch House," and the oldest house in Dedham (Massachusetts). Comparable examples can be found among scenic cartes of England, France, and Germany.

Mortuary and Mourning

Death or post-mortem portraits are relatively common, particularly of infants and young children. Often such a picture was the only likeness that the family could have. The high incidence of child mortality made death so commonplace that these portraits did not convey the feeling of morbidity or gruesomeness we might experience today. There are even photographs of

324. Mortuary. Funeral Procession, The assassinated Thomas D'Arcy McGee, Montreal, April 13, 1868. James Inglis photo. This carte a pirated issue by Wm. A. Lyon, Toronto, without credit to Inglis.

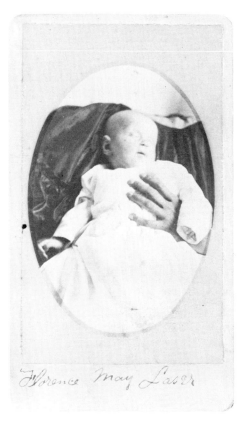

323. Mortuary. Portrait of an infant, "taken while dying, August 17, 1874." E. L. Tompkins, Holden, Mo.

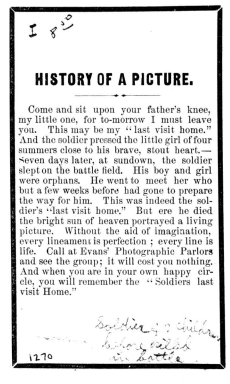

325. Mortuary. Mourning carte for a Civil War Soldier killed seven days after the portrait was taken. Both sides of card bordered in black. C. Evans, Philadelphia, ca. 1863. Courtesy of Henry Deeks.

Name, *Thomas Feeney*

Alias,

Crime, *Larceny*

Age, *43* Comp., *Lt.*

Height, *5.10¾* Weight, *150*

Hair, *Red* Eyes, *Blue*

Nose, Face,

Marks, *Scars back left hand*

Born, *Boston, Mass*

Married, *No*

Trade, *Teamster*

Date of Arrest, *Oct "7/98.*

Officer, *Abbott & Gilmore*

Remarks,

326. "Mug Shot" Thomas Sweeny, convicted of larceny, arrested in Boston, 1898. Card stock anachronistic. From same criminal file as Figure 86.

infants with a note: ". . . taken while dying." Figure 323.

The body of an infant is often tucked in a crib or placed on a pillow, occasionally held by a parent. Older children and adults are usually laid out as if asleep. The casket or coffin is rarely shown excepting those of celebrities.

There are many mourning cartes, of which there are three fairly frequent types: (1) the obituary notice, printed in gilt, on a black card mount, with or without a portrait; (2) the memorial card, usually with an oval portrait, surrounded by a printed wreath, generally with the name of the deceased and dates of birth and death, sometimes with a vita printed on back; (3) a portrait mounted on a card with a rectangular or oval heavy frame printed in black, usually with name of the deceased.

The Graver Collection includes a mourning portrait series showing the deceased Miss Catherine Ditmars (1879) at various ages. The photographer, G. A. Flagg of Ovid, N.Y., copied the portraits which were distributed by members of the family.

An unusual "In Memoriam" card of Charles J. Darbishire, Esq., first Mayor of Bolton, 1835–1838, was presented to members of the city corporation by Kay, the photographer, (Galvani Collection).

Occasionally families wished to have photographs of the wreath, floral pieces and floral arrangements at the funeral. There are also many images of family cemetery plots. Views of funeral corteges of famous persons are rare, the best known being that of Abraham Lincoln.

Burial customs of American Indians are recorded by several photographers, most notably Whitney and Bennett who issued cartes of tribes inhabiting the western Great Lakes region.

Attention is directed to mortality notations commonly found on the backs of carte portraits. The portrait of a child three or four years old may have written on it "died age 4 years 4 months, twelve days," or of a young woman, "died age 23." These are vivid reminders of the acceptance of the nearness of death in a nineteenth century family.

Mug Shots

Portraits of criminals for police records have been described on page 40. The type of information entered on the mug shot carte is shown in figure 326. See also figure 86.

Occasionally portraits of felons most often murderers were published commercially. Figure 327 shows both a confession and a sermon.

Story of GUSTAVE OHR. (Written in Canton Jail, while under death sentence.)

My name it is Gustave Ohr,
The same I'll never deny,
Which leaves my aged parents
In sorrow for to cry.
It's little did they ever think,
While in my youthful bloom,
They brought me to America
To meet my fatal doom.

In bad houses of liquor
I used to take delight,
And consequently my associates
They used me there invite.
It was on a certain day,
As you shall quickly see,
I was enticed into Mann's company
By a bottle of whisky.

It was in the town of Alliance,
As we were traveling,
Mann picked up an iron,
Commonly called a coupling pin.
As we got into Webb's sugar camp,
We all laid down to rest,
When Mann steps up to me and says,
Our chances are now the best.

He says now let us stun him,
And take his things away,
And we will go to New York city
And spend fourth of July day.
To Beloit then we quickly fled,
Thinking to escape, but
The hand of Providence was against us,
Ineeed we were too late.

Then we were taken prisoners,
And brought unto our doom,
To die upon the scaffold,
All in our youthful bloom.
Our trial came on quickly,
Condemned we were to die,
A death upon the scaffold,
All on the gallows high.

I am thankful to the Sheriff
For his kindness to me,
Likewise my noble lawyer,
Who tried to set me free;
And also to my clergymen
Who brought my mind to bear,
That there is a good and holy judge
Way up in heavenly sphere. MARCH, 1880.

Kell & Brown, Photographers, Canton, O.

327. "Mug Shot" A commercial issue, portrait of a convicted murderer awaiting execution. Poem written by the prisoner. Kell & Brown, Canton, Ohio, 1880.

Music and Musicians

There is marvellous documentation of musicians and composers. Portraits of virtually every composer and performer between 1860 and 1885 are known. The most famous, of course, were photographed by Reutlinger, Nadar, Gurney, The London Stereoscopic Company and other masters.

As with other categories of celebrities, pirated issues abound. Warren, Boston, for instance, published a

P. FAIRCLOUGH PHOTO.   NEWCASTLE

328. Musicians. Family Quintet. P. Fairclough, Newcastle, England, ca. 1873.

pirated portrait of Johann Strauss by Luckhardt, ca. 1871.

Performing artists were also extensively photographed for carte images, particularly operatic singers. Under P. T. Barnum's management Jenny Lind made her grand tour of the United States before the carte was introduced. Brady copied his daguerreotype portrait of Lind and issued many cartes of it. There were engravings copied from the Brady portrait which were also published in carte format. Famous instrumentalists, such as the violinist Ole Bull, were also photographed.

There are large numbers of portraits of minor performers and amateurs, with their musical instruments.

Various musical groups were photographed. Most common are small ensembles and family companies. These cartes record groups from the countries of Western Europe and many of the United States. Among the American cartes are bands, orchestras, singing groups, including large choruses.

All of the standard wind and string instruments known in the nineteenth century can be found in cartes de visite.

Several manufacturers of organs and pianos advertised their instruments by cartes. Both Savage and Carter issued views of the great organ in the Mormon Tabernacle in Salt Lake City.

There is extensive documentation of native and primitive musical instruments of every culture, including those used symbolically in religious ceremonies.

Naval

Warships of both the Union and Confederacy were extensively photographed. There are cartes of individual ships and river boats of all classes. The strategic importance of inland waters in the Civil War was recorded in many views of the boats used on the Mississippi River and its tributaries.

329. Musicians. U.S. regimental Army Band. George H. Johnson, Austin, Nevada. Card also bears the imprint of Savage & Ottinger, Salt Lake City, ca. 1868. Courtesy of Henry Deeks.

330. Musicians. Guitar players. Townsend, Poughkeepsie, N.Y., ca. 1866. Courtesy of Henry Deeks.

A sketch of the Confederate cruiser *Alabama*, destroyed in battle with the *Kearsarge*, was reproduced as a carte de visite, which was used for the illustration in *Battles and Leaders of the Civil War*.[6] Figure 191.

There are many wartime portraits of officers and sailors and montages of the admirals, both Union and Confederate.

Peacetime tours of duty of United States naval ships to distant parts of the world are documented by many cartes, usually photographed as mementos for members of the crews. See Page 55. Figure 331.

Scenes of naval yards, especially those in Boston, Brooklyn, Washington and Philadelphia are not rare, but the subjects are generally of limited interest, being mostly shot parks, gun parks, anchor parks, etc.

The United States Naval Academy was photographed several times for carte images. Midshipmen, buildings and parade formations are the usual scenes.

Cartes of foreign navies are seldom seen although harbor scenes occasionally show a patrol boat or a small gun ship. Cartes of training ships are also known.

Negro and Black Culture

Cartes de visites related to black people are summarized in Chapter Six. A brief list of the major types of subjects will suggest the range:

1. natives of Africa, particularly south and southwest Africa;

[6]Vol. 4, page 601. "This sketch was made from a photograph (of a drawing) which Capt. Semmes gave to a friend . . . " Carte in R. Cauthen collection.

331. Naval. "Officers of the *U.S.S. Sacramento*: Russell, paymaster; Dean, Surgeon; Brooks, Chief Engineer." S. B. Barnard, Cape Town, South Africa, 1867.

2. blacks in the United States, Central and South America, and the West Indies;
3. freed slaves in the Southern States, commonly shown at work in many occupations, especially cotton growing and processing, sugar cane, tobacco growing, and stevadores;
4. blacks serving as soldiers or civilian employees in the Civil War;
5. portraits of individuals and small groups including minor notables, clergymen, performers, and those who became economically and socially successful. Groom, Philadelphia, issued a street portrait of a blind beggar, ca. 1872.
6. propaganda and collateral subjects, such as solicitation of funds for charitable activities. For example, McAllister & Bros. published a photograph, *The Scourged Back*, showing the scars caused by cruel lashings (1862). Rare anti-black sentiment in cartoons by pro-slavery interests are known. Figure 332.
7. Humorous, most commonly as cartoons, generally comical, rarely derisive.

Novelties

This miscellaneous category includes unusual subjects that are not easily classified. There are hundreds of extremely diverse titles. Ten examples are cited here to suggest the range:

1. Marriage bans and wedding announcements printed in carte format, usually without a

332. Negro. "The Scourged Back," showing the scars of whippings. Copied from a photograph taken in Louisiana and sent to the Surgeon General of Massachusetts, April 1863. Issued by McAllister & Bros., Philadelphia, 1863. Courtesy of Nicholas Graver.

portrait. Similarly there are lists of births and deaths. The Centaur Photographic Company of Bromley, Kent, was the most prominent publisher of cartes of this type. For almost ten years it reproduced weekly lists of marriages and deaths published by newspapers.

2. An ingenious cage for a pet mouse or hamster.

333. Negro. Jamaica Missionaries. Villiers & Sons, Newport, England, ca. 1874.

3. A bird trained to fire a toy cannon. This image has been erroneously attributed to Brady. An 1875 issue bears the Eisenmann imprint. There are also cartes of talking birds. Figure 334.
4. A dance program printed on the card back with a portrait of the two floor managers. Figure 337.
5. Merry Christmas—Happy New Year cartes, 1870s and early 1880s; also Valentine greetings, ca. 1880.
6. An ornately decorated cake in the shape of an altar and canopy surmounted by an American

334. Novelty. Trained canary firing a toy cannon. Charles Eisenmann, New York, ca. 1878.

335. Novelty. Cage for a pet mouse or hamster.
M. M. Mallon, Bridgeport, Conn., 1865.

337. Novelty. A dance carte. Portraits of John Powers
and James Conway in the image. Locality and photographer not indicated, ca. 1868.

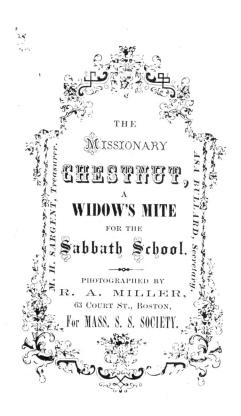

336. Novelty. "The Widow's Mite"—arrangement of a
chestnut in a glass decanter placed upon the New
Testament. R. A. Miller, Boston, 1864.

338. Novelty. Contrived double portrait, a popular trick,
1863–1868, practiced by many photographers.
J. W. Black, Boston, 1864.

flag "presented by Mrs. D. C. Painter and Mrs. Hattie Potter," photographed by B. F. Card, Emporia, Kansas, ca. 1866.

7. Still life arrangements, seldom seen in carte format. Andrews, operator for Davis & Co., Boston, ca. 1864, photographed a dozen partially opened flowers of the native water lily. The arrangement includes an ordinary pottery kitchen bowl placed on a stand covered with a cloth with a floral decoration. A folded newspaper was placed between the bowl and the cloth. Possibly the arrangement was made solely to photograph the water lilies. The newspaper is incongruous and likely was used to protect the cloth.

8. "Milo Gardner wearing Esquimaux suit of his father, Silas Partridge Gardner," ca. 1874, unidentified photographer.

9. A silver loving cup, trophy for a foot race, E. Crew photographer, Alliance, Ohio, ca. 1872.

10. "A piece of wood from John Brown's Coffin," no photographer's imprint.

Attention is also called to such carte de visite oddities as copies of the Lord's Prayer, poems, mug-shots of criminals, identification cards, etc. which are described elsewhere in this book.

Occupations

Occupational images are among the most eagerly sought collectibles. They can be conveniently grouped in seven categories:

1. Primitive industries practiced by native peoples, such as agriculture, hunting, fishing, weaving, warfare, etc.

2. Tradesmen, such as butchers, carpenters, blacksmiths, potters, stone masons, shoemakers.

3. Organized industries, in which different operations are performed in sequence: mining, factory workers, silk industry, iron and steel.

4. Merchants and vendors.

5. Professional and highly skilled physicians, dentists, clergymen, lawyers, educators, surveyors, photographers, scientists.

6. Actors, entertainers, performers, musicians.

7. Service occupations: military, police, firemen, servants, waiters, teamsters, barbers, and many others.

The large-scale industries, especially in mining and manufacturing, employing many hands were often photographed while in operation. Such carte images usually show workers busy at their tasks. Images considered to be occupational must show people at work, posed with the products of their labor, or in characteristic uniform (policemen, fireman) or traditional costume (clerical, butcher's apron, baker's hat and apron).

One of the most unusual series was published by E. Hattorff (Hamburg, Germany). Each title illustrates a different occupation, butcher, carpenter, servant girl, etc. (ca. 1870). The staged portraits were usually sold nicely hand colored.

339. Occupations. Surveyors with transits. Locality and photographer unknown, ca. 1873. Courtesy of Robert Cauthen.

340. Occupations. Lutheran Clergyman. J. E. Smith, Springfield, Ohio, 1872.

150

341. Occupations. Fireman. Garrett, Wilmington, Del., 1866. Courtesy of Henry Deeks.

There are many portraits of the young children of English civil servants stationed in various colonies photographed with their native nursemaids. There are also portraits of English "nannies," and American black nursemaids with white children.

The most glaring lack in occupational cartes is the almost total absence of photographs of the housewife and homemaker at her daily work. Rather surprisingly, among travel series, there are images showing women grinding flour, baking bread, and drying skins and weaving, but almost none in European and North American communities.

Pastimes

There are many cartes of games and amusements such as chess, checkers and card-playing. These were usually staged in the studio, sometimes merely as a device to suggest activity.

Occasionally a game may escape notice because it is inconspicuous, as for example a cribbage board with pins lying on a table in a portrait pose.

Views of children's games are more common, but were nearly always carefully staged whether indoors or outdoors. There were no spontaneous "snap shots." Games of croquet were frequently photographed, sometimes of families at home, more often of adult parties at summer resorts. "Bite Apple," an Irish version of bobbing for apples was depicted in a studio group of seven young adults engaged in the fun. The cards copyrighted Cork, 1867, have no photographer's imprint. Figure 343.

342. Occupations. Butcher, James M. French, Elizabeth, N. J. Frank H. Price, ca. 1868. Courtesy of George H. Moss.

BITE-APPLE.

Copyright.

343. Pastimes. A parlor game, "Bite Apple—Snap Apple Night, Hallow Eve." Cork, Ireland. Copyright 1866. Photographer not identified.

344. Petroleum. Pennsylvania Oil Region. "Flowing Well,
Tarr Farm, Oil Creek," no. 18 in a series. A. D. Deming,
Oil City, 1863.

Dancing is illustrated by many cartes, including costumed couples at parties, native groups, and humorous scenes.

See also: Sports.

Petroleum

The discovery of petroleum in northwestern Pennsylvania in 1859 ushered in a period of excitement and speculation as a new industry developed rapidly. Within a decade it had been rationalized and organized much as we know it today.

Great numbers of stereographs were produced as were a remarkable number of cartes de visite which are more scarce. While a score of photographers published stereos, I know of nine who issued cartes: John Mather, W. M. Deming, Goetschius Brothers, Copeland & Fleming, N. G. Johnson, F. Robbins and Wilt Brothers. Figure 344; see also Figures 234, 235.

The best series was photographed by Johnson, Erie, Pa., and published for him by the Philadelphia Photograph Company, ca. 1864, simultaneously in carte and stereo formats. The cartes are stereo halves, both images mounted as slightly differing cartes. The series is a travelogue of about sixty views, beginning in Titusville, descending Oil Creek and recording the "oil farms" in sequence to Oil City situated on the Allegheny River. This is the most complete "tour" of the early oil region known. Mather's cartes are also identical to his stereo images.

I have seen one scenic carte of a West Virginia oil well, ca. 1867, but the card has no photographer's imprint.

Pets

As would be expected, pets loved by their owners, appear in countless carte images. Commonly a child was shown with a dog or cat, when posed for a portrait. Men were often photographed standing with a dog by their side, especially hunters with their hounds.

Frequently the animal was photographed by itself, a portrait. There are beautiful examples which show great care by the photographer.

While dogs and cats are the most common pets, there are images of many other kinds—ponies, lambs, mice, rats, hamsters and various birds, especially canaries, pigeons and parrots.

Prize-winning animals (dogs, ponies) were photographed in carte format by Schreiber & Son, ca. 1868–1870.

Mascots of military units, bands, and fire companies are also known in carte images.

345. Pets. Child holding a cat. J. A. Whipple, Boston, 1872.

346. Pets. Girl with a dog. S. I. Masten, Boone, Iowa, ca. 1873.

347. Pets. Man with Dalmatian dog. George H. Tebbetts, Laconia, N.H., ca. 1866. Courtesy of Henry Deeks.

Philately

The federal government levied a stamp tax on photographs from August 1, 1864 to August 1, 1866, to raise money for the war effort. The photographer was required to place an appropriate revenue stamp on the mount at the time of sale and cancel the stamp with his initials and date.

The tax was graduated according to price, a one cent stamp on photographs selling for less than ten cents, two cents on those selling for ten to twenty-five cents, three cents on those from twenty-six to fifty cents, five cents on those selling from fifty cents to one dollar. Because very few cartes retailed for more than fifty cents only the one, two, and three cent denominations are usually found.

The act of 1864 required a tax of two cents on all photographs selling for twenty-five cents or less, but an amendment in response to complaints by photographers, provided for the one cent tax on cheap images. Photographers, with few exceptions, absorbed the tax rather than passing it to the customer.

Cancellation of the stamps was a nuisance to photographers. Many studios purchased rubber stamps commonly of circular or oval design to cancel stamps more rapidly. Many other photographers simply penned an X or a stroke across the stamp. This was fully acceptable to the authorities and was not considered to be illegal. Some photographers autographed their names as cancellation.

The various denominations and varieties of revenue stamps employed for this tax are described in Scott's Standard Postage Stamp Catalogue, and more fully in Scott's Specialized United States Catalogue, both of which are published annually.

All major varieties of the first general revenue issue, 1862–1871, from R1–R19, are known to have been used on cartes de visite.

Extremely rarely the regular postage stamp two cent black Jackson (Scott no. 73), was used. I have seen two examples, in the same family album, both photographed by D. B. Hall, Litchfield, Ill., cancelled "Hall," without date. This was probably an illegal use, but considered acceptable if no revenue stamps were available at the time of sale.

A carte de visite was sometimes sent through the mail, simply with an address and a one cent postage stamp. I have examined three examples mailed respectively in 1884, 1885, and 1889. Figure 348.

Photographica

One of the most remarkable aspects of the history of photography, is photography's record of itself. This has excited the curiosity of collectors who have recognized the unique significance of views showing studios, equipment, techniques, self-portraits, etc.

Many photographers used various small objects as properties for posing sitters. Commonly the carte album, or framed photograph is held in the hand or displayed on a table. Occasionally a stereoscope is used.

In the latter 1860s and early 1870s photographic jewelry was popular in the United States. Occasionally a woman sitting for a portrait wore a pendant containing the portrait of her husband or fiancee. The carte image sometimes records the minute likeness in detail. Figure 352.

Cartes of studios, indoor especially, show vividly how the photographer operated. Views of outdoor portable galleries, of great variety are known. Pictures of photographers with their cameras are highly prized, especially when identified. Figure 349.

Self-portraits, usually autographed, of many photographers are known. Commonly photographers had their portraits taken by an employee.

The head rest and other properties can usually be recognized as a regular studio device.

Many cartes are more important for the imprints and information on the backs than for the mounted images. A great number of logos used the camera, sun, radiant light, etc. as a symbolic device. Commonly the imprint includes information about succession, preservation and transfer of negatives, patent numbers, instructions to prospective sitters, and types of work done.

Unusual types of prints are often identified such as wortleytype, woodbury types, platinotypes, etc.

See Part III, Documentation and Interpretation of Cartes de visite: imprints.

Political

The most common cartes de visite related to politics are the portraits of men and women holding public office. Such portraits were published by the first-rate photographers in every country.

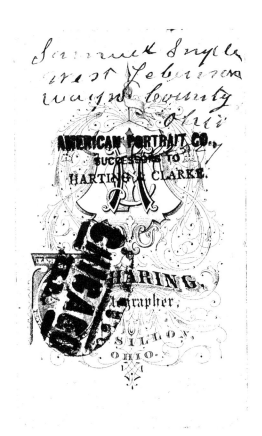

348. Philatelic. Carte mailed from Chicago to West Lebanon, Ohio, 1889. Image is still, in 1981, in excellent condition.

349. Photographica. Studio of F. M. Yeager, Reading, Pa., ca. 1866. Courtesy of Robert Cauthen.

350. Photographica. Self-portrait, H. L. Bixby, autographed on back. Burlington, Vt., 1871.

351. Photographica. Table stereoscope. O. H. Park, Clarinda, Iowa, ca. 1882.

353. Photographica. Boy with a carte de visite album. Melancthon Moore, Hastings, England, ca. 1878.

In England, members of Parliament, and in the United States members of Congress and the state legislatures were regularly photographed. References to montages of cabinet officers and state legislators have previously been made.

Certainly the rulers of a country benefitted by favorable publicity through widespread circulation of their likenesses and those of their families. If nothing more the citizens became acquainted with a human side of their leaders.

I have not been able to find carte images of candidates campaigning for office, particularly for the presidency of the United States. Very probably such were issued in the campaigns of 1868, 1872 and 1876.

Political cartoons in carte format were widely distributed in the 1860s, infrequently in the 1870s. The most common subjects were related to the war effort, such as "copperheads", satirizing Jeff Davis, vilifying proponents of slavery, etc. The crimes of Boss Tweed were also publicized in cartoons.

Scenic cartes and reproductions of paintings published to encourage patriotism are included under Propaganda, q.v.

Presidents of the United States

The period of the carte de visite spanned the administrations of six presidents: Lincoln, Johnson, Grant, Hayes, Garfield, and Arthur. Portraits from life, of all of these men and their families, were published commercially, those of Lincoln and Grant being the

352. Photographica. Brooch enclosing portrait of a man, probably the lady's husband. Jacob Shew, San Francisco, 1872.

155

most common. Buchanan was photographed by Brady who copied the portrait for carte images.

The rising popularity of portraits of celebrities in the early 1860s led to the publication of portraits of all of the presidents from Washington to Lincoln, copied from paintings, engravings, and daguerreotypes. Many of the issues were direct copies from the original rendering. In many cases the likeness was more or less accurately copied by camera lucida or simply redrawn by hand. The Brady, Anthony, and Appleton issues are best known.

Portraits of Grant, the soldier, are more common than as president. There are also, however, cartes of the aging Grant and his family after retirement.

The assassination of Garfield prompted publication of several cheap copy issues, including a montage with Lincoln titled "The Martyred Presidents" and another of Garfield, members of his family and the assassin.

There are scattered scenes of the homes of the presidents (Washington, John Adams, Jefferson, Monroe, Lincoln—Springfield, Ill.—etc.). Mount Vernon was especially well photographed, in large part due to the efforts of the Ladies Mount Vernon Preservation Association who engaged, in turn, Gardner, N.G. Johnson and Luke Dillon to issue carte and stereo images for the support of their work.

Propaganda

By definition, propaganda refers to the promotion of a particular opinion or doctrine, a persuasion toward a point of view. The word does not imply anything objectionable, "propagation of the faith" being, for instance, a proper use of the term.

Actually the most common propagandistic cartes de visite were published for or by religious organizations. Many Sunday School and Missionary Societies distributed cards to raise money to support their projects. Frequently the image was a scene showing a mission school or church, a group of pupils or converts, or a portrait of a native boy or girl, less commonly a religious scene copied from a painting.

Political propaganda in cartes de visite is much less frequent. The most interesting examples are the malicious or bitter attempts to degrade a public figure in cartoons.

Social propaganda in carte format was also very limited. As a means of raising funds for the support of orphans or the education of black children and orphans, cartes were published by a variety of organizations from the early 1860s into the 1880s. Figures 354, 355.

There were limited attempts to encourage social reforms. There are anti-slavery scenes, many of which are drawings; temperance, or anti-alcohol cartoons; and a few anti-women's suffrage posed groups and cartoons.

See also: Montages, Religions.

Railroads

Railroads were so extensively stereographed that every important line and its rolling stock was fully illustrated. Great series of images were published,

LEARNING IS WEALTH.
WILSON, CHARLEY, REBECCA & ROSA.
Slaves from New Orleans.

354. Propaganda. "Learning is Wealth," freed slaves from New Orleans. Charles Paxson, New York, 1864. Courtesy of Henry Deeks.

TRUE SYMPATHY.

"Whose little faces are these?"
"Inmates of the Orphans' Home, located at Mt. Vernon, Ohio."
"Bright faces! Pretty, intelligent children! Very much so! Many such children in the State homeless?"
"Hundreds of such!"
"What a pity! I do pity them!"
"How much?"
"I have not put any price upon my sympathy."
"It will not be worth anything to them till you price it and pay the price. But when your pity is valued and the price paid, it can be used for their good. And Solomon says, Prov. 19, 17: 'He that hath pity upon the poor lendeth unto the Lord, and that which he hath given will He pay him again.'"
"Why were these pictures taken?"
"To raise money for the support of the children. Do you wish to help a little? If you give Twenty-five cents or more, you can keep this picture."
The work is supported by charity, and is not sectarian, and homeless children are admitted from any part of the country.

G. W. McWHERTER,
Superintendent.

355. Propaganda. Reverse of portrait of two orphan boys. An appeal for contributions. Fred S. Crowell, Mount Vernon, Ohio, ca. 1880.

156

356. Railroads. Alpine cog railway, Rici, Switzerland.
A. Gabler, Interlaken, ca. 1872.

many of them in cooperation with the railroad companies. In sharp contrast, with the exception of the Union Pacific, cartes de visite are seldom seen.

In stereo, the Pennsylvania and Union Pacific Railroads are beautifully documented by great series of views. Purviance published some of his stereos of the Pennsylvania Railroad as cartes but they are quite rare. Savage (successor to Savage and Ottinger) likewise issued the same scenes in stereo and carte formats, including the famous sub-series of the joining of the Central Pacific and Union Pacific.

There are scattered views of smaller railroads as well as large lines like the Erie and the Delaware, Lackawanna & Western. Railroad bridges and tunnels (Hoosac and Mt. Ctenis) were photographed for carte images.

Not to be neglected are the local views of railroad stations, which sometimes show waiting passengers or standing trains. Occasionally the scene shows a junction of two railroads.

There are views of narrow gage railroads used in mining and lumbering, also of alpine, inclined railroads. Rolling stock, especially freight cars of many types, have been recorded.

Cartes of scenery along a rail line were also published in England, France and Germany. Such views in stereo format were produced extensively in the United States but less frequently as cartes. L. E. Walker issued a series along the route of the Erie Railroad.

Religions
The carte de visite coverage of the major religions of the world is extensive. The three most abundant types of religious cartes de visite are:

1. Churches, temples and other places of worship can be found in every travel series.
2. Portraits of religious leaders and clergymen and group portraits of them.
3. Scenes showing gatherings of the faithful, in-

357. Railroads. Station at California, Missouri. D. B. Watts,
ca. 1873.

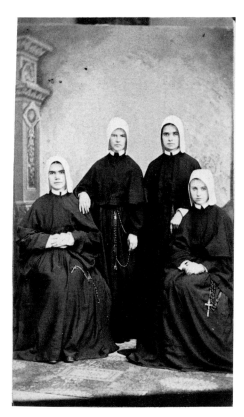

358. Religious. Roman Catholic nuns, St. Joseph, Missouri. Rudolph Uhlman, ca. 1876.

359. Religious. First Communion. Note painted background depiciting a church interior. A. Kruse, Chicago, ca. 1882.

360. Religious. Shaker Village, Canterbury, New Hampshire. W. G. C. Kimball, Concord, 1873.

cluding congregations, processions, pilgrims (Mecca, Rome, Jerusalem).

To these there may be added seven types found less frequently:

4. Distinct religious groups, culturally set apart from their neighbors: Shakers, Amish, Mormon, et. al.
5. Members of religious orders, such as Roman Catholic nuns.
6. People in ceremonial dress, such as for first communion in the Roman Catholic Church.
7. Religious statuary, shrines and symbols, often as features in a scene.
8. Reproductions of religious paintings intended for sale to the faithful as a memento, or as a symbol for veneration (The Sacred Heart of Jesus, The Crucifixion, The Virgin Mary and Child). Cartes of a Shrine and of related religious subjects were usually sold to pilgrims (Lourdes, St. Anne Dupre) as keepsakes.
9. Reproductions of panels of The Lord's Prayer, The Ten Commandments, etc.
10. Religious propaganda.

In 1867, the Lutheran Publication Society, Philadelphia, distributed the well-known portrait of Martin Luther on the occasion of the Seventh Jubilee of the Reformation. The chronology of Luther's life was printed on the back. During the next six or seven years, the same portrait, or the bust only copied from an enlargement, was published for the use of Lutheran organizations, usually without the biographical sketch.

Many American Sunday School and Missionary societies sold cartes de visite to raise funds for the support of their projects. There is a considerable variety of subjects, predominantly for the work in foreign missions.

See also: Architecture, Propaganda.

Resorts

The popular resorts of the United States and Europe were extensively photographed for carte images. Such pictures were of two general types: series or selections of scenic views from which the guest or tourist could

361. Resorts. The "Glen House," White Mountains, New Hampshire, E. Kilburn, Littleton, ca. 1864.

LUZERNE.

S. R. Stoddard   Glen's Falls. N. Y.

362. Resorts. The "Wayside," Luzerne, Glens Falls, New York. S. R. Stoddard, ca. 1874.

purchase souvenirs of his visit, and views of the hotels or inns presented or sold by the management to the guests as advertising. Generally the latter bore printed information describing the facility, names of the proprietors, etc. Sometimes rates for lodging and meals were given.

In the United States, the White Mountains, Adirondacks, Catskills, Delaware Water Gap, and the Glens of New York were the most patronized resort areas. By the mid-1870s the Colorado parks region, such as Colorado Springs and Manitou, and in California, the Geyser Springs and Yosemite, had become popular attractions. Stereos and cartes of all of these are numerous. By the late 1870s Florida had attracted winter tourists. Many Florida hotels distributed cartes of their establishments.

England had its famous resorts in the Isle of Wight and Brighton, while on the Continent, the spas of Germany and Austria had become renowned vacation sites. The Alpine hotels of France, Switzerland and Italy were also famous tourist attractions. Most of these were shown in carte de visite images. The European views were nearly always scenic, avoiding the direct advertising so characteristic of many American issues.

Schools & Colleges

Every town that boasted a public school with four or more rooms had it photographed. Commonly each spring the teachers and pupils were lined up and photographed in front of the school. The nation-wide movement to provide universal education through six

or eight grades and optional high school instruction, was in no way better shown than in the hundreds of photographs of the buildings erected to achieve the ideal.

The graduating classes were always photographed as a group and commonly each student had his portrait taken individually for exchange among classmates. For many photographers this business became a substantial factor in their annual incomes. Accordingly, many photographers openly competed for the work. For instance, two photographers for more than a decade produced the individual portraits of the graduates of Fall River, Mass. High School. The class was large enough to justify a special imprint such as "F.R.H.S., Class '83," with a motto in Greek, Latin, or English.

Many colleges distributed among prospective students cartes de visite of the buildings and montages of the faculty and administrative staff. Information about the college was usually printed on the backs.

Quincy College (Illinois) distributed a carte of the college and giving the faculty and calendar for the academic year 1867–1868. The 1867 graduating class of Augustana College, Paxton, Illinois, was portrayed in a montage photographed by P. A. Burggren. Figure 364.

As with high schools, college graduating classes were often photographed as a group, or a montage carte, and for individual portraits. Larger institutions, for example, Yale, Cornell, Harvard, permitted a local photographer to publish a small series of scenes of the college buildings and campus and then offer them for

363. Schools and colleges. Cook College, Havana, New York. G. M. Marsh, 1872.

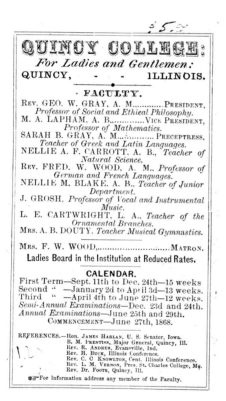

364. Schools and colleges. Quincy College, Illinois. Carte back with names of faculty and academic calendar. The image shows the college building. Photographer not identified, 1867.

sale to students, family, and visitors. Peck issued a large number of photographs of Yale. A few schools designated an official photographer, such as H. H. H. Langill for Dartmouth, ca. 1880.

There are many views of European universities and schools—Cambridge, Oxford, Eaton, Harrow—and of students in academic gown.

Among portraits of minor celebrities, there are many of college presidents, professors who achieved some fame in a field of scholarship, and those faculty members who were locally admired and highly respected.

Sculpture

The educational impact of the reproductions of paintings and photographs of sculpture as fine arts has already been discussed (page 107). The subject is included here to suggest the range of subjects in the rich iconography of notable sculpture.

The statuary displayed in the museums of Europe was systematically photographed for the carte de visite between 1861 and 1873. By then, virtually every notable carving and statue had been recorded. The great monuments in stone and bronze were also documented.

The popular interest in contemporary sculpture encouraged the inclusion of statuary exhibition halls in the various world expositions, beginning with the first in 1851.

William England published a superb series of more than seventy pieces displayed at the International Exhibition of 1873. There are also fine series of sculpture of the 1877 Vienna Exhibition and of the Philadelphia Centennial Exhibition, 1876.

The United States had few sculptors of note. Hiram Powers, the most outstanding, had settled in Florence where he accepted students and his sons established a photographic studio. Hiram Powers and his famous works, *The Greek Slave, America,* were beautifully photographed by L. Powers. The Powers Brothers also photographed the works of their father's students, for example, a bust by Pierce Connelly, ca. 1865.

David C. French, who had studied with Powers, produced the famous *Minuteman* erected in 1875 at Concord, Mass. Cartes of the statue and the dedicatory ceremonies are known.

There was a growing appreciation of fine sculpture in America. The statues placed by each state in the Capitol building, the great equestrian statues in Washington, and the memorials demanded by cities and public institutions contributed to the advancement of sculp-

365. Sculpture. Tomb of St. John Nepomuk. Prague series no. 62. F. Fridrich, Prague, ca. 1867.

relations, death, friendship). Portraits which were affectionate family mementos are not considered to be sentimentals.

The series of drawings by Soule, the New York Publishing Company, and Tomlinson, were largely of this genre (see page 113). S. P. Christmann, ca. 1867–1873, published several series of staged sentimental scenes, chiefly for the pleasure of children. These tinted images include incidents in daily life, pastimes, minor mishaps, occupations, and fairy tales. More than four hundred titles are known.

Grotecloss, New York, ca. 1864, published several posed pictures of children costumed as characters in fairy tales. *Little Red Riding Hood* is illustrated here.

Many American photographers produced occasional sentimental cartes, mostly posed but in some instances reproductions of paintings or sketches by local artists. For example, W. C. Benedict, New Boston, Ill., issued a scene showing a girl watching three dolls asleep in a canopy bed, ca. 1867.

This type of picture was favored by many Italian photographers. There was a wide variety, including many clever and enchanting situations. Giorgio Conrad, Naples, published a large series of tinted views. A girl at confession, no. 183, is an example of the simplicity of his staging techniques. He also produced lively studio "street" scenes with gamins. Figures 366, 367.

ture. Both Bell and Jarvis produced cartes of many of these.

The popular taste, however, turned to the sentimental work of John Rogers, whose figures were produced as plaster casts and sold in great numbers. A dozen publishers issued carte and stereo images of the Rogers Groups.

Somewhat less popular were the "Palmer's Marbles" also well illustrated in the carte format.

Details of stone carvings around the doors of cathedrals, of gargoyles and human figures were frequently illustrated by cartes.

There had developed a fashion for placing elaborate monuments on family burial plots in the new spacious cemeteries, such as Greenwood and Mount Auburn. Well known sculptors were commissioned to produce the memorials. Some of the splendid pieces, which were illustrated commercially in stereo and carte formats, represent much of the finest nineteenth century work done in America. Most of the cartes, however, were photographed for the families, not for general sale.

Sentimental

It is difficult to categorize the huge variety of cartes de visite that were commercially published as sentimental images, i.e., intended to arouse emotions, tender and gently humorous. Most were produced for children but many were quite sophisticated, dependent upon experience for the reaction (love, marriage, family

366. Sentimental. *The Prayer*, studio staged, no. 718. S. P. Christmann series, Berlin, ca. 1868.

367. Sentimental. *Confession*, studio staged. Note "partition" between priest and child. Giorgio Conrad series, no. 103. Naples, ca. 1865.

368. Sentimental. *Childhood's Prayer*, studio staged. J. Chapman, New York, 1865.

J. Chapman, New York, 1865, published a charming pose of a young girl kneeling by her bed, *Childhood's Prayer*, which is unusual for its natural manner. Figure 368.

There are occasional mawkishly sentimental cartes which seem much overdone.

Ships and Shipping, including boats on inland waters

Ships of every description are illustrated in cartes de visite. The most informative images are of busy harbors, especially Hamburg, Harve, New York, Hong Kong, Rio de Janeiro, and Valpairaiso. Coastal steamers, most notably plying between New York and Halifax are well recorded. Views of naval ships, passenger ships and freighters are moderately common.

Boats used on inland waters can be recognized in many scenes, especially river steamboats on the Mississippi and its tributaries. Lake steamers, many of which were primarily used in the tourist trade, are quite common: Lake Erie, Lake George, Winnipesaukee, etc.

The picturesque steamboats of the Mississippi River

369. Ships and Shipping. Fishing ships, Scheveningen, Holland. A. Jager, Amsterdam, ca. 1865.

370. Ships and Shipping. Harbor scene, Hafen, Germany. Hermann Priester, Hamburg, ca. 1870.

371. Shipwreck. Prussian War Ship *Americus* and English merchant ship *Chancellor*, off Callao, Peru. Ricardo Villaalba, ca. 1872.

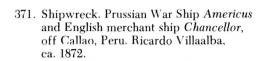

LAKE GEORGE, N. Y.

372. Ships and Shipping, Steamer *Minnehaha*, Lake George, New York. S. Beer, New York, 1862.

and its navigable tributaries were an important link in the transportation system of the United States, moving great cargoes of cotton, wheat, other agricultural goods, lumber, ores and manufactured goods. The riverway was also a strategic factor in the Civil War.

Canal boats and traffic in Holland were beautifully photographed by Jager and Braun. The Erie Canal was documented by several photographers.

There are fine cartes of shipbuilding in Connecticut and Maine. There are also images showing shipwrecks and vessels beached in a storm. Figure 371.

See also: Naval.

Sports

There is a considerable carte documentation of sports, although there are relatively small numbers of titles of any one sport.

1. Team sports; groups of ball players, cricket, rowers.
2. Individual competitive sports: running, swimming, boxing, wrestling, fencing.
3. Spectator sports, other than the above: horse racing.
4. Outdoor leisure sports: riding, hunting, fishing, archery, mountain climbing.
5. Indoor leisure sports: billiards.

WHITEMAN   HASTINGS

373. Sports. Cricket player. E. Whiteman, Hastings, England, ca. 1874.

374. Sports. Archer. John Bull, Weymouth, England, ca. 1865.

A majority of portraits of sportsmen were photographed in studios, the subject usually dressed in the suits characteristic of the activity. In many cases he is posed against a suggestive painted background—a forest, lake, or seashore.

Eisenmann published portraits of famous boxers, wrestlers, and strongmen. Similar portraits of pugilists were published in England and Germany, mostly after 1875.

There are occasional views showing native sports in travel series, as for example, Japanese wrestlers and swordsmen.

Theatrical

The most important cartes are, of course, the incredible gallery of portraits of actors, actresses and playwriters. Scarcely a well known name cannot be matched with a likeness. The most celebrated actors were photographed many times, such as Mrs. Scott-Sidons, Maggie Mitchell, and Joseph Jefferson.

There are fascinating portraits of actresses and actors in costumes of their popular roles. Sarony was the outstanding American photographer of theatrical celebrities, publishing his prints mostly in cabinet format but a good selection of them as cartes. The London Stereoscopic Company and Fritz Luckhardt in Vienna also produced portraits of actors in the costumes of the most famous roles.

There are scenes from plays and operas posed for the photographers.

There are also cartes of well known theaters and opera houses, mostly however exterior views. Insufficient lighting prohibited the photographing of large interiors. Cartes of artist's sketches were commonly produced as by Georgio Sommer, Naples, ca. 1870.

Among the more unusual theatrical subjects in carte format are Punch and Judy shows (Brighton, Scarborough, England), vaudevillians, and blackface minstrel groups. At least two Passion Plays at Oberammergau were photographed for cartes de visite in the 1870s. The series include portraits of the principal actors. Jacob Steigenberger photographed the earlier of these series, ca. 1871.

Tintype Cartes

The tintype is a distinct style of photograph which was made in many sizes and issued in many formats, very commonly mounted as cartes de visite. In the United States as early as 1861 the tintype carte was popular.

The vast majority are family portraits, rarely produced for commercial sale.

The most interesting aspect of the tintype carte was the search for methods of mounting the image to enhance its appeal. S. Masury, Boston, in 1863, patented a card mount with an open window bordered by a printed or embossed wreath-like frame. The tintype was mounted on the back of the card with the portrait centered in the window. During the next five years, nearly fifty distinct frame designs were applied to similar card mounts. Some of these were devised to

display the small gem portraits, which were usually less than one inch square.

There are tintypes of famous persons, including Lincoln, Breckenridge, Grant, Lee, and Davis, all copied from albumen carte prints. Because the tintype is a unique image, many collectors are unaware that these portraits are copies, each one individually copied. Scenic tintypes in carte format are unusual.

About 1870, the open window mount was displaced by a larger image mounted in a two- or three-leaf paper folder of carte size. In the three-leaf folder, two form the pocket, while the third is a protective cover.

Tintypes produced in the 1860s have black backs; those after 1870 are brown; the difference resulting from changes in the japanning process used to prepare the sheet iron.

Toys

Portraits of children with toys are among the most delightful carte images.

Most commonly the toy is a doll, ball, or stuffed animal. Older children are often posed with a hoop, rifle, tricycle, pull cart, or whip, or seated on a hobby horse.

The dolls are of infinite variety. Some are costly, life-like, and beautifully dressed, while others are simple, home-made rag puppets. Toy furniture and dishes show a similar variety. One can also follow the chronologic sequence of new types well into the 1890s.

375. Tintype. Portrait taken with Wing's Multiplying camera and mounted on a Wing type card. George W. Godfrey, Rochester, N.Y., 1865.

376. Tintype. Portrait of a child, "Frank Baker." N. R. Rider, Brunswick, Maine, 1869.

377. Toys. Girl holding a doll. Metcalf and Welldon, Boston, 1874.

378. Toys. Girl with a doll and doll carriage. N. Baldwin, Wichita, Kans., 1873.

380. Toys. Girl holding a rifle. Note sash tying the child to the posing chair. Milne, Hamilton, Canada, ca. 1867.

379. Toys. Boy with a velocipede. S. Clark, Springfield, Ohio, ca. 1880.

381. Toys. Hobby horse. Maull & Co., London, ca. 1865.

382. Toys. Boy with a hoop. A. W. Sheppard, Brooklyn, N.Y., 1865.

sledges. V. G. Silva, Funchal, issued a carte of an enclosed passenger sledge drawn by two oxen.

Whitney, St. Paul, published an unusual view of a *Dog Train from Pembina, 49 degrees N. Latitude*, ca. 1864. Figure 384.

Camels as beasts of burden and carrying riders are shown in many views of North Africa and the Near East (Bonfils, Beato, Hammerschmidt).

Canal and river traffic are illustrated in many European and American cartes.

See also: Horsedrawn, Railroads, Ships and Shipping.

Wars

There were only two major military conflicts during the era of the carte de visite, the Civil War and the Franco-Prussian War. The tremendous importance and social impact of Civil War photography has been discussed in Chapter Seven.

The Franco-Prussian War, 1870–1871, decisive as it was, was brief and localized. There were stereo and carte issues, including scenes of destruction of bridges, bombardment of towns, groups of soldiers, and postwar monuments. These are seldom found in American collections.

Portraits of military leaders, more of German than of French officers, and of soldiers are fairly common in Europe. There are spectacular scenes of the destruction of Strassburg by Varady & Co.

Hobby horses and stick horses are shown in great variety. Some have handsomely carved and painted bodies with genuine hair manes and tails.

The toy rifles—girls as well as boys were often posed holding one—range from crude wooden pieces to realistic models that appear to be workable.

Among the more unusual cartes are Christmas trees surrounded by toys, children amusing themselves with a paint set, or a set of blocks, a little girl posed as if jumping rope, boys playing marbles, and an occasional close-up of a toy such as a Noah's Ark with its animals arranged in parade formation.

Photographers who specialized in portraits of children usually maintained a variety of properties including stuffed dogs (some amusingly crude), a dog cart, a hobby horse and small toys to achieve both pictorial effect and the child's cooperation in posing.

Transportation

In addition to the busy street scenes showing carriages, wagons and lorries drawn by horses and the views of railroads, there are many cartes illustrating unusual modes of transportation.

Typically travel series include rickshaws (Japan) pulled by man power closed carriages (China) borne by two or four men and various kinds of litters. Uses of the elephant and water buffalo are shown in fine views by Bourne and Shepherd and Sache and Murray, (India).

Oxen were used in many countries for various purposes: drawing carts and wagons, sleighs and

383. Transportation. Baby carriage. Floyd and Power, Minneapolis, Minn., ca. 1875.

384. Transportation. "Dog Train from Pembina, 49 N. Latitude." Whitney, St. Paul, Minn., ca. 1865. Courtesy of Robert Cauthen.

Views of the Ruins of Paris during the Commune that immediately followed the Franco-Prussian War were issued by several photographers.

The Modoc Indian War, 1872–1873, which hardly deserves the name, was photographed by L. Heller and Muybridge for scenic stereos and cartes. Heller also issued portraits of the Indian prisoners. The Modocs camped in the lava beds near Tule Lake, California, bravely resisted attempts to move them to a reservation.[7]

There are thousands of portraits of military leaders who owed their fame to war service. The majority were American because of the timing and magnitude of the Civil War, but there are great numbers of portraits of European military men, British, French, German, Austrian, Italian, many of whom were in charge of troops stationed in colonies and forts located around

the world, such as British in India and Afganistan.

There are many war-related carte images as, for example, battlefields Waterloo, Bunker Hill, historic cannon, monuments, and relics found at various battle sites (Ticonderoga).

See also: Military, Naval.

Zoology

Carte de visite coverage of zoology was not comparable to that in stereo. Haes' remarkable experiments photographing animals in the London Zoological gardens resulted in two fine series of stereographs. At least a few of the titles in the earlier series were also issued in carte format.

Systematic photographing of the animal kingdom, from protozoans to anthropoid apes was not attempted until Underwood & Underwood prepared their sets of educational stereographs about 1900.

Excluding pets and domesticated animals, cartes of animals are quite rare. Most common are the circus

[7]For an excellent illustrated account of the photographers and their work see Palmquist, P., *History of Photography 2* (3): 187–205, 1978.

385. Transportation. Ox-cart, St. Jean de Luz, France. Ladislaw Konarjewski, ca. 1865.

Buffalo Tram.

386. Transportation. "Water Buffalo Team," Colombo, Ceylon. Slinn and Co., ca. 1865.

animals, either caged or on display. Elephants, bears, lions, tigers and giraffes are most frequently shown.

Public interest in the birth of "Young America," to "Hebe", an elephant in the Philadelphia Zoo, encouraged A. W. Rothengatter to photograph mother and baby in 1880 (two issues are known). Figure 387.

Rattlesnakes in nature were photographed by Savage and cobras with snake charmers by several Asian photographers.

There are close-up views of the luna moth and the mourning cloak butterfly published by Tilton, ca. 1863, who issued various natural history series. Other specimen views in carte format include mollusks such as the chambered nautilus by Lambert, Singapore, ca. 1870, and by Moulton, Salem, Mass., ca. 1868. G. W. Tomlinson published (possibly imported) various small series of natural history cartes, each with eight or ten titles, in the early 1860s, including "Foreign Birds," a set of ten for fifty cents.

The existence of occasional tinted images of song birds and wild flowers of several types of mounts, suggests that there are other series illustrating natural history which have not been recognized by collectors.

Attention is called to color printed and hand tinted lithographic images of birds and mammals on thin white cards cut to carte size. Some of these are actually older than the carte de visite, having been popular in the early 1850s. Such prints were manufactured sporadically into the 1900s for scrap book collections. Personally, I do not consider these as cartes de visite although examples are found occasionally in family albums assembled in the 1860s.

387. Zoology. *The Mother Elephant "Hebe" and her baby "Young America."* First elephant known to have been born in captivity. A. W. Rathengatter & Co., Philadelphia, 1880.

PART THREE:
THE DOCUMENTATION AND INTERPRETATION
OF CARTES de VISITE

This section is intended to provide technical information which will be useful in the identification, description, dating, and interpretation of cartes de visite.

In order to interpret an image it is necessary to analyze and describe it. What is the subject? Who photographed and published it? When was it produced? How was it made? Why, or for what purpose, was it made?

An accurate description can thus be a catalogue entry which will inform a potential user if the image will be helpful. Few people, even professional historians, realize that before an image can be accepted as a reliable historical document it must itself be verified and documented.

Frassanito, in his pioneering *Gettysburg—A Journey in Time* (1977), has shown how untrustworthy long-accepted Civil War photographs can be. Photographers misidentified locations, moved objects including human bodies to improve pictorial effects, and introduced other errors such as failing to credit or miscrediting the actual photographer.

Every collector wishes to know the nature of the specimens in his collection just as every archivist and scholar needs to know precisely the nature of the object under investigation.

Because the carte de visite is a specific format or style of photographs, description is relatively standardized.

The Carte de Visite Format

The carte de visite is immediately recognizable by its size and mount. The card mount measures approximately 2½ × 4 inches or 63 × 100 mm. The image size is somewhat variable but is usually about 58 × 90 mm. The length of the print is more variable than the width.

The distinguishing characteristic is size of the card. Although originally intended as a mount for paper prints, several other types of images were commercially published in carte format: photomechanically reproduced, reproductions ink press printed, tintypes mounted as cartes de visite, etc. All of these are considered legitimate.

In addition to the mount and the image, the imprint or logo is an integral part of the format. Any carte without an imprint is suspect of being a copy, probably a pirated copy, although it may be—and often is—an original issue. The imprint includes the name and location of the photographer (or publisher) plus any supplementary information printed on the card. The imprint is ordinarily placed on the card back but it is often on the front.

The relations of the carte de visite to other formats.

In the early 1860s there were only two styles of commercially produced card mounted photographs, the stereograph and the carte de visite. As noted on page 88, many cartes are identical to members of stereo pairs. The 4/4 camera was used to produce negatives with four or eight images which could be printed and mounted as four or eight cartes or two or four stereos.

Several new formats were introduced in the 1860s and 1870s. The earliest and most successful of these was the cabinet card. The mount measured 4¼ × 6½ inches, thereby accommodating an image area nearly three times larger than the carte. The large head or bust portrait was far more pleasing and gradually overshadowed the carte in portraiture.

Technically, the cabinet card was little more than a large carte. It was produced in the same styles of posing, printed by the same methods, mounted on the same card stocks, and identified by similar imprints.

The date of introduction of the cabinet card is uncertain although it has been credited to F. R. Window (Window & Bridge) in England in 1866.[1] Certainly Window's promotion of the format was responsible for its immediate success in England, the Continent and the United States. Several American photographers, among them McClees, Warren, and Whipple, had produced card mounted images of this size (approximately half plate) as early as 1862.

In the United States the cabinet view was moderately popular in the large eastern cities in the late 1860s but today these early images are quite rare. By the mid 1870s they became more common but not until the 1880s did they overtake the carte de visite.

A second new format, the victoria card, was introduced about 1870–1871. It too was intended for portraiture. The card mount measured 3½ × 5 inches and thus was intermediate in size between the carte and the cabinet formats. It never achieved much success although many images, portrait, scenic and novelties, were published as victoria cards.

Identical or nearly identical scenic images may be found in more than one format, carte, stereo, and large plate, for example. Most commonly the images were produced with two or three cameras positioned and operated at the same time. The stereo and carte images could be obtained from a single negative.

In many cases whole or part of a negative or positive

---

[1]*Photo. News 10*: 385–386, Aug. 17, 1866. See also, *Phila. Phot. 3*: 357, Nov. 1866, which reports that "Wilson and Hood are making Bregner cutters (for prints and cards) as fast as possible. Anthony is already producing albums."

image was copied by enlargement or reduction, often only a portion (such as the head) of an individual.

The only relation between tintypes and cartes de visite was the tintype image mounted on a card or in a folder with the dimensions of the carte. These were produced as cartes so that they could be placed in albums or be conveniently kept with cartes (see page 164).

During the 1870s and early 1880s at least twenty formats of card-mounted photographs were patented under fanciful names: Trilby, LaFavorita, Sans Pareil, Boudoir, Promenade, etc.—each one distinguished only by size. The majority of these mounts bear photographers imprints.

Card Stock

The card stock used for mounts is the most important single feature that will indicate the date of a carte. Specifically, it will date the mount, not necessarily the image. The prints may have been produced from a negative several or many years old. Generally, however, the mount and image are of nearly the same age.

The card stock is extremely variable with two progressive chronologic trends: the thickness of the stock increased gradually from 1860 to 1885 and the ornamentation was marked by continuously changing styles involving increasing elaboration from 1860 to 1885.

From 1860 to 1866 bristol board or its equivalent was used almost exclusively for mounting. This thin white card, having an average thickness of .014–.016 inch was used almost universally. Occasionally similar card, but with brown or gray color, was used. A very few photographers cut any white card stock that was available.

Until late 1860, the photographer usually purchased the board in sheets and cut his own mounts or obtained them from a stationer who cut the cards to specifications. The rapid popularization of cartes de visite quickly led to the manufacture of pre-cut cards. By mid 1861 a variety of mounts were available commercially.

The plain white card was soon decorated by a border, commonly of a single or double gilt lines. Sometimes these lines form a design in the corners. Occasionally these lines were printed in red, blue, green, purple, magenta, or black—named in order of frequence. This type of card mount was used throughout the 1860s, but faced considerable competition from other types of mounts after 1866. Figure 20.

The bristol card was normally quite smooth but was sometimes calendered, i.e., rolled to increase smoothness and stiffness.

This thin card was ideal for album cards because they could be easily inserted in the pockets of the album leaves. Under repeated handling such mounts, however, became dog-eared, bent or cracked. To improve durability, by 1870 two different types of thicker stock were introduced: paste board and press board.

In paste board the thickness was increased by pasting together three or more sheets of paper. The finished cardboard contained one to many inner layers ("inners") and a face and back ("outers") which were of better quality. The most common types used for carte de visite mounts were five or seven-ply, with the face white or colored, usually enameled, and the back, coated or uncoated, receptive to ink printing.

"Enameled" in cartes de visite has two meanings. The word here is used in its technical sense in the paper industry, i.e., sized with talc, dextrinized starch, or other coating. In the period 1868–1871 especially, but with other scattered instances as early as 1861, the image was sometimes coated with a clear varnish which was brushed over the print surface to give it a highly lustrous finish. This was widely known as enameling. There were many patented mixtures and special instruments for varnishing the image.

True cardboard or press board is a single matte, the matrix compressed by rollers into the desired thickness. Commonly it is made of wood pulp, sometimes of other fibers, mixed with a binder in the matrix to improve mechanical strength. The development of heavy machinery made the manufacture of high quality cardboard economical after 1875. Although plain pressboard was used to some extent for cheap cartes from about 1872 to 1885, it was usually covered, at least on the face, with a thin sheet of white or colored paper.

Better grades of pressboard were made from chemically bleached pulp. Cheaper grades were gray in color, quite porous, and brittle, with brittleness and discoloration usually increased with age. Cheap cardboard was often used by publishers for mounting pirated copies of portraits of celebrities when the lowest possible cost was desired.

There were at least thirty distinct kinds of card stock used for carte de visite mounts, differing in number and types of ply, fiber composition of the matrix, and method of finishing the outers. These basic kinds were cut, colored or ornamented in various ways so that approximately eighty widely used types of mounts are readily recognized. These types account for about 90% of the cartes issued between 1860 and 1885. A complete list would be of too limited use to justify inclusion in this book.

The varieties and variants given here are American types but the similarities between European and American mounts, 1860–1880, are astonishing. A. Marion, Paris and London, the largest manufacturer of mounts in Europe, sold them throughout the world, including many in the United States. By 1872 A. M. Collins & Son of Philadelphia (est. 1866) had succeeded in attracting more than three-quarters of the card trade in the United States. Their catalogues from 1872 to 1882 boasted "Every conceivable variety of photographic cards" including three hundred kinds of pre-cut carte de visite mounts.[2] A wide selection of imprint designs was also available. The photographer chose one he liked and the dealer imprinted the cards.

The huge number, 300, includes for instance, cards with a red face with pink back, with yellow back, with

---

[2]See also Collins' advertisement (1872) in Estabrooke, E. M., "The Ferrotype and How to Make It."

gray moire back; beveled edge with gilt; beveled edge with red, without beveled edge—i.e., six variants of one type.

Occasionally novel and imitative card mounts were offered to the trade but none of these persisted more than two or three years. Card mounts with printed oval frames are of this class.

Between 1865 and 1868 cards with printed frames, sometimes called a cartouche, usually in gilt or black, were intended to provide a style of mounting similar to the open window card for tintype cartes. About a hundred variants are known. These may be grouped in four basic types:

(1) simple oval frame of one or more lines, one of which is heavy.

(2) oval frame with decorative motifs.

(3) oval frame, decorated and with tassels and a hanging cord.

(4) an ornate rectangular instead of an oval frame.

Each basic type was available in three oval sizes: small, less than 1½ inches high; medium, about two inches; and large, more than 2¼, often 2¾ inches.

A cheaply made related type was used briefly, 1867 and 1868. The front of the mount was covered by a background and an oval frame to receive a portrait, printed by woodcuts. The printing was usually brown or blue, but green and gray were also used.

The virtual monopoly of the manufacture and distribution of carte mounts by one company, of course, standardized the styles and fashions. The same types of cards, colors, and imprints were used everywhere.

Collins introduced new designs every year, sometimes more frequently, often with some fanfare. These constantly changing styles represented a deliberate attempt to stimulate business. Since most photographers purchased only a four or six month supply of mounts they were always able to buy the latest style. This accounted for the rapidity with which a specific card type spread over the United States and provides the basis for the reliability of chronologic dating by card stocks alone.

Beginning about 1872, many photographers offered their customers a choice of several styles of mounts, sometimes at different prices. Other photographers finished or reworked the images in two grades, regular and deluxe, mounting them on different card styles. The photographers, therefore, were using more than one kind of mount at the same time but the imprints were uniform.

There were, of course, many photographers who resisted fadism, whether it be in card mount or imprint style. For example, Henry Ulke, Washington, D. C., continued to cut his own bristol mounts until 1869, but fortunately consistently between 1866 and 1871 printed the year on each card. E. S. Dunshee, Boston, used the same logo from 1872 to 1884, but changed the card stock four times during that period. Dunshee, beginning with 1873, like Ulke, printed the year on every card.

The Imprint or Logo

One of the remarkable features of cartes de visite is the photographer identification which normally appears in an imprint. No other photographic format has ever been so richly identified. Some stereographs were imprinted as early as 1851–1852[3] and the majority after 1856.

The term imprint is to be preferred over the word "logo" which commonly implies a trademark design, or vignette, whereas most carte imprints are typeset and the same design was used by hundreds of photographers. While the card stock is the prime criterion for dating a carte de visite, the imprint is the most informative feature.

The Importance of Typographic Variations

All of the cards purchased in an order were imprinted identically, that is with the same typography, etc. Additional orders very frequently show variations in typesetting and card stock.

Identical images mounted on cards with differences in typography represent distinct issues, i.e., printed at different times.

Evolution of the Imprint

The earliest photographer indentifications found on American cartes de visite are small labels, usually oval or rectangular pasted on the backs of the mounts (1859–1861): Rockwood, Fredricks, Anthony, Broadbent, Whipple, et al. Rarely, such labels were used by photographers as late as the early 1880s, but the card stock will at once indicate the correct age of the mount.

The earliest imprints are simple one liners as by George C. Rockwood; Rintoul & Rockwood; Bogardus, New York; and Southworth & Hawes, Boston.

"Blind imprints" or blind stamps were impressed names and addresses placed on the face of the mount without ink. Such imprints were used occasionally on stereographs from about 1856 until 1870. In cartes de visite they were most commonly used in the early to mid-1860s. There are many examples, e.g., Lawrence & Houseworth, C. Seaver, Jr., Schoonmaker, R. E. Mosely.

By late 1860, two and three line imprints became typical. In these the name and location of the photographer are given, often with the notation "artist," "photographist," "ambrotypes and photographs."

Almost immediately there was added a line stating that the negative was preserved and duplicates could be had at any time. Except for various embellishments, this basic type of imprint remained in use for ten years.

Spontaneously many photographers devised personalized imprints commonly with a vignette. Card suppliers responded by offering a wide variety of cuts (designs) which proved to be very popular. The most common devices were eagles, "Columbia," cornucopias, patriotic symbols and ornate scrolled vignetted, or framed name. Hundreds of clever and attractive logos can be found on cards of this period.

[3]Darrah, *World of Stereographs*, 1977, p. 7.

January. 1862.

Sarah Clark.

CARTES DE VISITE,
BY
SILSBEE, CASE & CO.
PHOTOGRAPHIC ARTISTS,
299½ Washington Street,
BOSTON

CASE & GETCHELL,
From Dec. 3, 1862.

390. Early imprint noting succession. Case and Getchell, Boston, 1862.

388. Imprint rubber-stamped, commonly dated. Used from the early 1860s to about 1870. H. Glosser, New York, 1862.

J. J. HAWES,
Photographer:
19 Tremont Row,
BOSTON.

389. Simple imprint, one to three lines, type set, 1862–1864. J. J. Hawes, Boston, 1863.

391. Imprint a vignetted name. Hundreds of designs were used, 1862–1865. A. Bogardus, New York, 1862.

173

Died Oct 16th 1869
Saturday Morn -
Aged 30

Mr. Ellwanger

All Negatives preserved and extra Copies made
if desired.

392. Vignetted name. Imprint of G. K. Warren, Lowell
and Cambridgeport, Mass., 1862–1863.

394. Patriotic imprint, note succession. J. W. Maser,
Rochester, N.Y., 1863.

Daniel Stearns
Aged 64 years 20 ...
1864

Additional Copies from the plate from which
this picture is taken can be had if desired

393. Vignette imprint, with more extensive information
concerning the photographer and studio. A. Bogardus,
New York, 1863–1864.

395. Imprint decorated with curved lines. Common
1863–1865. Note preservation of negatives. Burrows
and Bundy, Middletown, Conn., 1864.

In the late 1860s the imprints began to diversify in several directions, increase in size ultimately covering the whole back, the addition of a wide range of information, and the quest for a greater measure of individuality.

If one has available for study a large number of cartes, a hundred or more, from a single photographer, and these span more than a decade, it is easy to arrange the imprints in chronologic sequence and thus establish a reference time scale. Such a sequence can be used to date any carte produced by that photographer within an accuracy of one year.

To express this in another way, with experience, about 95% of the cartes issued between 1860 and 1885 can be dated with reliability of plus or minus one year. After 1885 the card mounts and types of imprints change little as the format is slowly displaced by other types of images.

For most practical purposes dating cartes in five year increments, ca. 1865, ca. 1870, ca. 1880, is sufficient. The reliability in this range is virtually 100%.

Rubber stamped imprints

The use of rubber stamps to imprint the card mount extended from 1861 to 1890. B. Glosser, New York, stamped his cards with a circular design similar to that usually used for postal cancellations, 1861–1862. The practice was more prevalent in small communities than in cities. During the period of the revenue tax on photographs many photographers used rubber stamps of many designs to cancel the stamps as required by law. Figure 388.

J. W. Black used a rubber stamp with date to identify proofs submitted to his customers. Figure 448.

Between 1874 and 1885 many photographers purchased rubber stamps of varied designs to imprint their cards because it was cheaper than ink-printing. One of the more common designs was of a girl holding a canary in her hand.

Types of Information in the Imprint or Logo

The Photographer's Name

Although the name printed upon a card mount appears to be a self-evident fact, the name itself frequently presents problems.

Most photographers, at least for a part of their careers identified their studios and work by their names in full or with initials: J. J. Hawes, C. D. Fredricks, E. & H. T. Anthony, John P. Soule. The identity of the *studio* or *publisher* is obvious, but not necessarily the *camera operator*.

Many photographers at one time or another used only the family name in the imprint: Bogardus, Brand, Black. In the cases of such masters the identity is certain. When the imprint gives Brown, Johnson, Smith, or even Dunshee (there were at least eight with this name), identification, without a town location, may be nearly impossible.

396. Ornate vignetted imprint. Many designs were used 1864–1867. Note tax stamp. E. W. Buel, Pittsfield, Mass., 1865.

397. Ornate oval-framed imprint, a very common style early 1864 to late 1867. J. R. Roberts, Clyde, N.Y., ca. 1865.

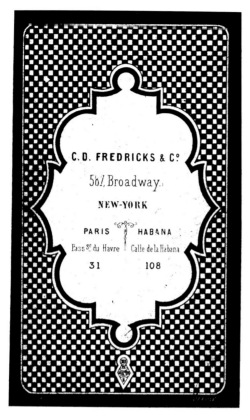

398. Ornate groundwork on back, bilateral ovoid area for imprint. Many variants of this popular style were used 1864–1870. C. D. Fredricks, New York, 1866.

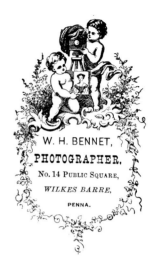

400. Camera and cherubs motif used world-wide from about 1866 to 1874. W. H. Bennet, Wilkes Barre, Pa., 1872.

1874.

C. R. B. Claflin,

At No. 377 Main Street,

Worcester, Mass.

399. Imprint set with larger type, usually placed lengthwise on mount, 1870–1883, most commonly 1870–1875. C. R. B. Claflin, Worcester, Mass., 1874.

No. 71 Broad Street,
Lynn, Mass.

401. National Photographic Association logo, applied to cartes by more than a thousand photographers, 1871–1875, especially 1872–1873. At least six variants are known. Bushby and Hart, Lynn, Mass., 1872.

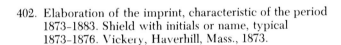

402. Elaboration of the imprint, characteristic of the period
1873-1883. Shield with initials or name, typical
1873-1876. Vickery, Haverhill, Mass., 1873.

403. Elaboration of the imprint. Many designs, commonly
printed in 3, 4, or 5 colors. 1875-1878. Proctor,
Salem, Mass., 1876.

Some photographers changed the spellings of their names: Chr. Engell of Spring Grove, Minnesota, became Chr'n Engle. Schellhaus changed his name to Shellhouse. Many photographers exchanged initials. P. A. Brown became A. P. Brown.

Not the least problems result from mis-spellings in typesetting. Some photographers corrected such errors with pen and ink, but others simply ignored the mistake.

Fancy script letters (f, s, i, j, k, h) are easily confused and misread. Contemporary publications, such as business directories, often perpetuate these mistakes. Business directories and newspapers are also notorious for careless errors in the typesetting of personal names.

Rarely on cartes, but commonly on stereos, the photographer identified himself by initials rather than by name. This practice was particularly widespread in France, 1850s and 1860s, less so in Germany and England. Approximately fifty sets of French initials have been identified.

In the 1870s, very occasionally earlier, many American photographers used logos designed around initials but in most cases an imprint with name and address accompanied the vignette.

The imprint often includes a note, "successor to" or "late with." Successor means that the photographer has purchased the studio of the person named. Commonly such cards have a statement "negatives of (Mr. Weaver) are preserved. Copies may be had at any time."

Generally, succession implies that the new and former proprietors operated the same studio at the same address. Typically, the successor notice was used for six months to a year or until the new owner believed he was well established.

"Late with" indicates that the photographer was formerly employed by or was in junior partnership with the person named. It implies a degree of endorsement or recommendation. Usually it also implies that the photographer has established his first independent studio. Rarely, the term was used instead of "successor."

One of fairly frequent practices during the first few weeks of transition between owners was over-printing the logo on the cards on hand. Because such imprints were used very briefly, they are relatively rare. There are many variations, such as a true overprint blocking out the name of the former owner, incorporation of the old in the new imprint, autographically signing the card and crossing out the former owner's name, etc.

Partnerships and Family Succession

These are often helpful in dating cards. Partnerships were usually of short duration, lasting for only a few years, e.g., Silsbee & Case, Case & Getchell, Black & Case, Rintoul & Rockwood, etc.

Blind partnerships are identified by "—and Company," e.g., W. H. Tipton & Co. This usually means that the relationship is a financial interest in the studio, not

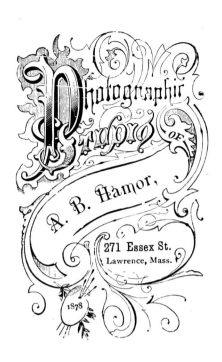

404. Imprint nearly filling the card back. Photographers
name on scroll or panel, commonly with printed
year 1877–1883. A. B. Hamor, Lawrence, Mass., 1878.

406. Floral imprint; photographer's name usually on scroll
or panel, typically 1881–1886. S. Piper, Manchester,
N.H., 1882.

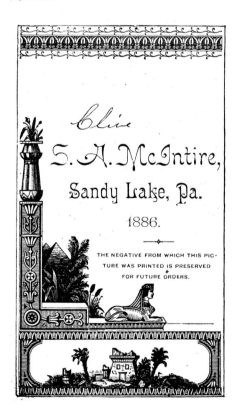

405. Back of card ornamented with small geometric or
floral designs. Imprint of photographer frequently at
bottom of card face. Common 1880–1886, rarely to
1888. Taylor and Preston, Salem, Mass., 1885.

407. Egyptian and Japanese motifs, widely used 1882–1888.
S. A. McIntire, Sandy Lake, Pa., 1886.

Frankly E Morgan
to his Aunt Nettie.

Buchtel *Feb 18/7*
10 months old,

PHOTOGRAPHERS

119 AND 121 FIRST ST,

Portland, - - - Oregon.

ALL NEGATIVES PRESERVED.

No.

Duplicates from this Picture may be had
at any time.

Mary E. Wayne
Jan. 1893

Phillips'
Photographers
1206 Chestnut Street,
Philadelphia.

408. Return to plainer imprints. Some photographers avoided ornate mounts, others used them briefly. Buchtel and Stolte, Portland, Ore., 1876–1878.

410. Typical imprint of the early and mid 1890s. Phillips, Philadelphia, 1893.

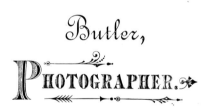

Butler,

PHOTOGRAPHER.

Corner Main & Centre Sts.

MARSHALLTOWN, - IOWA.

1883.

NEGATIVES RETAINED FOR FUTURE ORDERS.

Exposition Universelle
PARIS 1900
MÉDAILLE D'ARGENT

Mme Vᵉ Hermann
M.

PHOTOGRAPHE
SPÉCIALITÉ DE PORTRAITS D'ENFANTS

PARIS
20, Chaussée d'Antin, 20
8ᵉ 1903 B P GRIMAUD PARIS

411. Imprint of the early 1900s, used chiefly in Europe. Reproductions of the photographer's signature were used from 1862 into the 20th century. Mme. V. Hermann, Paris, 1903.

409. Plain imprint, typical of the 1880s. Butler, Marshalltown, Iowa, 1883.

professional participation. When young W. H. Tipton purchased the studio of C. J. Tyson, for whom he had worked for nearly ten years, he had little money. Tyson permitted his protege to pay off the indebtedness over a period of many years. This was a fairly common practice, especially when a photographer decided to retire for reasons of age or illness, turned to a different occupation, or when the heirs of a deceased photographer assisted a new owner in continuing an established family business.

Family imprints are also revealing. F. Charnaux, Charnaux & Sons, Charnaux Brothers (Geneva, Switzerland) span a period of forty years. In hundreds of instances, sons worked with, and often succeeded, their fathers.

Along with social mobility, i.e., moving from learner and assistant to independence to employer and master, there was also extensive geographic mobility. Moving from a small to a larger studio, from one town to another, from one state to another, was a characteristic aspect of American restlessness. Nearly 28% of the 11,000 American carte de visite photographers known to me operated studios in more than one town and 8% in more than one state.

Gallery Names

The use of fictitious names such as "Elite Gallery," "New York Gallery," "Sunshine Gallery," "Home Gallery" often give no clue to the identity of the proprietor or photographer. When a city is given,

checking city directories will usually provide identification. If no location is given, a search is usually fruitless.

Slogans

These were used frequently enough to deserve attention. Many symbolize the importance of light in photography. "Fiat lux" and its translation, "Let there be light," "Light is my servant," "Silver Sunbeams." Others made extravagent claims such as, "the world's largest movable gallery."

Services Offered by the Studio

In the early 1860s many imprints informed the public that the photographer also produced daguerreotypes and ambrotypes.

One of the most common advertisements with the imprint was copying services, especially of daguerreotypes. These old family portraits, unique images, could be reproduced as cartes de visite in multiple copies. Tremendous numbers of these copies were produced for delighted customers.

Many imprints mention that the photographer will do outdoor work, enlarging, will make "life size" portraits, can produce portraits in "all finishes," copy maps, and photograph machinery.

To augment income many studios sold stereographs and cartes de visite, albums, stereoscopes, opera glasses, telescopes, and novelties. Picture framing was a

412. Card mount with notched edges, 1890–1895. H. E. Cutler, Morrisville, Vt., 1892.

413. Card mount with notched edges, front lustrous white with pebbled border around space for the image. Imprint usually embossed, 1894–1900. Albee Bros., Machias, Maine, 1898.

common service, partly because large portraits were usually framed.

The growing professionalism in photography in the latter 1860s and 1870s was shown in various ways. The National Photographic Association's logo, a vignetted NPA, was enthusiastically applied to the backs of the mounts by hundreds of members. Wilson, Hood and Co. sold three sizes of the cut or printed the design on the mounts purchased from them.

The display of examples of work in exhibitions and competitions served both to publicize fine photography and achieve personal recognition. Although beginning with the early 1860s, the imprint was often accompanied by claims of patronage, awards and medals, picturing them was more often a practice of the latter 1860s and 1870s.

Price Schedules

The prices charged for carte de visite are frequently printed on the mount. Less often, the prices for different formats are given. In such cases the actual price paid for the carte can be determined.

Although the average price was generally standard throughout the United States, at any given time, there were outstanding studios that charged much higher prices, intentionally discouraging cheaper trade. There were also cut-rate operators, commonly itinerants, whose prices were only half the average price.

Throughout the 1860s the price of a dozen cartes ranged from $1.50 to 3.50 per dozen, with the usual price $2.00. In 1872–1873 the range was the same but the average had dropped to $1.50.

The highest prices for standard mounts with retouched images known to me, range from $5.00 to 6.00 per dozen, 1875–1878 by various Boston and New York photographers.

The remarkable price stability over a period of more than twenty years was due largely to the actual decrease in cost of chemical and paper supplies and the improved portrait business that paralleled the growing population of the United States and general prosperity (despite the economic depression of 1873).

Instructions for the Sitter

Although relatively rare, there are imprints which instructed the prospective customer as to suitable dress for portrait sittings: what colors to wear, which are poorest, the time of day, etc. In the period before artificial illumination was available, such suggestions were mutually helpful.

Other Types of Information in Imprints

The types of information described above do not exhaust the variety although they include the most prevalent; less frequent, yet common enough to deserve notice are:

1. date of establishment of the business
2. identification of the style of portrait—such as Rembrandt, Berlin Head, Holbein, Russe
3. patent number or license to use a patented process
4. use of electrical lighting

171, 173, & 175 MAIN STREET

STOCKTON, CAL.

414. Autographed photographer's name and address. Seward, Utica, N.Y., ca. 1866.

415. Camera motif. Photographer's name in rebus writing on camera back. J. Pitcher Spooner, Stockton, Calif., ca. 1877.

L. E. Jackman,

Springfield, Vt.

416. Camera motif. L. E. Jackman, Springfield, Vt.,
ca. 1872.

5. names of retouchers ("artists" after 1868),
   operators, etc.
6. second occupation of the photographer—medical doctor, dentist, clergyman, jeweler, fly-tier,
   etc.
7. fraternal affiliation, most commonly Masonic
8. religious affiliation, most commonly Roman
   Catholic
9. national origin, most commonly German, Norwegian, Swedish

The purpose of revealing fraternal or religious
affiliation or nationality was most likely to seek the
patronage of those of similar viewpoints.

The Photographer
The most obvious purpose of the imprint was the
identification of the photographer. Although it follows
logically that the photographer named produced the
negative of the mounted print, this presumption rests
on very uncertain grounds.

417. Camera motif. Carl Forell, Galesburg, Ill., ca. 1873.

418. Camera motif. Arthur A. Glines, Newton, Mass., 1881.

Pictures enlarged and finished in Ink,
Oil or Water Colors.

419. Cherub and palette motif. This design was used by hundreds of photographers throughout the United States, 1875–1882. V. V. Leonard, Plattsmouth, Nebr., ca. 1880.

421. Individualized imprint. Nadar (= Felix Tournechon), Paris. Printed signature and list of some of his correspondents, ca. 1870.

420. Individualized imprint. With Canterbury Cathedral. J. Bateman, Canterbury, England, ca. 1867.

To be sure, vast numbers of small-scale studios were operated as one-man businesses, perhaps with family help or a young assistant to do routine chores and clean-up. The mounted images produced in such studios were the personal work of the photographer.

Likewise, the wealthy, famous, or influential client, was given the personal attention of the photographer-proprietor in the largest studios. There were hundreds of renowned studios which employed six, eight or more cameramen who did the routine portraiture, but who were never credited for their work. The finished, mounted images rightfully bore the imprint of the studio and proprietor. The imprint was a mark of reputation, not of authorship.

Every careful observer has found inferior work among the issues of the masters, chiefly because the master was not the actual photographer. We cannot, categorically, lay the blame on assistants, however.

Some studio proprietors did credit their operators, especially if there were managing branch studios. In such cases the operator would be identified: "S. B. Heald, in charge" or "Under the superintendance of Mr. S. B. Heald" (Warren's Studio, Boston, Mass.).

Staff photographers, employed by manufacturers, construction companies, federal and state bureaus, and hospitals who were paid a salary were not ordinarily identified on imprints. Rarely a photographer was able to reserve the right to imprint his private work (Smillie, Smithsonian Institution, 1870s).

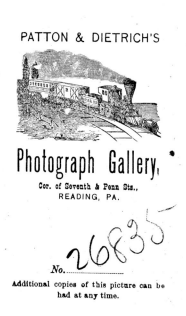

422. Individualized imprint. Railroad Train. Patton and Dietrich, Reading, Pa., 1868–1874.

424. Individualized imprint. Beehive motif. Note services offered by the studio. Savage and Ottinger, Salt Lake City, Utah, 1869.

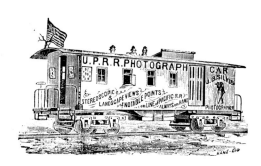

423. Individualized imprint. J. B. Silvis' Union Pacific Railroad Studio, 1874.

425. Advertisement of medal award. Bradley and Rulofson, San Francisco, 1876–1877.

426. Imprint with medal awards. Landy, Cincinnati, Ohio, 1879.

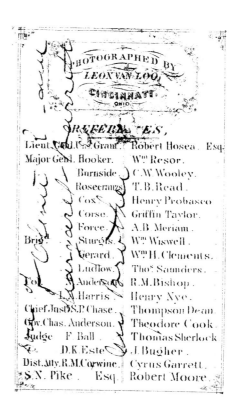

428. Individualized imprint. Listing distinguished references. Leon Van Loo, Cincinnati, Ohio, 1865.

427. Imprint with medal awards. A widely used practice in Europe from 1862 into the 1900s. Marshall Wane, Douglas, Isle of Man, ca. 1876.

C. G. BLATT'S
PHOTOGRAPHIC EMPORIUM,

Isn't this a good old treat,
Where the public fears no cheat,
They know his pictures have no beat,
In finish, excellence—and cheap.

Your faces made so sweet,
And the style so nice and neat,
Besides they are so very cheap,
That the poor man need not squeak.

And all this you will find,
If you only come in time,
To C. G. BLATT, you see,
Who will still in Bernville be.

He knows that you must laugh,
Fifteen pictures for one and a half
Duplicates fifteen for one dollar,
That's the way the people holler.

429. Individualized imprint. Boastful doggerel poem. C. G. Blatt, Bernville, Pa., used 1870–1876.

All negatives saved. Additional copies at half price, sent by mail postage paid.
RETAIL PRICES.
$3.00 *per half doz. Best.* $5.00 *per doz. Best.*
7.00 " "   " *Cabinets.* 10.00 " " " *Cabinets.*
5.00 *each 7x9 Photographs.* 7.00 *each 8x10 Photo.*
Duplicates at half the above prices.
Wholesale or Club rates, half the above prices.

430. Imprint including price list. James W. Turner, Boston, 1876.

Attribution

We should attribute an image to the photographer who claims it, but not without question, until proven otherwise.

Family portraiture seldom presents problems of attribution. The major exceptions are copies of old images, or reprinting from old negatives that passed to a successor.

Portraits of celebrities are another matter. Copying was so easily done and piracy so widely practiced, that any image that lacks a good degree of sharpness is suspect. Only a few great photographers are not known to have pirated portraits, e.g., Sarony, Mora, Moser of Chicago.

Purchased negatives, with rare exceptions, were appropriated as one's own and claimed as such, even by the most famous photographers—Brady, Gurney, Carbutt, Notman.

Identifying the Photographer

Merely to associate a photographer's name with an image is seldom enough. Who was he or she? Where did he work? When? What did he accomplish? How did he learn photography? Even a thumb-nail sketch of the photographer imparts some life to the image before us.

To locate information about a photographer it is necessary to search. Published information has been accumulating rapidly since 1970, making the task simpler, but it still requires ingenuity and persistence.

The three critical facts which are necessary to begin are. a name, a location, and an approximate date.

There are now available checklists recording the names of upwards of 25,000 American photographers, about half of whom operated in the 19th century.

The World of Stereographs includes an index of approximately 4,000 American and foreign photographers arranged alphabetically and geographically. Other lists for Colorado, Illinois, New Mexico, Chicago, St. Louis and various other states and cities have been published[4] and many other compilations are in progress.[5]

The search for personal information begins with the imprint and, most conveniently, local business directories. United States decennial census records and local town, county and court records are also useful. Most photographers advertised in newspapers, which occasionally reported comments upon the photographers' activities. Obituary notices sometimes include a sketch, usually with errors, of the individual's life.

The census enumerations of 1860 and 1870 are seriously incomplete in identification of photographers. For twenty Pennsylvania cities and towns, 26.3% of the photographers actually operating at the time of the census were not recorded as such (some are identified as "artists," some as "merchants," and one well-known photographer "occupation none").

Photographers operating in intervening years, 1862–1867, 1872–1874, etc., were, of course, not included in any census.

Available business directories for these same communities 1860–1885, fail to list 15.5% of the photographers who were active at the time of compilation. The limitations of *all* printed lists must be recognized.[6]

Descendants living today may have memorabilia, images of and by the photographer, more rarely account books and correspondence.

Only when a considerable body of work has been examined is it possible to judge or evaluate the stature or significance of a photographer. One famous image may have established or preserved his name, but hardly his stature.

The Publisher

The importance of the publisher in commercial photography is gradually being appreciated. Originally the photographer who wished to sell prints to the public was his own publisher, and advertised himself as such.

The portrait photographer whose trade consisted chiefly of custom work was not a publisher because he did not offer prints for general sale. On the other hand,

[4]Richard Rudisill, Museum of New Mexico, has compiled bibliographies of works listing photographers and of unpublished works in progress. These bibliographies have been reprinted in *Photographica 13* (4): 11, 12, and *13* (5): 11, 12; 1981.
[5]In press, *Index of American Photographic Collections*, by James McQuaid, project director, Paulette Wilson assistant, will list 19,000 photographers whose works are preserved in 500 institutional collections.
[6]Darrah, *World of Stereographs*, 1977, p. 237.

the local photographer who produced scenic cartes or stereographs for sale was a publisher. Identification and attribution of such images seldom presents problems, because they were usually imprinted by the photographer.

The commercial publisher of photographs commonly produced no original negatives. He functioned as a manufacturer of mounted images, his photographic operations were concerned with making prints. Many publishers marketed or otherwise assisted in the distribution of the cartes, especially if the images were "published for_____".

The large volume publishers usually purchased negatives, considered them as their own, and imprinted the mounts, e.g., Stinson, Taber, O'Kane.

Photoprinters who provided a service, that is printing and mounting for customers, were not publishers. The imprints they applied to the mounts were always those of the photographer and publisher. Organizations of many kinds (see page 64) published cartes but had no facilities for producing them, thereby requiring the services of a photoprinter.

The Card Without an Imprint

The cost of imprinting a thousand card mounts was so little that few photographers produced cartes without a logo of some kind. Sometimes a small-town or village photographer or a cheap itinerant did not believe it was necessary to identify his work. One might be disappointed that a beautiful portrait cannot be attributed to a photographer, but research on such a carte would seldom be justified.

By far the greater number of cartes without an imprint are copies, usually pirated. Any portrait of a celebrity or other popular subject without a logo is, beyond reasonable doubt, a pirated copy issue. They were produced as cheaply as possible for a quick profit. Few photographers who issued original marketable cartes failed to claim credit for their work or publication. During the Civil War many camp-following photographers did not imprint their cards.

As noted earlier, an imprint does not automatically authenticate the image. It may still be a pirated copy. With patience the suspected copy can usually be matched with the original issue from which it was taken.

A copied print always shows some loss of detail. Especially when compared with an original issue the differences are considerable. Fine detail in the face and background is lacking or blurred, sharpness is diminished. As noted earlier, page 18, the nearly universal practice of commercial printing from copy negatives sometimes resulted in great variation in the quality of prints. The method of first printing a glass positive and then using it to produce many copy negatives was usually carried out with strict control but second-rate publishers of cheap prints were less careful.

Scenic views without imprints are usually copies but many are original issues. Fine scenic views of the White Mountains by E. Kilburn, of Washington by Alex Gardner, and of New York by Anthony are known without their usual imprints. There is no satisfactory explanation for this inconsistency.

Occasionally cartes of local events and disasters bear no imprints even though the image obviously has the sharpness of an original. Some of these were probably produced by amateur photographers who happened to reside in the vicinity. Many college professors, high school teachers, medical doctors, engineers, and amateur scientists were capable photographers. It would have been a simple matter to purchase the supplies necessary to issue a modest number of cartes.

Another possibility was that the issue was custom-made, i.e., a photographer was hired to take the picture and produce cartes for a customer, who intended to distribute them himself.

Some cartes without imprints were sold wholesale to jobbers and retailers, such as print dealers, stationers and novelty vendors. The dealer could then imprint them. There are many common such imprints, as by Joseph A. Ward and New York Photographic Company. Generally these were copy issues.

There is a great variety of dealer imprints, including "blind stamps," and labels which were routinely applied to all images produced by other publishers.

Fraudulent Cartes de Visite

As yet fakery in cartes is very rare, primarily because the monetary value of most cartes de visite is too small to encourage deception.

The only cases known to me are Civil War scenes. A good stereograph sells for 20 to 40 dollars, or less. An equivalent carte de visite sells for 40 to 75 dollars or more. The fake is produced by separating the stereo pair and remounting them on authentic contemporary cards from which a trivial portrait has been removed. The deceiver could therefore more than treble his investment.

As prices for rare carte images advance, there will likely be attempts to market fakes, probably skillfully copied and processed prints.

The Image

The image of course is the photographic print, the subject. There are thus two approaches to it: the technical methods involved in its production and the visual content.

The photographic processes used in the production of carte de visite images were remarkably standardized from 1860 to 1885. Basically and almost universally the albumen print was made from a wet collodion glass plate.

There were some hybrid processes ca. 1857–1861 and 1880 to 1885. A few salt prints were mounted in carte format but these were prepared from glass negatives hence are not true calotypes. Gold toning of the image was almost universally practiced.

In the 1880s a number of innovations in processing were applied to carte de visite. Some of these, such as the gelatin dry plate which was widely used after 1883, were of great help to photographers but did not materially alter the nature of the print image.

187

431. Carbon print, "Permanent Chromotype," Swan process, widely used 1874–1883. Maitland, Stratford, England, ca. 1880.

433. "Porcelain" finish. Soft focus, ground glass negative. Balch, Boston, October, 1874.

432. Carte Russe, "Russian style," Rembrandt-like illumination, portrait on a black background. G. I. Canfield, Bay City, Mich., 1876.

434. Mezzo-tinto, Meinerth process. Imprint indicating license to use the method. Henry Cushing, Woodstock, Vt., 1868.

The practice of portraiture encouraged experimentation with new processes of printing and finishing. Accordingly, platinum prints with their delicate gray uncoated finish are occasionally found among cartes de visites of American and European origin ca. 1890–1900, rarely earlier. Unusual toning, such as with uranium salts in the wortleytype, are almost always identified as such ca. 1867–1870. Figure 440.

Bromide prints, characterized by a soft, slate gray to black color are found among English cartes of the 1880s and fairly commonly in American cartes produced in the 1890s and early 1900s.

Despite these various types of prints and the many kinds of images produced by photomechanical methods, for all intents and purposes, the collector of cartes de visite is concerned with albumen prints. Nevertheless, familiarity with various styles is helpful.

A useful chart for identifying and correlation of the various photographic processes used in producing images was published in The Society of Archivists, London, 1976, and reprinted in the *History of Photography*, 1978.[7]

Chromotypes, "Permanent Carbon Prints"

Throughout the nineteenth century photographers searched for ways to overcome the nagging problem of image fading. Any new technique that seemed to offer some improvement was certain to undergo fair trail. One of the most widely used methods to produce "permanent" pictures was the carbon print process devised by J. W. Swan.

These carbon prints are images in pigmented bichromated gelatin produced on special tissue paper. The image was transferred to a supporting paper and given a glazed finish. These were popular, especially in England and France in the latter 1870s. Figure 431.

The method of preparing the carbon tissue and making the prints is described in W. E. Woodbury's *Encyclopaedic Dictionary of Photography*, 1898, pages 80 and 83.[8]

The cartes made in this style were priced about fifty percent higher than the standard kinds. Nadar refused to make any chromotypes (nor to enamel or glaze any photograph), while Jabez Hughes developed his own variation of the chromotype and for portraiture used it exclusively.[9]

Many fine examples are to be found, especially by Sawyer and Bird, who were also the manufacturers of carbon tissue, Albert Sachs (Bradford), G. W. Griffin (St. Helens), Lejeune, and Appert (Paris).

Chromotypes made by the Swan method were produced by many American photographers between 1876 and 1883, but larger styles were more popular. These were usually called lambertypes. Leon Lambert had acquired American rights to the process. The British rights were held by the Autotype Printing and Publishing Company, of which Swan was a part-owner.

A. Braun had the French rights and Hanfstangl the German. American chromotypes are quite rare.

The chromotype had a tendency to curl, the thicker the glaze the more severe the subsequent curling.

Cartes Russes, Russian Cartes

The origin of this type and its name are uncertain. The style was briefly popular in Paris in the latter 1870s. It was occasionally imitated in the United States. The image is a vignetted bust photographed with strong side lighting ("Rembrandt") against a black background. There are striking portraits of women in this style. Figure 432.

Opalotypes or Opal Prints

This name was occasionally improperly used by photographers to identify portraits with a soft image, similar to that in a true opalotype. Strictly, the opal print is an image produced on opal glass which had been finely ground to give the soft effect. As used for carte de visite and cabinet portraits, the designation implies the use of a ground glass negative. Some photographers preferred to call these cartes porcelain prints. Figures 433, 435.

The Mezzotinto or Mezzotint, Meinerth Patent

Carl Meinerth (Newburyport, Mass.), U.S. Patent 66726, 1867, produced a soft portrait image by placing a plate glass or thin sheet of mica, between the printing

PATENTED OCTOBER 19, 1869.

PORCELAIN PHOTOGRAPHS,

Made only by the Patentee and
J. H. Young, in this City.

Any quantity of these Pictures can be
had by sending the Number.

465 W. Baltimore Street,

BALTIMORE, MD.

[7]See Gill, Arthur T., "Recognition of Photographic Processes," *History of Photography 2* (1): 34–36.
[8]See also Pritchard, 1882, loc. cit., pages 30, 33, 35, 133, 136.
[9]Pritchard, loc. cit., page 133.

435. Imprint advertising porcelain photographs. J. H. Young, Baltimore, Md., 1869.

paper and the negative.[10] The resulting diffused focus gave the soft image which resembled the so-called porcelain finish, somewhat similar to the opal print.

Meinerth licensed his process to more than four hundred photographers. Brewster in 1845 had experimented with a similar technique, inserting sheets of paper or glass between negative and print (see page 29).

Portraits produced by Meinerth's method are almost always identified as mezzotints in the imprint because the license agreement required that the photographer print his license on the back of the mount. Figure 434.

The Cameo Portrait

This style is recognized by the oval-shaped convexity on which the portrait is displayed. The effect was achieved by placing the card mount in a press and die with the desired size. Various devices were manufactured and sold under the name "cameo press." The earliest examples have an oval convexity with a length of 1¾ inches and date from about 1868. The greatest popularity in the United States occurred in the early and mid-1870s. This style was never very popular in Europe although many fine examples were produced, especially tinted portraits by the London Stereoscopic Company, ca. 1872.

The Chute Cameo Press had interchangeable dies, two sizes for cartes and another for cabinet prints. The inexpensive Ewing Cameo Press accommodated a carte, while the Barker press could be used for a carte or a "tintype without breaking the edges."[11]

There are many other named types of finishes and styles. Some of these were merely slick names intended to persuade the public that the photographer used a secret or superior process. Others, which were patented or copyrighted, seem to have been used by the patentee only. These were so rarely applied to the carte de visite as to be unimportant.

Lighting techniques to produce portraits with so-called Rembrandt, Holbein, and Raphael effects have been mentioned earlier, page 28.

Photomechanically Produced Images

Photomechanical processes include all methods in which a photographic image is formed upon a printing surface from which multiple copies can be made directly, that is, without further dependence upon light.

There are two main types: first, those processes in which the image is moulded in pigmented gelatine, and second, those in which the image is printed in ink.

The moulded image is best typified by the *Woodburytype*, invented by W. B. Woodbury and used extensively in England for the production of cartes de visite ca. 1875-1882. In this method a bichromated gelatine is exposed under the negative. Poitevin in 1854 had discovered that light would harden the gelatine

mixture. An exposed sheet was washed to remove the unexposed gelatine which remained soluble.

The image, which thus stood in relief, was next used to make an intaglio mould. The intaglio mold was placed in a specially constructed press with a heavy lid. A small quantity of warm pigmented gelatine, of any desired color, was poured into the mould, a sheet of paper placed over it, and the lid closed. The paper was pressed against the mould and the gelatine adhered to the paper, thus transferring the image to it. Hardening of the image was accomplished with an alum rinse.

The transferred image, which also stands in relief, is remarkably brilliant, ideally suited for portraiture. The Woodbury Permanent Printing Company (Kent Gardens) with a battery of seven presses could print 30,000 cartes per day.[12] The Woodbury Company produced great numbers of fine portraits of celebrities from many countries, in carte format. Earlier issues credit the original photographer, English, French, and German, but later issues often lack this information. Figures 128-131.

In the United States the Woodburytype was produced by John Carbutt (Philadelphia). The prints were used chiefly for book illustration but there are very rare carte portraits, probably custom made for persons whose portraits were to be included as book illustrations.[13]

Most photomechanical processes are of the second type, involving reproduction of images with ordinary printing inks. The original image was copied, usually on bichromated gelatine spread upon glass, wood, stone, metal, or other material, in relief or intaglio. There were many variations of each process.

In the *collotype* (or *albertype*, *lichtdruck*) the basic process involved the preparation of a reversed image on a thin film of bichromated gelatine on a thick sheet of plate glass. When the image had been washed and hardened, the glass plate was fastened in an ordinary lithographic press. The gelatine image was moistened with a wet sponge before a roller inked it. When a sheet of paper was pressed against the image, the ink was transferred to it. Albert, the inventor of this method, used it extensively for the production of cartes. In the United States the process was seldom used for cartes de visite. The best known examples were printed by Albert Bierstadt who also produced stereographs. The collotype process was used chiefly for printing large quantity issues.

Reworked Images

Retouching an image, negative or print, was practiced from the beginning of the albumen positive-glass negative methods. At first this involved only covering up holes and other defects in the negative but was soon extended to "improving" the image.

Retouching, as commonly understood, was not introduced until the mid-1860s in Europe and 1867 in

[10]Darrah, W. C., 1980, "Carl Meinerth, Photographer," *The Photographic Collector 1* (4): 6-9.
[11]Wilson, Hood & Co., Catalogue, 1873, p. 51.

[12]Pritchard, loc. cit., pages 97-101.
[13]Fine examples of carte size portraits by Carbutt were mounted in Henry, J. T., 1973, *The Early and Late History of Petroleum*, Philadelphia.

the United States.[14] The larger head in the image especially in the cabinet size, made it desirable to improve shadowing and half tones by lightening or darkening areas of the negatives, and to remove blemishes from the face.

Nevertheless retouching the carte negative in crude and superficial ways was done from the earliest 1860s. Most commonly, in the vignetted portrait, a thin line was drawn to sharpen the border between neck or face and background. Often the face on the lighted side blended into the background. Commonly the hairline on the forehead was strengthened or the blonde hair itself separated from the background. Occasionally the mouth, eyes, or ears were touched up.

The progressive improvement in retouching skills and their more extensive use can be followed in carte portraits from 1860 to 1873. By this time, trained retouchers, who were called "artists," used patented tools and special machines to do the work.

About 1870 a portrait produced from a retouched negative became known as a "Berlin Head" or sometimes as "the German style". Many photographers imprinted the mounts to advertise the new popular style. It is difficult to distinguish the Berlin Head from images printed from ordinary retouched negatives of the late 1860s. The chief difference is to be found in the background and shadowing, more attention being given to the whole picture than touching up only the face of the subject.

Tinting the portrait was quite common in the United States in the early 1860s but more or less abandoned by 1865. A few photographers continued to rouge cheeks on paper prints and tintypes in the latter 1860s.

Sarony, Mora and the London Stereoscopic Company produced superbly tinted portraits as custom work, in the mid-1870s.

Portraits of celebrities were rarely issued tinted, the chief exception being the many images of Pope Pius IX sold to pilgrims in Rome.

Tinting views of native peoples in costume was common in Europe and Japan, infrequent elsewhere. Many examples of exquisite workmanship are known. Images in tinted issues were always available untinted.

Tinting of scenery was rarely done except some village scenes with colorful ruins and cityscapes. A few photographers, for example Hattorff, tinted street scenes showing colorful activities.

On the other hand, tinting of sentimental and allegorical subjects was common. Again the images were always sold tinted and untinted.

All coloring was done by hand with pigments that were translucent or nearly so.[15] Commercial publishers sometimes had production lines in which each operator applied only one color.

There were various other methods of "improving" a portrait that enjoyed limited popularity between 1867 and 1873. The most striking was the pencil, pen, or crayon portrait. Figure 438.

[14]See Taft, Robert, 1938, *Photography and the American Scene*, pp. 323-329.
[15]Darrah, W. C., *World of Stereographs*, p. 43.

436. Imprint identifying a "Berlin Head," from a retouched negative. Woodward and Son. Taunton, Mass., November 1870.

437. Typical retouched negative of the 1870s. Head, face, sleeves and cuffs outlined. No other reworking of the image. W. H. Abbott, Little Falls, N.Y., ca. 1878.

191

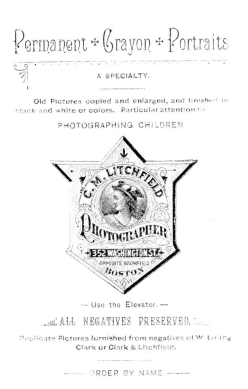

438. Crayon portrait. Negative reworked with a graphite pencil and the silver image removed chemically. H. G. Smith, Boston, 1873.

439. Advertisement of crayon portraits. Note also preservation of negatives by predecessors. C. M. Litchfield, Boston, 1877.

The "artist" carefully traced the features of the face, lined the hair and shaded by stipling as needed with a pen or medium hard graphite pencil. The silver image was then removed by chemical treatment. This could be done to a print or to a negative from which multiple prints could be obtained. The inked negative was usually used for cartes de visite.

For unknown reasons the inked carte portrait was popular only in the Boston area about 1870–1873, although it was occasionally produced elsewhere. I have examined examples by eight first-rate Boston photographers, including Black, Whipple and Warren, and by several New York and Philadelphia photographers.

The charcoal portrait was made in the same manner but only on enlarged prints, not for cartes de visite. The surface was sprayed with protective thin varnish.

The crayon portrait was, as its name implies, sometimes colored over by pastel or wax crayons. It was therefore a reworked print, very rarely used for special gift cartes de visite.

The Issue

The term "issue" (used as a noun) refers to the total number of copies of a print produced at one time for commercial distribution. It may have been for 50 or 50,000 copies. Many popular subjects were kept "in print" for many months. The quantity of an issue is seldom known, although for many well-known titles, a crude estimate can be made.

Some titles were sold for ten years or more, being reissued from time to time—nearly always on mounts and with imprints differing in detail from the original issue and from preceding issues. "Issue" when used as a verb, is synonymous with "publish."

The Series

It is usually helpful to know if a carte or stereo is one of a series, that is, a sequence of images related to a single subject or theme. Stereographs were usually published in sequential manner in series, "subseries," or sets, from as few as three or four to as many as twelve hundred titles. Cartes de visite were often published in series, but seldom extensively.

Major publishers identified the images in a series by a uniform series title and individual subject titles.

There are many examples:
"Brady's Album Gallery"
Jex Bardwells, "Views of Detroit and Vicinity"
Johnson's "Views of the Pennsylvania Oil Region"
Herbruger's "Isthmus Views" (Panama)

The cartes by Bardwell, Johnson, and Herbruger are identical to their stereo images and bear identical serial numbers.

The Trade List

The trade list is the total number of titles published commercially, i.e., of those images offered for public sale. It does not include custom work intended for private use.

The term as used in the history of photography had its origins in references to trade catalogues by stereographers published in the 1850s but was soon accepted to mean the list of all titles published commercially.

Trade catalogues are important research tools. Some photographers issued catalogues of only their stereographs. Others listed only special series, such as cabinet portraits of theatrical celebrities. Some photographers listed a variety of titles and indicated in what formats the image was available.

Successive catalogues issued by a publisher over a period of years invariably show the addition of new titles and deletion of old ones. Other changes may also be evident: a title may be renamed or reworded; a new title may be substituted for an old one; a new negative replacing an old one; etc. Thus no single catalogue recorded the total trade list.

Catalogues of cartes de visite titles are extemely rare despite the fact that many imprints bear a note "a catalogue will be mailed upon request."

Whereas stereographs in a series or list are usually numbered, cartes most often are not. European publishers of scenic cartes—which were identical to stereos—numbered them: Bedford, Blanchard, Wilson, Braun, to name only a few. So did a few Americans like Soule and Houseworth. In contrast, Bierstadt, Kilburn, Anthony, Whitney, Savage and Carter numbered their stereos but not their cartes. Reconstruction of a trade list of cartes de visite is much more difficult because there is no clue as to how many "missing" titles may have been published.

Interpretation of the Image

Interpretation as used here refers to the study of information available in the detail that may be helpful in establishing the date, location or attribution of the image, especially when other reliable information is lacking. Interpretation does not include artistic criticism or appreciation but does include such technical aspects as method of toning or other processing.

Visual Information in the Image

The visual content of an image can sometimes be used to date the negative. Especially when a large image is without an imprint or is unmounted, the picture may be the only source of information. The use of visual content is seldom necessary in establishing a date for a carte de visite because the mount and imprint are far more reliable.

Nonetheless there are images that are instantly recognized as anachronistic. Generally these are copied daguerreotypes, the costume being of the 1840s or 1850s.

Of course, the subject of an untitled image can often be identified by details in the picture.

The most obvious opportunities to determine the approximate date of a portrait are found in the dress of the subject, costume, hair style and accessories. It is first necessary to recognize a distinction between high fashion and serviceable garments made at home or by a local seamstress. High fashion, with its constantly changing styles, is a reliable guide which can be documented. There is a fairly good pictorial record of American ladies' fashions after 1870, but it is neither complete nor detailed.[15] As yet there is no handy reference for American women's or men's fashions pre-1870.

The latest fashion was worn by the well-to-do and the prominent. A new style spread from Paris, London, and New York into the hinterlands with remarkable rapidity. There was a strong desire to imitate but there was always some time-lag. Home-made copies are easily recognized. See, Costume, page 127.

Parades and public gatherings can usually be dated and referred to a holiday or other celebration. Once an approximate date has been determined, a newspaper search can be made. Such features as trees in leaf, or bare; flowers in bloom, spectators with light or heavy clothing will usually indicate a season of the year.

Fire ruins and other types of destruction, excepting a single burned house, can almost always be identified and dated if the town is known. Occasionally a sign giving the name of a factory, a bank or a newspaper office will be a very promising lead.

Technological inventions, especially those related to the telegraph (poles, cross-ties, insulators), railroads

[15]Blum, Stella, 1974, *Victorian Fashions and Costumes from Harpers Bazaar, 1867–1897*, New York.

440. Wothleytype. Uranium-silver image. Imprint of the United Association of Photography, London, ca. 1868. Courtesy of Geo. H. Moss.

(box cars, locomotives, coupling devices, signal systems), bridge building, etc. are often reliable indicators.

Ingenuity and painstaking observation are indispensable in the search.

Dating a Carte de Visite: Recapitulation

The criteria helpful in dating a pre-1890 carte may be summarized in three keys: card mounts, imprints and portrait images. Because of the enormity of the variations in each category, these keys should be used independently. When the conclusions based upon the three keys are compared, the approximate date should be determined.

The individual characteristics are indicative, not diagnostic. When combined, the results are reliable.

Principal card stocks in chronologic sequence
A Thin Card .010″ - .020″, generally .014″ - .017″°
   Square corners°°   1858–1869
     Color white
         plain   1858–1866, rarely later
         with border of one or two
            lines   1861–1869
         with oval frame for
            image   1863–1868
         face of card with printed
            background   1866–1868
     Color gray or tan, plain 1861–1866
B Medium Thick card .020″ - .030″
   Square corners
     Color yellow or white
       .020 - .026   1869–1871
   Round corners
     Color yellow or white
       .020 - .026   1871–1874
     Color gray .024 - .028   1872–1880
     Cards variously colored,
       red, lavender, green, blue; back of
       card of same or different
       color   1873–1880
     Cards chocolate, or
       black   1877–1887
     Cards with beveled edges, usually in
       gilt or red   1875–1881
C Thick card, greater than .030″
   with or without beveled edge; colors
   as above   1880–1900
   Back covered with faint geometric
     designs   1881–1888
   Back with border of Egyptian or
     Japanese motifs   1881–1886
   Thickness exceeding .040″ to
     .050″   1890–1910

°Thickness refers to the card alone, not the mount and image; measured near one edge, conveniently with a micrometer caliper.
°°Square cards were occasionally used throughout carte de visite history, but the card thickness and color will immediately approximately date the card.

Card with lustrous front, edges
   notched or incised   1894–1900
Card soft gray, corners cut
   square   1902–1910

Principal Types of Imprints in Chronologic Sequence
A Simple typeset imprint,
     small type   1860–1866
   Single line   1860–1862
   Two or three lines   1861–1866
     without "negatives preserved" or
     "duplicates can be had" 1861–1862
     with "negative" or
     "duplicate"   1861–1866
   With a vignette (eagle, shield, Liberty,
     etc.)   1862–1866
   With name vignetted   1862–1865
B Larger typeset imprint
   Usually three or more lines, commonly
     with other information 1863–1867
C Background of reverse side of card
     ornamented ovoid shape 1864–1868
   With box to hold revenue
     stamp   1864–1866
   With cherub and camera above
     imprint space   1865–1872
D Photographer's name printed lengthwise,
   in large type, back plain 1868–1882
E NPA logo printed on the
     back   1871–1874
F Elaborate designs, of great
     variety   1872–1885
     monochrome   1872–1885
     polychrome   1872 rare, 1873–1880, rarely later
G Geometric designs (refer to
     illustrations)   1877–1884

After 1885 the sharp decline in the popularity of cartes de visite was accompanied by less attention to the imprint. Many photographers simply used a rubber stamp while others devised highly individualized logos.

Typical Portrait Styles in Chronologic Sequence
A Head or Bust, plain background
   Vignetted head
     image smaller than ¾ × ¾
       inches   1860–1864
     image ¾″–1¼″ × 1″–1½″ 1860–1867
     image larger than 1¼″ × 1½″ 1866–1870
   Bust covering half the area of the
     print   1870–1875
   Large head, image covering ¾ of
     print   1874–1890
B Seated figure, three-quarters to full length
   Plain background   1860–1868, rarely later
   Background a drape, simple
     furniture   1860–1866, rarely to 1868
   With accessories, such as vases, books,
     furniture, urns, etc. 1860–1870
C Standing, full-length
   Background plain,
     uncommon   1860–1870

441. Mounting style. Portrait on card with open window, surrounded by an embossed frame. McCormick, Boston, 1866.

443. Finishing style. Portrait framed in a shadow design, 1872–1875. C. L. Lovejoy, Utica, N.Y., 1873.

442. Mounting style. There are several sizes of frames and many designs of each, 1864–1868. Wm. J. Baker, Utica, N.Y., 1866.

444. Finishing style. Oval portrait in an ornamental background, common 1873–1878. Jos. A. Fancy, Boston, ca. 1875.

Background a drape and/or
 column   1860–1868
Background with accessories, including
 balustrades, steps, etc.   1860–1870
Background of painted scenery, of
 infinite variety
 See illustrations   1861–1890
 (Note: compare card stocks)
With rustic accessories   1875–1885
With papier mache props   1875–1888, chiefly
                                            after 1880

Note: Many photographers adopted favorite types of posing, especially of children, women with beautiful faces and elderly sitters. With experience, a collector can recognize the work of many photographers without seeing the imprint.

Custom Copied Portraits

All photographers who produced cartes de visite advertised their ability to copy old portraits, especially daguerreotypes. Some refused to copy tintypes.

The approximate date of the original daguerreotype can, in many instances, be determined by the style of the mat, which was a thin brass frame placed between the image plate and the glass cover plate. The styles of the mats of the early to mid 1840s were simple designs, whereas in the latter 1840s they were more ornate. In the 1850s another element, a thin brass protector was introduced. This protector held together the image, mat, and cover. The protector became increasingly ornamented into the early 1860s.[16]

Throughout the 1860s, thousands of daguerreotypes were copied as cartes and distributed by the families who wanted them. Many photographers identified these as "copied March 6, 1863;" "This is a copy not up to our usual quality;" "copied at Reed's Gallery," or similar notation. Figures 445, 447.

Occasionally the photographer preferred not to imprint his copy work because of the inferior nature of th print.

Other Anachronisms - 1860s images on 1880s mounts.

Some collectors are needlessly disturbed by finding identical images on mid-1860s, early 1870s, and even late 1880s mounts. These are nothing more than family mementos, obtained from a local photographer who reproduced an old carte so that newer members of the family could have copies of the likenesses.

Classification and Description of Cartes de Visite

A collection of cartes involve some form of systematic storage, a data file, and a procedure for recording the data.

A system for classifying and indexing collections of fewer than a thousand images can be conveniently and economically based on metal file drawers of 3 × 5 or 4 × 6 inch size.

For most collectors a subject system is most preferable. Specialized collections require individ-

ualized systems. Other systems will be considered briefly below.

The major headings will depend upon the nature of the collection, but will probably include:
 Portraits
  Individual
  Groups
 Scenic
 Historical Events
 Subjects

Portraits may be indexed alphabetically by names of persons and cross-indexed by area of celebrity: literary, military, musical, political, theatrical, etc.

Scenic are conveniently arranged geographically, either by region or alphabetically.

Collections of scenes in a single state are usually filed by county and county by township and under each alphabetically.

Historical events can be filed chronologically or in combination with geographic occurrence. Subjects can be designated in any system, typically as in that used in the encyclopedic section of this book.

Each image or group of related images should be indexed.

Provenance. The history of the image, including the succession of its owners, is of considerable importance. Unfortunately, the majority of cartes have for a long time been separated from the original owners, having been passed from dealer to dealer to collector. Nevertheless precious family albums have remained in the possession of descendants who can document the images. It will become increasingly important to record and preserve the lineage of ownerships.

When one is satisfied that as much information as possible has been obtained from careful observation, the image should be described and/or indexed.

Description of a carte de visite

The procedures are very similar to these used in bibliography. The image was produced by a photographer and publisher, using chemical processes. The mounted image involved purchase of cards, professional services and hand work.

All pertinent information should be recorded:
 Photographer: Publisher: (if different)
 Title or subject of image;   locality:
 Date of negative, if known:
 Date of mount:
 Image: type of print, tone, finish, etc.
 Series and series number: if given
 Comments:

Recording identification data and comments on the back of the card mount or photograph is generally considered to be acceptable. Some archivists recommend it. I have in some instances recorded on the back of a mount the identification of the subject, the name of the photographer, the word "copy," provenance, etc. as documentation of the image.

The descriptive information may be recorded in some standardized form, such as an index card, punch card, or entered into a data storage system.

[16]Welling, William, 1976, *Collectors' Guide to Nineteenth Century Photographs*, p. 24.

445. Finishing style. Portrait in a symmetrical frame, common 1874–1878. There are many designs. This image is a copied daguerreotype portrait. J. C. Haring, Massilon, Ohio, 1876.

447. Superbly copied daguerreotype portrait. Photographer unknown, carte ca. 1862. Courtesy of Henry Deeks.

446. Unusual card mount. Simulated wood grain back. Introduced 1874 but rarely used. 1874–1878. Gurney, New York, ca. 1874.

448. Photographer's proof. Sample print submitted for approval by the customer. Note rubber date stamp. J. W. Black, Boston, 1864. Courtesy of Robert Cauthen.

Indexing and data storing for large classified collections of cartes de visite poses many problems. My preference is for arrangement by photographers, alphabetically, with groupings by country or region.

Historians, indeed all scholars, would not quote a statement without crediting the author or source. Yet thousands of academic and serious books, even authors of historical treatises, use photographs without considering the identities of their photographers. The photographer is no less the original source than an author or discoverer.

Computerized data storage can be incredibly complete. The retrieval of a large volume of information is rapid and as accurate as the data stored. There are three limitations that should never be ignored: raw data is only the first step in research. Its function is to provide leads, names, multiple instances. The information in the printout is not research.

The second limitation is that only information put into the system can be recovered. If one desires to investigate a neglected area of photographic technique or history, it is very unlikely that any computerized index system would yield the data relating to specific images produced by the technique in question.

The third limitation is not with the data storage system, but rather with the investigator. To handle data observed and stored by others does not become personal knowledge and experience until the individual has actually handled images. There is no substitute for first hand knowledge.

Preservation and Restoration of Carte de Visite Images

The first step in preservation is proper physical storage. The chief requirements are a dry place, subdued light or darkness, and protection from abrasion.

The archivist responsible for preserving great rarities will have different requirements than a general collector who has few or no very rare images.

A dry place is only a compromise.

Polluted air contains many contaminants that are chemically injurious not only to the silver image but also damaging to the paper and card stock. Sulfur compounds released during combustion of fuels are the most serious atmospheric pollutant.

Careless handling, which includes finger prints on the images, must also be prevented. Many collectors, graduate students, and researchers seem to be ignorant of the liabilities of the photographic image to deterioration. It is fragile and self-destructible.

Many photographs of historical interest are believed to be unique, that is, only one copy is known to exist. An "original" print is not necessarily unique. It rarely is, especially if the format is one that was commercially popular. The very purpose of negative-positive methods was to produce multiple copies of the image.

Physical Arrangement of the Collection

The arrangement of a collection, that is, the classification of the photographs, depends first upon function, its intended use. The institutional collection, which potentially will serve many users, by necessity must have accessibility and sophisticated simplicity. Since we are concerned here only with cartes de visite, relations to other formats, or storage integration with them, need not be discussed.

The private collection, whether it is intended for research or pleasure, obviously should be arranged for the collector's convenience.

There are two equally logical systems: arrangement by photographer or arrangement by subject. Archival collections, such as by a state, university or industrial company may require arrangement by departments or divisions. Such subdivision is really a subject system.

The accessibility of a collection depends upon the catalogues and indexes, i.e., data storage, as much as upon physical storage. The rapidity with which an image can be located, or the specific resources in a collection can be recognized, determines the degree of usefulness of the collection.

The more complete the "cross indexing," the less handling of the images and the less curatorial assistance required.

Storage of Images

Ideally a rare or historic photograph should be preserved under carefully controlled conditions: acid free, constant humidity, constant temperature, in darkness or subdued light, in a dust-free atmosphere. The image should also be protected from abrasion and careless handling, especially from finger prints.

Such storage conditions are impractical if not unattainable by private collectors. Nor does the cost permit most institutions to provide these protections. Common sense dictates that individual images and collections should be given the best care possible under a given set of circumstances.

Restoration

Under no circumstance should a non-experienced collector attempt to clean, chemically treat, or touch up a photographic image. While a soiled image can be cleaned, or a chemical bath may intensify a faded image, expert knowledge about the operations involved is needed. Most experts hold the opinion that an original paper photographic image, especially a very rare one, should NEVER be restored. Copy prints and copy negatives can often be manipulated and greatly improved, thus preserving the original as it is.

For those interested in the problems of restoration, the following sources are recommended:

Kodak, *The Preservation of Photographs*, 1979.

Ostroff, E. *Conserving and Restoring Photographic Collections*, 1976.

Reilly, James, *The Albumen and Salted Paper Book*, 1980.

Zigrosser, C. & Gaehde, C., *Guide to the Collecting and Care of Original Prints*, 1975.

Photographic Conservation, published quarterly by the Graphic Arts Center, Rochester Institute of Technology.

Common Types of Defects and Damage

The most obvious and common damage to cartes de visite is trimming, either the top and bottom of the mount or the corners have been removed. This was done to fit the mount in the pocket of an album. Many albums contained a template to be used as a pattern for trimming. In this sense the mutilation was necessary because the album required it.

The albumen print was susceptible to several problems, especially fading, spotting and mildewing.

Fading resulted from incomplete washing of chemicals or prolonged exposure to light. Poor processing, of course, was a fault of the photographer. Cartes housed in albums for generations are often in mint condition, having been protected from light, dust, and handling.

Mildews are populations of microscopic fungi that are living on organic substances such as the albumen, dextrin paste, gelatin, or binder in the card fiber matrix. These microorganisms, which are universally distributed in air, can begin to grow and attach themselves on a damp substrate. As long as the card remains in a damp situation, mildewing will increase until it invades the fiber, discolors both image and card, and develops a characteristic musty odor.

Many books, magazines and documents, like photographic images and mounts, show various degrees of mildew and damage caused by it. Minor mildew effects are manageable. Under dry conditions, they are not harmful to other images in a collection. Under damp circumstances they will contaminate adjacent specimens quickly. Severely mildewed images are a hazard, but the fungi will remain dormant under conditions of very low humidity.

Spotted images may result from many different causes, of two main types: inherent in the print itself, especially reactions between silver and sulfur or due to accidents subsequent to mounting.

Clear spots on the print may have been caused by a dirty camera lens, such as dust particles or finger prints, or because of a defect in the emulsion on the negative.

Chemical reaction between the silver image and the adhesive used to mount the print is an occasional cause of spotting. The use of such nonreactive substances as gum arabic or dextrin for pasting the prints, generally avoided this problem.

Spillage of water, ink, or other substances that might wet the image surface usually stained or spotted the print.

While such spots can be removed or minimized by proper technique, this should never be attempted without expert knowledge and full awareness of the risks involved.

Damage Caused by Handling

The majority of carte de visites, because they are nearly a century or more old, show the effects of repeated handling. Most obvious is soiling, primarily resulting from dust, human skin oil, and moist fingers. Less apparent, but in most cases there is some evidence of abrasion—scratches by movement of one card or image against others, even those preserved in albums. With every handling, unless the viewer takes special care, there is additional wear, however slight.

Fine images can be protected by placing them in polyethylene plastic envelopes or sleeves. These are commercially available in quantities of one hundred or more. The sizes useful for cartes de visite are 2¾ × 4½, or 3 × 5 inches. Polyester (Dupont mylar) envelopes, much more expensive, are recommended for very rare images.

Two other types of damage occur subsequent to the distribution of the cartes, separation of the print from the mount and splitting of the card mount.

Cartes that have been stored in a damp place or have been moistened accidentally may show curling of the print, due to softening of the adhesive. When drying occurs, the print and card may have separated. After 1866 many card mounts were finished with a dextrinized surface that would receive a wet print. The resulting bond was exceptionally durable, but under unfavorable conditions the print and card could separate. With great care the print, if not varnished, can be removed and remounted. A thin gum arabic or dextrin mucilage should be used.

Splitting or exfoliation of the multiple ply card is an occasional problem particularly with very thick cards used in the 1890s and 1900s. In most cases the splitting has been caused by storage in dampness, the binder between the plys alternately hydrating and drying. In some instances the cards were poorly manufactured, allowing them to swell and shrink with seasonal temperature and humidity changes, thus pulling the plys apart. (Such cards show the construction and method of manufacture clearly.)

Images painted over by children must be considered to be damaged or mutilated. Tinting by publishers was sometimes carelessly done. However, the translucent colors indicate their original nature. Even when commercial tinting was done with an opaque pigment, such as cinnabar or ochre, the color was applied so thinly that the detail in the image was not obscured.

In contrast, the pigments used by children were nearly always opaque. Some children painted quite skillfully, producing deceptively pleasing effects. Comparison between a commercially tinted and childishly painted-over image will show the differences immediately.

Summary

A very considerable body of information can be derived from a careful study of a carte de visite: the photographer and/or publisher, its age, the photographic processes used in its manufacture, and the visual content of the image. The image, card mount, and imprint should be considered as a unit.

Each image is more than a picture. It is a document, however trivial, of the historic past. A scholar would not quote from the work or publications of others without properly crediting the source. Yet, most scholars, even experienced historians, do not hesitate to use a photograph without attempting to attribute it to the photographer. The photographer, as observer and historian, is still a vague concept.

These vintage images, as it has become fashionable to call them, are fragile, self-destructible, and liable to many kinds of deterioration. Thus proper care and preservation, no less than documentation and data storage, are imperative. There are no rules, no established procedures, only the combined experience of many persons and the recommendations growing out of their experience. The whole field of photographic documentation and preservation is still in its infancy.

In this light the information summarized here should be helpful, but it is only a guide.

BIBLIOGRAPHY

General Remarks

The books and articles included in this bibliography provide information about cartes de visite and background to nineteenth century photography.

Books and articles cited in the narrative are given as footnotes. Most of these references are not repeated in the bibliography.

Anthony, E. & H. T., 1862. *Catalogue of Card Photographs published by E. & H. T. Anthony Company.* 12 pp. New York.
> Probably the earliest comprehensive catalogue of cartes issued in the United States.

Anthony, E. & H. T., 1865. *New Catalogue of Card Photographs.* 19 pp. New York.

Beaton, Cecil and Buckland, Gail, 1975. *The Magic Image: The Genius of Photography from 1839 to the Present Day.* Little, Brown & Co., Boston.

Boye, Else M. & Nyquist, F. P. (eds.), 1969. *Norsk familie-album, 1894–1969.* Grondahl, Oslo.
> Overlaps the closing decade of the carte era.

Braive, Michel F., 1966. *The Photograph: A Social History.* McGraw Hill, New York.

Burgess, N. G., 1863. *The photograph manual; a practical treatise, containing the carte de visite, etc.,* 8th ed., Appleton, New York.

Coke, Van Deren, 1972. *The Painter and the Photograph.* rev. ed., University of New Mexico Press.

Crawford, William, 1979. *The Keepers of the Light: A History & Working Guide to Early Photographic Practices.* Morgan and Morgan, Dobbs Ferry, N.Y.
> A most informative and understandable book.

Darrah, William C., 1964. *Stereo Views: A History of Stereographs in America and their Collection.* W. C. Darrah, Gettysburg, Pa.

Darrah, William C., 1977. *The World of Stereographs.* W. C. Darrah, Gettysburg, Pa.

Disderi, A. A., 1862. *Essai Sur L'Art de la Photographie.* Disderi, Paris.

Estabrooke, Edward M., 1872. *The Ferrotype and How to Make It.* 1st ed. Getchell & Hyatt, Cincinnati, Ohio. Morgan & Morgan reprint edition, 1972.

Frassanito, William A., 1975. *Gettysburg: A Journey in Time.* Charles Scribner's Sons, New York.
> The pioneering critical work on the documentation of Civil War photographs.

Freund, Gisele, 1980. *Photography & Society.* David A. Godine, Boston.
> First published in France, 1974 as *Photographie et Societe,* du Seuil, Paris.

Gernsheim, Helmut & Alison, 1955. *The History of Photography,* Oxford University Press.

Gosling, Nigel, 1976. *Nadar.* 298 pp. Alfred A. Knopf, New York.

Gower, H. D., Jast, L. S. & Topley, W. W., 1916. *The Camera as Historian.* Samson Low, Marston & Co., London.
> Arno reprint edition 1973. A landmark in methods for recording data about historical images.

Greenhill, Ralph & Birrell, Andrew, 1979. *Canadian Photography, 1839–1920.* Coach House Press, Toronto.

Ives, Wm. M., 1953. *Prints and Visual Communication.* Harvard University Press, Cambridge.

Jackson, Wm. H., 1876. *Descriptive Catalogue of North American Indians.* U. S. Dept. Interior, Hayden Survey, Misc. Publ.

Jay, Bill, 1979. *Negative/Positive: A Philosophy of Photography.* Kendall-Hunt Co., Dubuque, Iowa.

Jussim, Estelle, 1974. *Visual Communication and the Graphic Arts.* R. R. Bowker Co., New York.

Maas, Ellen, 1977. *Die Goldenen Jahre der Photoalben.* Dumont, Koln, Germany.

Mathews, Oliver, 1974. *The Album of Carte-de-visite and Cabinet Portrait Photographs, 1854–1914.* Reedminster, London.

McCauley, Elizabeth Anne, 1980. *A. A. E. Disderi and the Carte de Visite Portrait Photograph.* Ph.D. Dissertation, Yale University.

McCauley, Elizabeth Anne, 1980. *Likenesses: Portrait Photography in Europe, 1850–1870.* Art Museum, University of New Mexico.

Mayer and Pierson, 1862. *La Photographie consideree comme art et Industrie.* Hacette, Paris.

Newhall, Beaumont, 1949. *The History of Photography from 1839 to the Present Day.* Museum of Modern Art, New York.

Newhall, Beaumont, 1961. *The Daguerreotype in America.* Duell, Sloan & Pierce, New York.

Newhall, Nancy, 1952. "The Caption, the Mutual Relation of Words/Photographs." *Aperture 1* (1) 19–23.

Ostroff, E., 1976. *Conserving and Restoring Photographic Collections.* American Association of Museums, Washington.

Ovenden, Graham, ed., 1975. *A Victorian Album. Julia Margaret Cameron and Her Circle.* DeCapo Press, New York.

Pollock, Peter, 1958. *The Picture History of Photography.* Harry N. Abrams, New York.

Pritchard, H. Baden, 1882. *The Photographic Studios of Europe.* Piper & Carter, London. Arno Press reprint edition, 1973.

Reilly, James M., 1980. *Albumen & Salted Paper Book: A History and Practice of Photographic Printing, 1840–1895,* Light Impressions, Rochester, N.Y.
> An excellent source of technical information.

Robinson, Henry P., 1860. *Pictorial Effect in Photography.* Piper & Carter, London.
  Helios reprint edition, Pawlet, Vt., 1971.
Robinson, Henry P., 1892. "Paradoxes of Art, Science, and Photography." *Wilson's Photographic Magazine* 29: 242-245.
Root, Marcus A., 1864. *The Camera and the Pencil, or the Heliographic Art.* M. A. Root, Philadelphia.
  Helios reprint edition, Pawlet, Vt., 1971.
Rudisill, Richard, 1971. *Mirror Image; the Influence of the Daguerreotype on American Society.* University of New Mexico Press.
Taft, Robert, 1938. *Photography and the American Scene—A Social History 1838-1889.* Macmillan, New York.
Thomas, Alan, 1977. *Time in a Frame: Photography and the Nineteenth Century Mind.* Schocken Books, New York.
Towler, John, 1864. *The Silver Sunbeam.* Joseph H. Ladd, New York. Morgan & Morgan reprint edition, 1969.
Waldack, Charles, 1862. *The Card Photograph,* an appendix of 32 pp. to the 3rd ed. of *Treatise on Photography on Collodion.* Waldack, Cincinnati, Ohio.
  Also published separately as a pamphlet.
Weinstein, Robert A. and Booth, Larry, 1977. *Collection, Use, and Care of Historical Photographs.* American Association for State and Local History, Nashville, Tenn.
Welling, William, 1976. *Collectors' Guide to Nineteenth Century Photographs.* Macmillan, New York.
Welling, William, 1978. *Photography in America: The Formative Years.* Thomas Y. Crowell Co., New York.

Witkin, Lee D. and London, Barbara, 1979. *The Photograph Collector's Guide.* New York Graphic Society.
Woodbury, Walter E., 1898. *The Encyclopaedia Dictionary of Photography.* Scovill & Adams Co., New York.

*Periodicals
(noting years searched)*

American Journal of Photography (1852-1867)
Anthony's Bulletin of Photography (1870-1902)
Humphrey's Journal of Photography (1850-1870)
Philadelphia Photographer (1864-1888)
Photographic Art Journal (1851-1860)
Photographic Journal, London (1853-1875)
Photographic News, London (1858-1875)
Wilson's Photographic Magazine (1889-1895)

Current periodicals with occasional scholarly articles related to cartes de visites:

Fotogeschichte (Timm Starl, Frankfurt am Main, West Germany)
History of Photography (Taylor & Francis, London)
Image (George Eastman House, Rochester, N.Y.)
Northlight (Journal of the Photographic Historical Society of America), publication suspended, 1980.
Photographic Collector (Robert G. Duncan, Holyoke, Mass.)
Photographica (Photographic Historical Society of New York)
Stereo World (National Stereoscopic Association)

INDEX OF PHOTOGRAPHERS AND PUBLISHERS CITED

Names are given in the fullest form imprinted on cartes. Numbers in italics refer to illustrations. Geographic locations are given in the text. See also the geographic index by countries and states.

GEOGRAPHIC INDEX OF PHOTOGRAPHERS

Country names are given as imprinted in the nineteenth century.
Locations of studios are given in the narrative and legends with the illustrations; page references are to be found in the alphabetic index.

UNITED STATES

ALABAMA
Gerrish, E. A

ARIZONA
Bonine, E. A.

CALIFORNIA
Bonine, E. A.
Bradley & Rulofson
Durgan, Frank
Hart, A. A
Hayward & Muzzall
Heller, L.
Houseworth, T.
Howland, B. F
Kay
Lawrence & Houseworth
Miltz & Swart
Muybridge, E. J.
Reilly, J. J.
Shew, W.
Silvis, C.
Spooner, J. P.
Tandy, H. C.
Watkins, C. E.
Weed, C. C.

COLORADO
Chamberlain, W. C.
Collier, J.
Jackson, W. H.
Hook, W. E.
Thurlow, J.
Weitfle, C.

CONNECTICUT
Burrows & Bundy
Erekson, O.
Kellogg Bros.
Mallon, M. M.
Parmalee, S.
Peck Bros.
Phelps, G. C.
Scholfield, E. A.
Siebert, Christ

DELAWARE
Garrett, M.

DISTRICT OF COLUMBIA
Addis, R. W.
Bell & Bro.
Brady, M. B.
Child, G. F.
Dillon, Luke C.
Gardner, Alex.
Goldin, John
Holyland, John
Jarvis, J. F.

Smillie, T. W.
Ulke, Henry

FLORIDA
Engle & Furlong
Pierron, George

GEORGIA
Pelot & Cole
Perry & Leveridge
Riddle, A. J.
Wilson, J. N.

HAWAII
Chase, H. L.
Dickson, M.
Montano, A. A.

ILLINOIS
Benedict, W. C.
Brand, E. L. & Co.
Burggren, P. A.
Butler, T. H.
Carbutt, John
Clark, L. W.
Cole, H. M.
Copelin
Fassett, S. M.
Forell
Greene, P. B.
Higgins, Dr.
Hough, Joshua
Jones, J. Hanson
Jones, T. M.
Lovejoy & Foster
McMillan, Z. P.
Miltz & Swart
Mosher, G. D.
Pittman, J. A. W.
Pratt, D. C.
Tresize, J. Q. A.
Tresselt, R.

INDIANA
Baldwin, N.
Bulla Bros.
Butler
Clark, D. R.
Eppert
Evernden, Wm.
Fellows, E. G.
Mote Bros.
Wright, D. H.

IOWA
Buser, H. R
Card, B. F.
Carpenter, Lucelia
Elliott & Hill
Hughes Bros.

Kirk, II. P.
Masten, S. I.
Mooney
Park, O. H.
Sayre, J. R.
Warner, P. H.
Wetherby, I. A.

KANSAS
Barker, A. W.
Card, B. F.
Cosand & Musser
Henry, E. E.
Littleton, M. K.
Smith, Chas. T.
Whitaker, G. C.

KENTUCKY
Carpenter & Mullen
Klauber, E.
Webster, J. B.

LOUISIANA
Lilienthal, T.
Marmu, C.
Moses, B.

MAINE
Allee Bros.
Durgan, Frank
King, M. F.
Laroque, H.
Mills, II. A.
Pierce, William
Rider, N. R.
Stinson, Geo. & Co.

MARYLAND
Chase, Wm. H.
Chase & Bachrach
Holyland, J.
Schaeffer, R.
Spaulding, J. C.
Walzl, R.

MASSACHUSETTS
Adams, C. P.
Allen & Horton
Andrews
Balch
Battelle & Rankin
Bierstadt Bros.
Black, J. C.
Black & Case
Bouve, G. F.
Buchholtz & Hendrickson
Buel
Bufford, J. H.
Bushby & Hart
Butterfield
Case & Getchell
Chase
Chute
Claflin, C. R. B.
Cross, A. B.
Davis & Co.
Dunshee, E. S.
Eaton, A. B.
Everett & Soule
Fancy, Jos. A.
Fish, G. G.

Glines, A. A.
Hamor, A. B.
Hawes, J. J.
Heald, S. B.
Horton
Jones, J. W.
King, S. A.
Knowlton Bros.
Litchfield, C. M.
Loomis, G. H.
Marshall, A.
Masury, S.
McCormick
Meinerth, Carl.
Metcalf & Welldon
Miller, R. A.
Mosely, R. E.
Moulton, J. S.
Mumler, W. H.
Notman, J.
Notman Photographic Co.
Ormsbee, Marcus
Pollock, C.
Popkins, B. F.
Prang, L. & Co.
Proctor
Putnam, J. C. G. J.
Randall
Reed, H. J.
Richardson, H. N.
Robie, H. R.
Robinson, H. N.
Russell, Frank
Schillare, A. J.
Seaver, C. Jr.
Silsbee, Case & Co.
Smith, Miss C.
Smith, M.
Sonrel, A.
Soule, John P.
Soule Photographic Art Co.
Soule, W.
Spooner, J. C.
Southworth & Hawes
Staniford
Story, Augustus
Sylvester, C. T.
Taber, Chas. & Co.
Taylor & Preston
Tilton, J. E. & Co.
Tomlinson, G. W.
Vickery
Ward, Jos. & Son
Warren, G. K.
Warren, W. S.
Whipple, J. A.
Wing, Simon
Woodward & Son
Wyman, Henry

MICHIGAN
Baldwin, S. C.
Bardwell, Jex
Brubaker, C. B.
Canfield, G. I.
Carter & Graham
Childs, B. F.
McInness, H.
Schellhaus, L. W.

MINNESOTA
Beal
Edwards, C. G.
Engell, Chr.
Fearon, R. N.
Floyd & Power
Illingworth, W. H.
Martin
Upton, B. F.
Whitney, J. E.
Zimmerman, C. A.

MISSISSIPPI
Barr, D. P.

MISSOURI
Fox, A. J.
Hoelke & Benecke
Hughes & Co.
Macurdy, J. C.
McConnell, C. H.
Scholten, J. A.
Tainter, G. W.
Taylor, L.
Taylor & Vohringer
Tompkins, E. L.
Uhlman, Rudolph
Watts, D. B.

MONTANA
Huffman, L. A.
Winter, Frank A.

NEBRASKA
Cross, W. R.
Hull, A. C.
Jackson Bros.
Leonard, V. V.

NEVADA
Johnson, Geo. H.
Noe
Tandy, H. C.

NEW HAMPSHIRE
Allen, W. F.
Desmarais, E.
Eaton, A. B.
French & Sawyer
Gregg, Sherman
Hamilton, S. C.
Jewell, J. Byron
Kilburn, E.
Langill, H. H. H.
Lindsley, H. O.
Piper, S.
Rowell, C. C.
Tebbetts, Geo. H.
Wilkins, J. & Co.
Williams, J. H.

NEW JERSEY
Douglas, Ranald
Forster
LaForge, J. E.
Marriner, G. K.
Pach Bros.
Rolfe, W. R.
Price, Frank
Wendt, Frank

NEW MEXICO
Bennett & Brown

NEW YORK
Abbott, W. H.
Alden, A. E.
Anthony, E.
Anthony, E. & H. T.
Appleton, D. & Co.
Baker, W. J.
Barker, G.
Barney, E. P.
Barnum, DeLoss
Barrett
Bauer, Mrs. J. F.
Beer Bros.
Beers
Bierstadt, Charles
Bogardus, A.
Brady, M. B.
Chamberlain
Chapman, J.
Coddington
Crum, R. D.
Dana
Dessaur, Fernando
Dow, James M.
Dunshee, E. S.
Eisenmann, Charles
Fay & Ferris
Fredricks, C. D.
Glosser, H.
Godfrey, G. W.
Grotecloss, Wm. G.
Gurney, J. & Son
Hallett & Bro.
Hinckley
Hollenback, O. A.
Holmes
Howland, B. F.
Jordan, I. H.
Kent, J. H.
Kertson, M.
Kurtz, W.
Lape, G. L.
Lovejoy, C. L.
Magnus, Charles
Marsh, G. M.
Maser, J. W.
Mead Bros.
Mills, J. C.
Mora, J.
Morand, A.
Moulton & Larkin
New York Photographic Co.
O'Kane, J.
Ormsbee, M.
Orr, A. Jr.
Pach Bros.
Paxson, Charles
Reilly, J. J.
Rintoul & Rockwood
Roberts, J. R.
Rockwood, Geo. C.
Russell, A. J.
Sarony, Napoleon
Schoonmaker
Seely, Charles

Semmendinger, August
Sheppard, A. W.
Slee Bros.
Smith, W. G.
Spencer, S.
Stacy, G.
Stoddard, S. R.
Towler, J.
Townsend
Turner, A. A.
Walker & Boyles
Weller, L. S.
Williamson, C. H.
Winans
Wood Bros.

NORTH CAROLINA
Cooley, S. A.

NORTH DAKOTA
Berg, J.
Bratlee
Haynes, F. J.
Walker, L. E.

OHIO
Alley, E. H.
Baker, L. M.
Battels, B. F.
Butler, Bonsall & Co.
Clark, S.
Crew, E.
Crowell, Fred. S.
Decker, Elias
Haring, A. L.
Kell & Brown
Kinnaman & Howell
Landy, J. M.
Liebich
Loveridge, J.
McMillan, Z. P.
Miltz & Swart
Oldroyd, W.
Tresize, J. Q. A.
Van Loo, Leon
Waldack, C.

OKLAHOMA (INDIAN TERRITORY)
Concannon, T. M.

OREGON
Britt, Peter
Buchtel & Stolte

PENNSYLVANIA
Allen, A. M.
Bennet, W. H.
Bishop, H.
Bishop & Zimmerman
Blatt, C. G.
Bonine, E. A.
Bretz, George M.
Broadbent, S.
Broadbent & Phillips
Brown, P. A. (A. P.)
Burnite & Welden
Centennial Photograph Co.
Choate, J. N.
Coonley & Wolfersberger
Copeland & Fleming
Cremer, James

Cummings, T. & W.
Daily, John
Deming, A. D.
Deming, W. M.
Dunshee, E. S.
Evans, C.
Germon, W. L.
Goetschius Bros.
Groom
Gutekunst, F.
Henderson, R. S.
Hough, G. S.
Hull, S. S.
Johnson, N. G.
Johnson
Kleckner, M. A.
Kunstman, Wm.
Lachman, Isaac
Langenheim Bros.
Lochman, W. H.
Lovejoy, C. L.
Martien, Wm. S. & A.
Mather, John
McAllister & Bros.
McClees, J. E.
McIntire, S. A.
Moran, John
Mumper, Levi
Newell, R.
Patton & Dietrich
Philadelphia Photograph Co.
Phillips, H. C. & Bro.
Purviance, Wm.
Ridgeway, Dr.
Robbins, Frank
Rogers, J. H.
Root, M. A.
Rothengatter, A. W.
Rothwell, J. Wesley
Sheaffer, S. G.
Schreiber & Son.
Schurch
Swords Bros.
Tipton, W. H.
Tyson, C. J.
Tyson Bros.
Weaver, P. S.
Wenderoth & Taylor
Wenderoth, Taylor & Brown
Wilt Bros.
Yeager, F. M.
Young, J. H.

RHODE ISLAND
Brown, S. B.
Hacker, F.
Manchester Bros.
Manchester Bros. & Angell
Russell, Frank
Scholfield, E. A.
Williams, J. A. W.
Windsor, G. E. & Co.

SOUTH CAROLINA
Cook, Geo. S.
Quinby & Co.

SOUTH DAKOTA
Baily, Dix & Mead

Delong, W. W.
Morrow, S. J.

TENNESSEE
Schlier, T. M.

UTAH
Carter, C. W.
Savage, C. R.
Savage & Ottinger

VERMONT
Bixby, H. L.
Cushing, Henry
Cutler, H. E.
Dunton, E. H.
Gage, F. B.
Hersey, S. O.
Houghton, G. H.
Kendall, W. P.
Styles, A. F.

VIRGINIA
Anderson & Co.
Ennis, George
Richmond Photograph Co.
Riddle, A. J.
Selden & Ennis

WISCONSIN
Bennett, H. H.
Curtiss, E. R.
Harman, H. S.
Kendall, R. D.
Manville, C. B.
Sherman, W. H.
Weller, L. P.

CANADA
Henderson, H.
Inglis, James
Lyon, Wm. A.
Maitland
McClure, J.
Milne
Notman, J.
Notman, Wm.
Notman & Sandham
Park, S.
Parks, J.
Vallee, E. P.

ALGERIA
Alary & Geiser
Geiser, J.
Portier, C.
Trappe

AUSTRALIA
Bell, E. C.
Bradley, William
Cherry, G.
Clark, J.
Farndell, E.
Lomer, Albert
Simco, George

AUSTRIA
Angerer, L.
Angerer, V.
Bohn, C. von

Carpentier & Ebeling
Chizak
Fridrick, F.
Jenik, Rosa
Kramer, Oscar
Luckhardt, Fritz
Malovich (Trieste)
Miethke & Wawra
Oprawil & Co.
Rabending, Emil
Rabending & Monckhoven
Rospini, C. J.
Unterberger, Fr.
Vienna Photographic Society
Wille, A.

AZORES
Silva, G.

BELGIUM
DeChamps & Co.
Ghemar Bros.
Tessaro, F.

BRAZIL
Henschel & Benque
Klumb, R. H.
Leutzinger, G.
Photographia Brasiliera
Pietsch & Dietze

CAPE OF GOOD HOPE
Barnard, S. B.

CEYLON
Andree, A. W.
Slinn & Co.

CHILE
Bischoff & Spencer

CHINA
Pun Lun
Schoenke, F.
Sidney, S. S.

COSTA RICA
Fortino, L. B.

CUBA
Fernandez, J. B.
Fredricks, C. D. & Co.

DENMARK
Hinrichsen, Chr.
Sorensen, Chr.

EGYPT
Beato, A.
Hammerschmidt, W.
Koumianos, Nicolas

ENGLAND
Annan, Thomas
Ashford Bros. & Co.
Bark, C. Vos
Bassano, Alexander

Bateman, J.
Beattie, J.
Bedford, F.
Blanchard, Valentine
Brewster, David
Bull, John
Burns, Archibald
Caldesi & Co.
Caldesi, Blanford & Co.
Cameron, Julia.
Centaur Photograph Co.
Chappius, P. E.
Claudet, A.
Cundall & Co.
Deana, Charles
Debenham, W. E.
De La Rue, Warren
Diamond, Hugh W.
Douglas, T. H.
Downey, W. & D.
Downie, D. C.
Duval, C. A.
Elliott & Frey
England, Wm.
Fairclough, P.
Fradelle & Marshall
Frith, Francis
Gade, R.
Gouptil & Co.
Griffin, G. W.
Grundy, Wm.
Haes, Frank
Hardy, Jas. W.
Hawke, John.
Henderson, A. L.
Hills & Saunders
Hughes, Jabez
Inskip
Jones, Daniel
Josty & Co.
Kilburn, Wm. F.
Lambert, Leon
Lock & Whitfield
London Stereoscopic Co.
Longley, F. E.
Lucas, Messrs.
Marion & Co.
Mason & Co.
Maull & Co.
Maull & Polyblank
Mayall, J. E.
Melhuish, A. J.
Moore, Melancthon
Negretti & Zambra
Newcombe, C. T.
Petschler, H.
Price, Lake
Robinson, H. P.
Robinson & Cherrill
Roger, G. F.
Russell, James
Sachs, Albert
Sedgfield, Wm.
Seeley, A. & E.
Southwell
Stuart
Swan, J. W.
Thrupp, R. W.

Titterton, John
United Association of Photography
Villiers & Sons
Wane, Marshall
Watkins, John & Charles
Whiteman, E.
Wilson, G. W.
Window, F. R.
Window & Bridge
Woodbury, W. B.
Woodbury Permanent Printing Co.
Worthley, Stuart
York, F.

FRANCE
Andrieu, J.
Appert
Bisson Bros.
Braun, A.
Carjat, Etienne
Collin
Delessert
Deplanque, Jules
Disderi, A. A.
DuFour, E. M.
Ferrier
Gouptil & Co.
Hermann, Mme. V.
Konarjewski, L.
Ladry, Ernst
Lamy, E.
LeGray, Gustave
LeJeune
Leon & Levy
Levitsky, S. L.
Liebert, A. Marion, A. & Co.
Maujean
Mayer
Mayer & Pierson
Nadar (Tournechon, F.)
Neurdein
Poucault, M.
Petit, Pierre
Petit & Trinquart
Pierson, L.
Reutlinger
Silvy, S. C.

GERMANY
Bonn, Wilhelm
Brandseph
Brockmann, F. & O.
Burger, W.
Christmann, S. P.
Deutsche Photographische Gesellschaft
Eckert, G. M.
Haase, L.
Hahn, Julius
Hammerschmidt, W.
Hanfstangl, L.
Hattorff, E.
Hofner
Holzamer, C.
Krone, H.
Kruse, A.
Kurtz
Linde, E. & Co.
Lindner, O.

Moser
Priester, Hermann
Rose, F.
Schoenscheidt, J. H.
Schumann, T. H. & Son
Sinner, P.
Steinberger, Jacob
Steuer & Hautzendorf
Williams, Sophus

GREECE
Constantine, D.
Moraites, P.

GUATEMALA
Buchanan, W. C.

HOLLAND
Jager, A.

INDIA
Bourne & Shepherd
Chintamon, Hurrychund
Lindley & Warren
Moses & Sons
Sache & Murray
Sache & Westfield
Schwartzschild
Westfield & Co.

INDOCHINA
Yu Chong

ITALY
Alessandri Bros.
Alinari Bros.
Anderson, James
Conrad, Giorgio
Degoix, C.
DeLuca Bros.
Emilia
Hodcend
Mang, Michel
Naya
Nessi
Noack, Alfredo
Perini, A.
Ponti, Carlo
Powers, L.
Powers Bros.
Rive, Roberto
Rossi, Julio
Schemboche
Sommer, Giorgio
Spithover
Ufer, Oswald
Van Lint

JAPAN
Suzuki, S.
Tamamura,K.
Uyeno, H.

MARTINIQUE
Morin, Felix

MEXICO
Clausnitzer, Carlos
Constant & Stephen
Crucis & Campa
Fahrenburg, A.
Moses & Co.
Zuber, L.

NATAL
Kisch, H.
Kisch Bros.
Sherwood, W. B.

NEW ZEALAND
Clark, W. H.
Corbett, J.
Rice, Thos. E.
Tait Bros.

NORWAY
Knudsen
Madsen
Olsen, Chr.
Selmer, M.

PALESTINE
Bergheim
Bonfils, F.

PANAMA
Herbruger, E.

PERU
Courret, E.
Maunoury, E.
Noble & Lopez
Richardson, V.
Villaalba, Ricardo

RUSSIA
Carrick, Wm.
Denier, A.
Lorenz, N.
Panov, M.
Posekin

SIAM
Chit, F.

SINGAPORE
Lambert, G. R.
Thomson

SPAIN
Clifford, C.
Joulia, E.
Laurent, J.
Masson, L.
Rojo, F.

SWEDEN
Dahlgren
Eurenius & Quist
Hansen, Mathew
Petterson, Otto

Roesler, A.
Vogel & Dienstbach
Wiklunds, A.

SWITZERLAND
Charnaux, F.
Charnaux, F. & Sons
Charnaux Bros.
Gabler, A.
Garcin
Lacombe & LaCroix
Rauch, J. F.
Varady & Co.
Vollenweider, M.

TRANSVAAL
Hesselson, J.

TRINIDAD
Morin, Felix

TUNISIA
Garriques, J.

TURKEY
Abdullah Bros.
Sebah, Cosmi
Sebah, P.
Shishmanian

INDEX TO SUBJECTS

COLOPHON

Composition, *Caledonia Composition*
Printing, *The McFarland Company*
Photography, *The McFarland Company*
    Paul G. Paponetti and Ray R. Deimler, Jr.
Text-Typeface, *Highland*
Paper, *Mead Black & White Enamel*
Binding, *Complete Books, Inc.*
Coordinator, *M. P. (Jim) Hartzell*